Visions of Reality

Visions of Reality

New Ways of Conceiving Old Problems

By Greg Nyquist

iUniverse, Inc.
New York   Bloomington

Visions of Reality

New Ways of Conceiving Old Problems

iUniverse books may be ordered through booksellers or by contacting:

iUniverse
1663 Liberty Drive
Bloomington, IN 47403
www.iuniverse.com
1-800-Authors (1-800-288-4677)

ISBN: 978-1-4401-0756-6 (pbk)
ISBN: 978-1-4401-0757-3 (ebk)

Printed in the United States of America

iUniverse rev. date: 12/16/2008

Contents

Introduction

This is a book about methodology. An intimidating subject, some might think; others might have worse names for it. Let me assure the reader from the outset: although the book is about methodology, there is little if any explicit methodology in it. This is not a book that will tell you *how to think* or *how to solve problems*. What it seeks to accomplish is merely to illustrate, in a series of essays on disparate topics, the consequences of following a specific methodological ideal. What is this methodological ideal? I call it *realism*, which simply means being honest, making the truth come first. If we apply all the zeal and intelligence at our disposal to remaining faithful advocates of fact and truth, it becomes less probable that we will spend our days feeding on illusions and wasting our lives in ignorance and despair.

It is easy enough to say one should be realistic and truthful, but how does one go about attaining this end? How does one make truth come first? The central premise of this book contends that the greatest obstacle to the attainment and understanding of truth is human pride. Arrogance and egotistical presumption constitute the great enemies of truth, because they cause us to believe our own lies. Human beings have enough trouble remaining honest toward others. But remaining honest to themselves poses difficulties that few can surmount.

As bad as it is to deceive others, it is even worse to deceive oneself. To know that something is a lie at least implies knowledge of truth. The case stands otherwise when we lie to ourselves. The lie we tell ourselves prevents us from ever knowing the truth. Through self-deception and a kind of "sincere" hypocrisy, the mind quarantines itself from reality. No longer can it distinguish fact from fiction and truth from error. Believing lies to be truth, the mind ends up becoming the victim of its own confidence scheme. The most dangerous lie is the lie we tell ourselves.

Unfortunately, human beings are little inclined to guard against the tendency toward self-delusion that exists in all of us. Individuals not only lie *to* themselves, even worse, they lie *about* themselves. Literally hundreds of experiments in social psychology have shown that most people think better of themselves than is warranted by the facts. (1997, 422) The human beast, far from being the rational animal that romantic enthusiasts imagine him to be, could more accurately be described as the mendacious animal.

Is there any remedy to cure the innate mendacity of man? If by remedy, we mean some trick or device to get rid of the predisposition altogether, the answer must be a resounding "No!" The limitations of human nature are congenital. Science ascribes the tragic fixity of these limitations to our DNA; theology blames them on original sin. Regardless of their origin, they are obvious facts that can be verified through everyday experience and the testimony of great literature.

Although human nature cannot be changed, various techniques and stratagems can be devised to mitigate its less propitious manifestations. Is not *that* the whole point of civilization—to blunt the sharp edges of human nature so that the inner core of baseness doesn't lead the struggling human soul to ignominy and despair?

Even though there exists no absolute remedy to cure the ills of self-deception, several stratagems can help us cope with the problem. The most important of these stratagems involves the individual's humble acknowledgment that he, just like everyone else, is prone to self-deception. Until the individual admits his common humanity, which includes admitting that he, too, is subject to the limitations of human nature, there is no hope for him. It is by noting these limitations that the individual takes his first tentative steps toward the kind of blunt honesty and truculent realism advocated in this book.

Another important stratagem is to recognize how our tendency toward self-deception can affect the way we think. We all have a tendency to rationalize what we want to believe, even when our will-to-believe plainly goes against the grain of the truth. How do we go about combating this fatal tendency in ourselves? There are two principles critical in this respect. The first principle is openness to criticism—the eagerness to expose our ideas to the most rigorous process of experimentation and testing. The second principle is respect for ideas and notions and usages that have stood the test of time.

At first blush, these principles may appear contradictory. After all, if all our ideas require the most rigorous process of experimentation and testing before we can accept them, why should ideas that have stood the test of time be respected above any other? Aren't all ideas so much grist for the experimental mill? *That* would be superficial way of regarding the issue. Any idea that has stood the test of time already has been rigorously tested: otherwise, it would have long ago become outmoded and forgotten. The fact that it is still around evinces its probable soundness. Moreover, not all ideas can in truth be rigorously tested. Some are based on very complicated judgments about the human condition—judgments so complicated that they could never be adequately justified on explicitly experimental grounds. Other ideas are based on incomplete information. Human beings are not omniscient. We can't understand everything, because either the circumstances confronting us are too complicated or we don't have access to all the relevant facts. If we could only evade the necessity of making a decision based on inadequate information, all might be well. Often, however, we are forced to act on incomplete information. What then should we do? In such circumstances, the best thing is to follow established usages, because at least these usages, even when they are not entirely understood, have proven useful to generations of men. There is probably something good in them and this something should be respected.

This does not mean that traditional ways of thinking and acting can never be challenged. Everything can and, when possible, should be challenged. The question involves whether, once a traditional norm has been challenged, it should be rejected. Since any long-standing tradition will probably have proven its usefulness and fecundity many times over, this in itself constitutes a very strong presumption in its favor. So before we reject any tradition with a long and distinguished track record, we better have very compelling evidence on the other side of the question. One should not, for instance, reject a long established custom or some incidental ancient usage merely because it isn't "perfect" or because it fails to accord with "reason." What one needs is very compelling *evidence* that the custom or ancient usage in question is pernicious, or could be replaced by something more effective. Without such evidence, one should be wary of messing with traditional ways of thinking and doing.

I have stressed the importance of *evidence*, because evidence usually constitutes the best way to get at the truth. Whenever some question arises over a matter of fact, the best way to settle the issue is to consult the relevant evidence. The worst way is to "reason" about it. What philosophers call "reason" is little more than clever rationalization. Knowledge of facts cannot be attained merely by reasoning about them. Reality is not a closed logical system; one fact does not logically beget another. Although conjectures about facts can be formed through logical speculation, such conjectures have little cognitive worth until they have been tested empirically.

To sum up: To get at the truth requires: (1) Awareness of the extent to which all of us fall prey to self-deception; (2) openness to criticism, particularly self-criticism, combined with an appreciation for established usages and venerable traditions; and (3) the realization that the best method of testing any claim about matters of fact is to consult the relevant evidence. If the individual allows these principles to help mold his attitude toward the business of getting at the truth, he will at least have a chance to see the world as it really is, free from the distorting influences of hubris, self-deceit, and wishful thinking. It is surprising how different the world looks once we have removed all the filters that human nature places in front of our minds. Once we no longer allow our shallow prejudices, our sterile ideologies, and our egotistical presumptions to confound and blind us, we begin to see things under the form of eternity, as God presumably sees them. And while omniscience must always elude our slender capacities, to enjoy even the merest glimpse of the aspect things wear within the sentience of the Deity constitutes an immense cognitive epiphany.

In the essays of this book I have attempted to apply the method sketched above, the method of realism, to some of the central issues confronting politics, economics, and philosophy in the modern world. In the first essay, "Conservatism True and False," I distinguish two types of conservatism, the realistic and the ideological. Conservatism, at least in its realistic variety, is fundamentally a practical philosophy: it draws its sustenance from man's experience of getting things done in ways that satisfy time-tested moral verities. Conservatism's practical orientation places it against any form of idealism, particularly of a moral or political nature. Contrast this with modern "liberalism," which masks the fundamental impracticality and egotism of its view of the human condition under a fig leaf of good intentions. But moral idealism, regardless of its form, too easily degenerates into moral solipsism. Belief in a moral ideal is taken as proof of that ideal's practical feasibility. Confusion of the moral with the practical insulates the idealist from any criticism about the means by which he proposes to attain his ideal. Liberalism has long been criticized as a manifestation of good intentions gone awry. This, however, understates the case against it. The liberal's refusal to consider the practical objections to his moral and political ideals—a refusal that is often buttressed by the utterly malicious and self-serving assumption that any criticism of his ideals must have its source in dubious motives—suggests something deeper and more pathological than merely good intentions thoughtlessly pursued. The liberal's pursuit of the ideal is more about himself and his own unbridled conceit than it is about helping others.

The egotism of moral idealism leads to another fallacy: namely, the illusion that political outcomes can be influenced by our espousal of them. In the essay "Politics and the Weather," I dissect this illusion. Since most of us, taken as solitary individuals, have little if any say in the political process, there is no point in becoming obsessed with what ought to be. Contrariwise, since all of us are very much affected by the consequences of political outcomes, we should be passionately concerned about what may or will happen. This shifting of our focus from what ought to happen to what will happen can help us develop a more realistic, one might say even "scientific," view of political reality.

5

The contention that most individuals have little if any say in the political process challenges common assumptions many people hold about democracy. After all, isn't that what democracy is all about? Doesn't "one man, one vote" give everyone a say in the political process, assuring that the "will of the people" always prevails? Hogwash, say I, and in the essay "The Democratic Farce," I provide a more realistic justification for democratic institutions. Democracy, I contend, is merely a game we all play so that we can amicably settle differences in political opinion. The only viable alternative to settling our political differences through farcical elections is to settle them through sanguinary violence. Farce, I suggest, is usually preferable to violence.

Some social problems can only be solved through "collective action," that is, by the state. Creating a society governed by laws rather than men, where the individual's life, liberty, and property are regulated and protected by an organized government cannot be attained merely through the random efforts of isolated individuals. Democracy is merely the method by which collective decisions are made. It is the *how* of collective action. But it doesn't tell you *why* a certain course should be taken rather than another. *That* depends on the judgment of the elected representatives. There exists a wide divergence of opinion as to the range or limits of "justified" collective action. Some believe in an activist state, interfering left and right in the affairs of men; others want to limit collective action as much as possible. As a contribution to this debate, I offer the essay "Moral Externalities," in which I argue that moral and social problems provide as great a pretext for collective action as do economic problems, since a moral externality (i.e., the effect of immoral personal behavior on innocent bystanders) can impose as great a burden on society as even the most costly economic externalities. If collective action (i.e., government sponsored coercion) is justified in cases of economic externalities, it is difficult to comprehend how it can be denied in cases of moral externalities as well. What should persuade the statesman and the legislator to proceed with utmost caution is the very real possibility that little can be done in either case and that the best way to deal with externalities, whether of the economic or moral variety, is sometimes to let things work themselves out on their own, so that practical solutions can emerge spontaneously from those most affected by problems at hand. In any case, it is most desirable that decisions about government sponsored coercion should be made free of ideological bias—which is merely another way of saying that the state should not be governed by rationalistic and rationalizing fanatics.

Of course, this is easier said than done. To be a human being is to be a rationalizer; and to be a rationalizer is to take the first headlong plunge into the vortex of fanaticism. The tendency toward ideology exists within most of us. It's in our very DNA. The only difference is that some people do a better job of battling this tendency than others. What accounts for this difference? Why do some people give way to their predisposition to ideology while others wage the valiant fight against it? This is a most interesting yet utterly perplexing question. It is particularly interesting and perplexing when applied to grossly implausible and even suicidal ideologies, such as those embraced by the radical left. Why would any human being allow his intellect and native good sense to sink so low as to believe the palpable absurdities eagerly embraced and expounded by so-called "progressives"? Normally, when people believe things that are not true, there is something in it for them. Yet at first acquaintance, there appears to be little advantage in believing left-wing ideology. Simply ruin and ignominy for everyone involved! So how can we account for these strange, counterintuitive opinions? In the essay "The Psychopathology of the Left," I take a stab at explaining why the left desperately adheres to an ideology that is neither speciously plausible nor practically efficacious. The least implausible explanation, I suspect, for the development and spread of leftist ideology is what the conservative philosopher Richard Weaver called the "spoiled-child psychology." Leftist beliefs evince a mental and emotional level that is comparable to that of a twelve year old. How can an individual whose level of maturity has hardly advanced beyond the dismal threshold of adolescence ever hope to mitigate, let alone control, the tendency toward fanaticism and mendacious rationalization that plagues and torments our species? Before a man can learn to know truth, he must develop the self-control necessary to master the baser tendencies of his inmost psyche; and this requires emotional and mental maturity. The man who never grows up is the man who will forever remain a fool.

Within the social science departments of American Universities, the Left has become dominant in every discipline *except* economics. *Prima facie*, this would appear a great boon for the development of economics.

Alas, it has proven otherwise. The so-called queen of the social sciences has not used its freedom from leftist intellectual oppression to any great advantage. Progress in theoretical economics has stymied on nearly every front, so that instead of a flourishing body of wisdom, all we find is a morass of pedantic shibboleths. In the essay "Machiavellian Economics," I suggest new foundations upon which to rebuild this once proud and distinguished discipline. Instead of bowing to the altar of quantity, economics should be founded on facts apprehended through a disciplined intelligence free of ideological bugbears. With this new approach in hand, I examine the problem of the business cycle. In the essay "Notes Toward a Theory of the Business Cycle," I outline a new theory based on the insights of Joseph Schumpeter and the Austrian School. In a final economics essay entitled "The Economics Profession: An Autopsy," I direct my attention towards the degeneration of contemporary economics. Those who, nowadays, pass themselves off as professional economists are sunk in the deepest ignorance. They have replaced understanding and wisdom with calculation and aimless statistical facility.

Politics and economics, though subjects of vital importance to the interests and well-being of *Homo Sapiens*, are hardly the most critical subjects of all. Of even greater importance is the relation of man and his spirit to the universe. Either there exists some sort of transcendent will or intelligence that takes an interest in the conduct of men and in their ultimate welfare, or we live in a universe utterly devoid of meaning or purpose in which our conduct and fate make no difference in the overall scheme of things. If we find ourselves infesting a universe utterly indifferent to us, then each of us will be inclined to only look after our own entirely self-contained yet thoroughly meaningless lives. After all, if all we have is one life to live with nothing after, around, or above it, then we would do well to make the best of it. If there exists more to the universe than dice and billiard balls going through endless fits of senseless gyrations; if, instead, there exists some vast meaning or locus of intelligence or transcendent spirit that cares about how we behave and what becomes of us: then a very different moral ideal of the good life would appear requisite. In that case, we would do well to figure out what sort of behavior is expected of us and to do our best to act accordingly.

With so much riding on the question, I thought it might be a good idea to apply the realist principles advocated throughout this book to finding a solution to this difficult and vexing issue. Hence the essay "Realism and the Spiritual Life," in which the question of God's existence is subjected to empirical and critical analysis. In the end, I discover that neither side in the debate over God's existence can make a slam-dunk case for its position, and that the question, like so many other vexing issues in life, can only be settled through a kind of intuitive judgment based on an appreciation of the relevant evidence. Yet this recourse to intuition itself could be questioned. What are we to think of such judgments? Can we rely on them? This suggests the need for some preliminary work. And so I have taken the liberty to insert, before the essay on realism and the spiritual life, another essay entitled, appropriately enough, "In Defense of Intuition," in which the scope and limit of intuitive judgments are delineated.

After investigating these profound issues involving man and his relation to the universe, I found that several important questions remain to be answered. When examining, for instance, the question of God's existence, I found convincing evidence that the principle of natural selection, which atheists urge as the ultimate explanation for life, explains a very great deal about the development of life, though it doesn't explain everything. At the same time, I found some evidence, though hardly conclusive evidence, of transcendence in the universe. Given these two collections of evidence, each pointing to diametrically opposed conclusions, how are we to come to any kind of unified theory of the universe? How do we reconcile the former body of evidence with the latter? In the final essay of the book, "Freedom and the Spontaneous Universe," I introduce a plausible conjecture aimed at integrating the evidence of naturalism with the evidence for transcendence, thus suggesting a unity out of which man's relation to the universe can be better understood and appreciated.

We live in a time when man's fundamental propensity toward superstitious belief has transferred from the religious to the secular sphere of life. The secular left's view of human nature, criminology, economic policy, and international relations is so riddled with palpably false notions that it takes one's breath away. Leftists live in a fairy tale world even more removed from reality than those occupied by the most reality-hating religious enthusiasts of the Dark and Middle Ages. Secular leftists refuse to accept all those painful lessons from mankind's melancholy history concerning the fragility of civilization and the necessity of using force to uphold civilized values. Instead, they blame the West for the barbarians who wish to destroy it and prescribe a medicine of appeasement and suicide. Through its dominance of centers of learning and the mainstream media, leftist modes of thought have so infested our culture that even ordinarily sensible people find themselves unwittingly influenced by them. Against this dark shadow of secular leftism which threatens to eclipse Western Civilization the methodology of realism serves as a bracing and even liberating antidote. To try to see things as they really are—as they would appear, presumably, to the mind God—rather than seeing them merely as the inveterate coward or the spoiled child would see them; to experience, in short, an authentic *vision of reality* (rather than a vision *against* or *contrary* to reality): *that* should be the *summum bonum* of all learning and wisdom!

Part 1: Politics

1. True and False Conservatism

There are few things more inconstant than political labels. Policies which in one decade are called "liberal" find themselves called "conservative" in another. Yesterday's liberal may become today's conservative; today's conservative may become tomorrow's liberal. Despite all the migratory propensities of these labels, there exists a certain consistency or core meaning in them which transcends the semantic fluctuations of the moment. That individuals such as Edmund Burke, David Hume, Alexander Hamilton, Alexis de Tocqueville, George Santayana, Joseph Schumpeter, Michael Oakeshott, and James Burnham are conservative hardly anyone would doubt. Nor would very many question the conservative credentials of Rush Limbaugh, Milton Friedman, David Frum, Sean Hannity, and Ann Coulter. Nonetheless, it should be clear to anyone who delves beneath the mere surface of things that the individuals in the former list are conservative in an appreciably different way than the individuals in the latter list. This is not to say that one group is better or worse than another, but simply to point out a few differences that deserve to be recognized and appreciated. And what, may we ask, are these differences? The individuals in the former list, the Burkes, the Hamiltons, the Santayanas, are *non-ideological* conservatives. Their conservatism is not a precise creed; it is a method of interpreting experience. The other conservatives, the Limbaughs, the

Hannitys, and the Kemps are *ideologues*. They believe in a precise creed which transcends experience. They are dogmatic and full of political zeal.

It is probably unfair to single out particular "conservatives" and accuse them of being ideologues, since they are rarely ideologues of the purest breed. Ideological purity and conservatism simply don't go together, because conservatism, at its core, is not an ideological philosophy. It is, rather, as Albert Jay Nock once put it, "a purely *ad hoc* affair; its findings vary with conditions, and are good for this day and train only." Conservatism "does not generalize beyond the facts of the case in point. It considers those facts carefully, makes sure that as far as possible it has them all in hand, and the course of action which the balance of fact *in that case* indicates as necessary will be the one it follows; and the course indicated as unnecessary it not only will not follow, but will oppose without compromise or concession." (1991, 265)

Edmund Burke made much the same point when he wrote: "I cannot stand forward and give praise or blame to anything which relates to human actions, and human concerns, on a simple view of the object, as it stands stripped of every relation, in all the nakedness and solitude of metaphysical abstraction. Circumstances (which with some gentlemen pass for nothing) give in reality to every political principle its distinguishing color and discriminating effect. The circumstances are what render every civil and political scheme beneficial or noxious to mankind." (1909, 148)

Non-ideological conservatism, then, seeks a more adequate view of political reality—one which captures all the nuances and subtleties of each particular situation. It is for this reason that conservatives in the Burkean tradition mistrust abstract political systems and "metaphysical" principles founded on "reason." Political reality, Burke would say, is far too complex to be summed up in a handful of bromides cogitated by pretentious intellectuals. "The science of constructing a commonwealth, or renovating it, or reforming it, is, like every other experimental science, not to be taught *a priori*," Burke gravely warned in his *Reflections on the Revolution in France.* "Nor is it a short experience that can instruct us in that practical science, because the real effects of moral causes are not always immediate; but that which in the first instance is prejudicial may be excellent in its remoter operation, and its excellence may arise even from the ill effects it produces in the beginning. The reverse also happens: and very plausible schemes, with very pleasing commencements, have often shameful and lamentable conclusions. In states there are often some obscure and almost latent causes, things which appear at first view of little moment, on which a very great part of its prosperity or adversity may most essentially depend. The science of government being therefore so practical in itself and intended for such practical purposes—a matter which requires experience, and even more experience than any person can gain in his whole life, however sagacious and observing he may be—it is with infinite caution that any man ought to venture upon pulling down an edifice which has answered in any tolerable degree for ages the common purposes of society, or on building it up again without having models and patterns of approved utility before his eyes." (1909, 198-199)

This, in a nutshell, tells us what non-ideological conservatism is all about. Particularly noteworthy is Burke's assertion that "the science of government" requires "even more experience than any person can gain in his whole life, however sagacious and observing he may be." Here we have the conservative defense of tradition. Tradition, for the conservative, is not good in and of itself. Only the good is a good in and of itself. Conservatives regard tradition as a sort of accumulation of wisdom of many people, both living and dead. Tradition is something "confirmed by the solid test of long experience." Or, as the historians Will and Ariel Durant put it: "No one man, however brilliant or well-informed, can come in one lifetime to such fullness of understanding as to safely judge and dismiss the customs or institutions of his society, for these are the wisdom of generations after centuries of experiment in the laboratory of history." (1968, 35)

This does not mean that all traditional customs and institutions are good. The conservative is well aware that some customs and institutions are bad, either because they were always bad or because they became bad over time. The conservative merely insists that you must have very good reasons before you decide to abolish or reform a custom or institution. You should not get rid of a custom or institution simply because it is imperfect. Human institutions, by the very fact that they are human, must always be imperfect. If their imperfections are severe, they can be reformed. But we should never abolish something because it fails to conform to "reason."

Non-ideological conservatism is intransigently anti-rationalistic. Knowledge, for the conservative, is based, not on words or ideas, but on practical experience. It contains a large intuitive component which defies precise articulation. The conservative believes that concepts and ideas never completely agree with the reality they represent. Articulate knowledge is symbolic, and hence flawed and inadequate. Reason is therefore regarded as limited. As Hume put it, reason "sees a full light, which illuminates certain places; but that light borders upon the most profound darkness. And between these reason is so dazzled and confounded, that she scarcely can pronounce with certainty and assurance concerning any one object." (1910, 438)

Thus speaks the non-ideological conservative. What about the ideological conservative? How does the one species of conservatism differ from the other?

This question cannot be answered without first understanding the nature of ideology. James Burnham defined ideology as "a more or less systematic and self-contained set of ideas supposedly dealing with the nature of reality (usually social reality), or some segment of reality, and of man's relation (attitude, conduct) toward it; and calling for a commitment independent of specific experience or events." (1964, 104) When Burnham describes ideology as a "self-contained set of ideas," he is identifying the dogmatic nature of ideological convictions. Ideologues are immune to experience. No fact or event will ever convince them that their ideology is bogus or flawed.

Since ideologues will never admit they are wrong, it is easy to devise a test to determine whether a given set of beliefs qualifies as ideological. All one has to do is ask the suspected ideologue if there is any conceivable evidence that might prove him wrong. If he says "No, nothing can refute my beliefs" (or the practical equivalent thereof), then he is an ideologue. Ideologies, because they cannot be tested by experience, are irrefutable. The ideologue believes this is a good thing, that irrefutability is equivalent to certainty and truth. Here he is mistaken. An ideology is not irrefutable because it is true; it is irrefutable because it is not testable.

From this, it can be gathered that an ideological conservatism is merely a form or species of conservatism that has been dogmatized and transformed into a rigid set of principles. The ideological conservative follows the letter of conservatism but ignores its spirit. In his hands, conservatism becomes, not a method of grasping the complexity of social reality, but a dogma used to simplify reality to the point of distortion. In any conflict between the facts and his conservative dogmas, the ideological conservative always sides with his dogmas. Under this view, principles become more real than facts, ideas more real than experiential observations. In philosophy, this "damn the facts" attitude is called "idealism." The philosophical idealist holds that external reality is primarily mental, that it is made up, not of matter and forces and facts, but of images, feelings, ideas, and propositions. The idealist tends to believe that our conception of things must take precedence over the things themselves.

Idealism usually (though not always) goes hand in hand with rationalism. The rationalist seeks to discover matters of fact through logical reasoning, as if the nature of the world were to be found through mere speculation, rather than through observation, study, and respect for the wisdom inherent in tradition and accustomed usage. Rationalism, like idealism, is a form of conceit or egotism. The rationalist regards the conclusions of his mind as having more cognitive value than all the traditional notions and values which arise spontaneously from the accumulated experience of society. He places his own private judgment above that of experienced statesmen, eminent scholars, and the great men of history, saying, in effect, that he is smarter than everyone else and that, through thinking alone, he can reach valid conclusions about subjects which he knows little, if anything, about.

Coupled with this arrogance one often finds intellectual laziness. The rationalist simply does not want to put in the hard work it takes to gain understanding of any complex social problem. He would prefer to reach his conclusions by playing verbal games with words. Instead of humbly going out into the real world and developing the intellectual skills necessary to undertake research into social phenomena, he prefers to sit in his room and read newspapers and concoct opinions on the basis of vague generalizations found in editorials and books of political propaganda. But nothing of any worth can be discovered in that way.

The very fact that rationalism can never understand the complexity of social reality makes it eminently suitable for the purposes of ideology. Since the ideologue is more concerned with dogma than with fact, he will find rationalism an excellent tool for defending his beliefs. Rationalism and rationalization are not merely similar etymologically, they represent more or less the same thing. The rationalist is nearly always a rationalizer; and the rationalizer is always a rationalist.

Ideology, then, leads to (or at least entails) idealism and rationalism. This is true even when the ideologue officially adheres to an anti-idealist or anti-rationalist philosophy. Since ideology, by its very nature, gives ideas a priority to reality and reason a priority to experience, the ideologue cannot avoid succumbing to idealism and rationalism when he goes about the business of defending his beliefs.

Now since conservatism has always given facts precedence over ideas and experience precedence over reason, it would seem that conservatism finds itself opposed to ideology. And so it is: conservatism, by its very nature, is anti-ideological. The conservative wants to see social reality as it really is, not as he might wish it to be. Conservatism always strives towards realism. That is why the conservative vision of social reality tends to be, as Thomas Sowell has pointed out, essentially tragic. (1987, 33) Reality is not a playpen for our wishes. If you want to understand the way things really are, you have to be prepared to accept many things that go against the grain of human desire. Unpleasant things exist in reality, and conservatism accepts this fact bravely, without resorting to cowardly evasion or rationalistic make-believe.

Reality is also immensely complicated. It is entirely out of scale with the human mind and can only be represented symbolically, in terms of metaphors, myths, and vague ideas. No rationalist conception of reality can ever be fully adequate. This is why humility in knowledge is so important. It is also why conservatives oppose rationalism in all its forms. Reason, by itself, can never grasp the complexities of life. It will almost always distort and misinterpret them. A rationalist view of society must inevitably be a subversive view. Anything in society that the rationalist cannot understand he seeks to overthrow. All uncritically accepted traditions, such as those found in religion or traditional morality, the rationalist mercilessly attacks, arguing that, since they are irrational, they need to be replaced by constructs devised by "reason." Never mind whether society requires these non-rational supports in order to cohere and survive. The rationalist would rather see all of society implode into a universal chaos than flourish on the basis of traditions he regards as "irrational."

Keeping all this mind, it should be clear that the very notion of an *ideological* conservative is a contradiction in terms. Ideologues who go about calling themselves conservatives are merely spouters of conservative slogans.

This false, ideological brand of conservatism is prominent among two camps within the broad "conservative" movement: first, among the so-called "economic" conservatives and, second, among right-wing conspiracy theorists. Both groups tend to be very dogmatic in their thinking and are incapable of grasping any fact or principle that falls outside the narrow parameters of their restrictive ideology. Being ideologues, they are prone to the two fatal diseases of ideology: idealism and rationalism. For anyone who does not regard this as a serious problem, perhaps an empirical illustration will persuade him or her to reconsider.

Although Ayn Rand was unceremoniously booted out of the conservative movement by Whittaker Chambers fifty years ago, she has nevertheless exercised a profound influence on the development of "economic" conservatism—an influence that has always been in an ideological direction. Rand, despite all the noise she made about being an uncompromising realist, was, if the truth be told, an ideologue of the purest breed, immovable in her dogmatism and fiercely rationalistic. Rand's "objectivist" vision of the ideal society represents a kind of *reductio ad absurdum* of secular economic conservatism. Here, in the words of Rand scholar Chris Sciabarra, is a description of Rand's ideal social order: "In an Objectivist society, the socialization process would aid, rather than hinder, the development of maturity, rationality, and self-responsibility. Parents and teachers would treat children with respect, encouraging them to think, rather than to evade. They would not deliver moral ultimatums or religious injunctions, but present the child with reasons and explanations within the context of his knowledge, for every rule.... People would not act on the basis of an uncritical acceptance of traditions and/or of tacit rules of behavior. They would understand the nature of their actions and the implications of their beliefs. Accepting their own uniqueness and potential, such people would have a benevolent attitude toward one another. Human communications, sexual relations, spiritual commitments, and material exchanges would not be masked by strategic lying and deceit, but by mutual trust and respect." (1995, 367-8)

Here we find as pure an example of social rationalism as we are likely ever to stumble upon. Everything in society would be placed under the dominion of "reason." All uncritically accepted traditions, including "moral ultimatums" and "religious injunctions," would be unceremoniously thrown in the trash. Everyone would be expected to "understand the nature of their actions and the implications of their beliefs" so that they would never act on the basis of "tacit rules of behavior."

This is a view of society that only an intractable ideologue could hold. It not only oversteps important social realities—it mangles and crushes them beyond recognition. If it were even possible to regulate the social order with such principles, the consequences would be disastrous. If you removed all uncritically accepted traditions and subverted, through rationalist criticism, all tacit rules of behavior you would create a positively inhuman society. For it is precisely these uncritically accepted traditions and tacit rules of behavior that provide the moral glue responsible for holding society together and rendering social relations civilized and humane.

We see this all too clearly in the social behavior of Rand's most scrupulous and dedicated followers. Those who are familiar with Rand's own life will immediately understand what I am suggesting. Yet it goes well beyond the dysfunctional relations that existed between Rand and her immediate disciples. Within the objectivist movement itself one finds a high degree of social displacement, alienation, and anomie. As is well known, Rand preached one of the most extreme forms of individualism ever inflicted upon the human race. Randian individualism is revolutionary and subversive in scope. It is incompatible with the sort of "social bond individualism" favored by conservative thinkers like Richard Weaver. Anarchic (i.e., Randian) individualism, as Weaver wisely notes, "is charged with a lofty disdain for the human condition.... It is not Christian to accept such a view; or, if that is too narrow, it is just not possible. Such a view ends in the extremism of nihilism." (1987, 102-103)

A good example of this nihilism is seen in Ellen Plasil's account of her experiences within the Objectivist social milieu. Plasil, on the recommendation of one of Rand's closest disciples, Dr. Allan Blumenthal, began therapy with Dr. Lonnie Leonard, a leading Objectivist psychotherapist. Leonard, as Plasil would soon discover, had his own agenda that went well beyond Rand's philosophy. By taking advantage of the psychological vulnerabilities of his female patients, he sought to manipulate them into giving him sexual favors. He exploited Plasil for nearly five years before she realized the harm he was causing her. When she learned that Leonard had also sexually exploited other female patients besides herself, she terminated her therapy. This move set off a storm of controversy within the Objectivist community.

Since her teens, all of Plasil's friends and acquaintances had been Objectivists—that is, diehard followers of the Randian ideology. These were the people that Plasil would turn to in times of need. They constituted, as Plasil herself put it, her "entire support system." If they abandoned her, she would have nobody. So what happened? In keeping with the heartless rationalism which is at the center of Rand's ideological philosophy, Plasil's Objectivist friends betrayed her. They all sided with Dr. Leonard. "I received innumerable phone calls, from men and women alike," she later recalled, "who *condemned* me for terminating my own therapy and for the reason they had learned was behind my doing so. In one call, I was accused of 'destroying the closest thing Man has ever had to a god.' In another, I was threatened with retaliation for causing the closing of Dr. Leonard's practice." (1985, 158)

Here we have an eloquent example of the subversive effects of rationalist ideology. Rand's morality of "enlightened selfishness" and excessive individualism had, like a corrosive acid, eaten away the tradition-based social bonds that hold a community of friends and acquaintances together. Without these social bonds, the individual must rely entirely on his own private judgment in dealing with the immense complexities of social reality. Since this is not possible, the individual, left to his own devices, has no choice but to attach himself to the first charismatic figure who is willing to fill the void left by the absence of all those uncritically accepted traditions that provide the sense of community people need.

Once this is understood, we can begin to grasp why all of Plasil's Objectivist friends abandoned her and sided with Dr. Leonard. They sided with Dr. Leonard because he gave them the emotional support they desperately needed and could not get in any other way. Bereft of any sort of religious or communitarian support system, they had no choice but to become abject followers of a common charlatan and sexual malefactor. This is frequently what happens when some ideologue or philosopher attempts to replace the common sense morality of traditional ethics with a "rational" morality of intellectualist speculation or "reason." Instead of liberty and independence, we find blind loyalty to this or that self-appointed messiah.

Ideology, if carried out consistently, leads to social or political totalitarianism. That is why even ideologies which advocate liberty and independent thinking, such as Randian Objectivism, must lead, if they lead to anything at all, to a loss of personal autonomy and a degradation of liberty. Most human beings cannot tolerate living without some sort of community-based support system. If that support system is subverted through rationalist criticism or an excessive reliance on personal judgment, the individual will turn to some cult or to the state for support. The end result will either be the flourishing of cults or government interventionism on a massive scale.

Now while it is true that the Randian ideology is so extreme that even ideological conservatives cannot accept it *in toto*, this does not mean that Rand's influence on the Right can be regarded as of minor importance. Most of the so-called "secular" or "economic" conservatives influenced by Rand are deeply enmeshed within the mire of ideology. Too many of them, under the influence of Rand and other "laissez-faire" ideologies, are guilty of placing too much emphasis on the market and the laws of supply and demand. Merely because the market leads to an efficient allocation of goods and services doesn't mean it can be made into the leading principle of society. The truth of this was recognized by Wilhelm Röpke, the important German economist. "Society as a whole cannot be ruled by the laws of supply and demand," Röpke warned, "and the state is more than a sort of business company, as has been the conviction of the best conservative opinion since the time of Burke.

Individuals who compete on the market and there pursue their own advantage stand all the more in need of the social and moral bonds of community, without which competition degenerates most grievously. As we have said before, the market economy is not everything. It must find its place in a higher order of things which is not ruled by supply and demand, free prices, and competition. It must be firmly contained within an all-embracing order of society in which the imperfections and harshness of economic freedom are corrected by law and in which man is not denied conditions of life appropriate to his nature. Man can wholly fulfill his nature only by freely becoming part of a community and having a sense of solidarity with it. Otherwise he leads a miserable existence and he knows it." (1958, 91)

It would appear from all that has been advanced here that anyone sympathetic with the broad tenets of conservatism really ought to take a close look at what he really believes and make certain that he hasn't slipped into ideological thinking; because to the extent that he does slip, he is betraying the better part of his conservative sentiments. An ideological conservatism must always be, to the extent that is ideological, a false conservatism. The rationalism and dogmatism implicit in most ideologies are contrary to conservatism's essentially anti-rationalist and practical point of view. Those who want to mature and deepen in their conservatism need to oppose ideology in all its manifestations, even in its putatively "conservative" ones.

2. Politics and the Weather

Charles Dudley Warner once complained, as a joke, that everyone gripes about the weather but no one ever does anything about it. The point of the joke, of course, is that no one *can* do anything about it. The weather cannot be controlled by human action. A hurricane cannot be abolished by a vote in Congress, or by protest marches on a University campus, or by indignant talk radio hosts. It will do as it pleases despite the sentiments and actions of those who would like to stamp it out.

I believe the same thing is largely true of politics. Beyond a handful of people who have access to the levers of power, politics remains inaccessible to human control. For the average citizen, the government he lives under remains as uncontrollable as the weather. The only difference is that, whereas most people recognize that they cannot control the weather, far too many live under the illusion that they can make a difference on the political stage. Even though they are but one vote among millions; even though they do not know a single soul in government; even though they hardly have enough influence to control what goes on in their own households: yet they still believe that, merely by *arguing* about politics, they can help make things "better." The irrationality of human beings is almost touching in its naïveté and faith. When has arguing about *anything*, let alone politics, ever made things better? About the most arguing ever accomplishes is

24

to exasperate and annoy those subjected to it. Otherwise, its net effect is so close to zero that it might as well be zero.

Why, then, do so many people continue to wrangle and squabble and dissent about politics? Why do they participate in noisy yet futile protest marches? Why do they make fools of themselves carrying placards with infantile slogans? Why do they plaster their vehicles with idiotic bumper stickers supporting one hopeless and insane cause after another? Why so much energy, so many resources devoted to vain political commitments? After all, people don't go around protesting the weather. You don't find them running about with placards reading "Down with the Rain!" or "Say No to Wind!" or "Mothers against Sunshine." Everyone acknowledges that it would be pointless to remonstrate against the weather. Few, however, are willing to admit that political remonstrations are nearly as pointless.

As one example, consider the website, *www.taiwanese.com/protest*, set up some years ago to remonstrate against the guided missile tests staged by China off the coast of Taiwan in March of 1996. The site urges its readers to "send your protest to Chinese President Jiang Zemin and the PRC embassy in your area. Send your appeal for support to Security Council members in the United Nations, US President and Congressmen, and policy makers in your country. If you are not a constituent in your area now, share your views with your local friends, teachers, and ask for their support in writing to express their concerns." While there would be no point in questioning the sincerity of these good people, the naivety of their enterprise is little short of appalling. Does anyone seriously believe that Jiang Zemin or anyone at the PRC embassy gives a rat's ass whether you or I agree with China's military policies? The communist oligarchy that rules China hardly cares whether you or I or anyone else approves of their policies. Even protests by their own people would little dissuade them. They would simply put them down by force, as they did in the brutal 1989 Tiananmen Square massacre.

Some would argue that not all protests are futile. This is true. But even when protests do have an impact, such as the antiwar protests of the sixties, they accomplish little more than reinforcing shifts in public opinion that would have occurred without them. To be sure, this very reinforcing is not something to be dismissed out of hand. It can be of critical importance—as was demonstrated in the sixties civil rights movement. Although the country as a whole was moving towards greater toleration of black Americans, the protests led by Martin Luther King and others certainly provided an impetus to the movement. Even here, however, an important distinction has to be made. While the people who participated in the movement, taken as an entire group, did exercise a very real effect on the country, the effect of each individual was very close to zero. This is one of the great paradoxes of democratic action. A large group of people, if well organized under shrewd leaders, constitutes a political force to be reckoned with. But each individual in the group, when taken as a single person, has no real power of his own and can no more control the direction of politics than he can control the movements of the planets.

The leaders of protest movements obviously don't want anyone to understand this, because it would discourage people from joining movements. Here we see the other side of the paradox. While it is indubitably true that the individual, taken in his own person, cannot possibly make the slightest bit of difference, if all ordinary people felt that way and no one ever participated in politics, the impresarios of protest movements would be left in the lurch. They have to make all their followers believe that each person can make a difference, even though this is not in the least true. Only as one large, well-disciplined mass can a political movement hope to have any chance of changing things. Even then, its chances aren't terribly good.

What is true of political movements is no less true of electoral democracy. Some consider voting a national duty, as if failure to go to the polls on election day were a kind of treason. Others seek to convince people that it is in their interest to vote, that democracy gives them the power to make a difference. Every vote counts, we are constantly being assured. Your vote (or mine) could, perchance, make a difference in who wins the next election. Such convictions, I would argue, aren't worth the hot air needed to voice them. In an election involving millions of people, the odds that the outcome will hinge on one vote is infinitesimal, if that. We all remember how narrowly George W. Bush prevailed over Al Gore in the 2000 election. Yet, according to the official recount, Bush won Florida, the key state in his electoral victory, by 537 votes. This means that 536 of Bush's supporters could have stayed home in Florida and Bush still would have won the election. And all of Gore's supporters, down to the very last one, could have stayed home and it would not have made the slightest difference in the ultimate outcome.

There is another side to this whole issue which illustrates the political impotence of the average citizen in strongest colors. The recount in Florida occurred because the election was very close. According to the pre-recount tally, Bush won Florida by 1,725 votes. That seems like a lot, but compared to nearly six million Floridians who cast votes in the 2000 election, it is infinitesimal—or .03% to be exact. The margin is so small, it falls below the margin of error. As we learned in Florida, many people, certainly more than .03 percent, screw up their ballots. How then, if an election is decided by a mere .03 percent, can we ever be sure who won? We can't be sure. That's what it means to say the margin of Bush's election victory in Florida falls below the margin of error. We don't really know who won in Florida. Hence the controversy of the result. Now if really close elections fall below the margin of error, then how can anyone argue that one vote can make the difference? It would seem that a really close election would be precisely the sort of contest when votes don't count, because the election's outcome falls under the margin of error. The Florida election was a toss-up—precisely because it was too close to call. The courts had to settle it. The Florida Supreme Court, which leans to the Left, tried to hand the election to Gore by supporting a set of recount rules that heavily favored the Democratic candidate. The U.S. Supreme Court overturned this ruling, putting its stamp of approval on the counting rules that had already declared Bush the winner.

It is sobering to consider how little most of us count in the political scheme of things. Our protests don't count, our votes don't count, even our letters to Congressmen and Senators count (or if they do, they count for very little). We are constantly being told that we do count, but that is a falsehood. We only count as part of a much larger group—a group so large that it could afford to lose a member or two without anyone noticing. Those of us who are mere average citizens, without any special influence or leverage, are, as political and social actors on the great stage of history, utterly without significance.

So what does this mean? What lessons should be drawn from this? Should we simply give up all interest in politics, recognizing the utter futility of political action? No, we don't have to go *that* far. Keep in mind the paradox of political action: that while the lone individual counts as nothing by himself, if everybody felt like that and nobody voted or took part in the political process, the consequences could be devastating. Recall what Edmund Burke said: "When bad men combine, the good must associate; else they will fall, one by one, an unpitied sacrifice in a contemptible struggle." Since bad men will always be combining, in one way or the other, the good must also combine. And they must combine in sufficient numbers to make their efforts count. This means in numbers large enough that an addition or subtraction of this or that individual won't make any difference. Nor should we allow the insignificance of the individual to demoralize us. We all have to obey the mad logic of the system, thinking we can make a difference even though, by our own measly selves, we count for nothing.

In a sense, you could say that political action, whenever it relies on masses of ordinary people to achieve a political objective, such as winning an election or protesting an abuse of government, must, to have any chance of success, make use of a falsehood. To achieve success in politics through mass influence, you must first convince each person that their participation will make a difference. Yet, as we have seen, this is a lie. Georges Sorel, the French political theorist, called such lies "myths." A successful myth accomplishes its objectives by motivating the masses of people toward efficacious political and social action. "Experience shows that the *framing of a future, in some indeterminate time*, may, when it is done in a certain way, be very effective, and have few inconveniences," explained Sorel in his *Reflections on Violence*; "this happens when the anticipations of the future take the form of those myths, which enclose with them, all the strongest inclinations of a people, of a party or a class, inclinations, which recur to the mind with the insistence of instincts in all the circumstances of life." (1906, 124-125) Thus a man anticipates that, if his party wins an election, the government will enact policies of which he approves. This belief provides him with the motivation to act: that is, to take the trouble to go to the polls and cast his one vote among millions.

Note that there is not one, but two myths motivating our poor delusional elector. First, there is the simple myth that his vote can make a difference—which is plainly not true. Then there is the second myth that, supposing his party wins, it will faithfully carry out all its promises. This is, as we know from experience, rather unlikely. The party may keep some of its promises. But the odds that it will keep all of them are very slim. Hence the scorn which all persons of sense regard political promises. Lies—the whole lot of them! Yet these lies are critical to motivating the masses. For this reason, they are not lies, but merely myths. As Sorel reminds us, "the myths are not descriptions of things, but expressions of a determination to act." That is really what a political promise is: an expression of a determination to act.

I have outlined the mythical, even mendacious character of the whole political scheme of things for one reason only: to prove the complete political impotence of the ordinary individual. Why is this important? Well, admittedly, for most people it is not important at all. As a matter of fact, it would be better if they continued to believe that their vote counts and that each individual plays a critical role in the evolution of society. This essay is not written for those good people. I address my thoughts solely to those who have seen through the veil of political illusion and realize the political impotence of the individual. This realization can both humble and liberate the spirit. Acknowledging our inability to affect the social order can be a blow to the ego. Yet by casting self-deception aside, we liberate ourselves from error.

To grasp how we can benefit from the liberation, let us return to our metaphor of the weather. The weather is not something that can be directly controlled by human will. It matters little what the forecast is, whether it will rain, snow, blow like crazy, or scorch like the devil, there is little that you or I or anyone else can do to prevent the weather from running its course. Yet this does not mean that we are entirely at the weather's mercy. If it rains, we can stay indoors; if it blows, we can close all the windows and take down any objects that might be exposed to the wind's mercurial rage; if it is warm, we can take pains to remain in the shade or go swimming. In other words, we can react to the weather, dovetailing our plans and our activities with its caprices. Thanks to the science of meteorology, we can make our plans several days in advance. If we want to go to the beach sometime in the next few days, we can check the forecast to determine which day will be most suitable for such a venture. If the forecast warns of rain, we can make sure we are provided with an umbrella and a raincoat. If the forecast warns of potential threats, such as hurricanes, tornadoes, floods, heat waves, ice storms, we can take the appropriate precautions. To know, for example, that a bad storm is headed in our direction gives us a chance to prepare for the worst. Since the deployment of weather satellites, which makes it much easier to predict the movements of dangerous storms, thousands of lives have been saved.

So the very fact that the weather cannot be controlled or abolished does not render us completely helpless, since we can control how we react to the weather. The same line of reasoning can easily be applied to politics. Although most of us cannot control what happens in politics, we can control how we react to political events. If, for instance, we note the appearance of political storms on the horizon, we can prepare ourselves for them, to minimize whatever injustices may be heading in our direction. Just as we can make rational preparations for the weather by consulting the science of meteorology, so we can also make rational preparations for political crises by making use of the scientific study of politics. If you can see through the cant and balderdash of partisan ideologues to the inner realities at the core of political action, then you can make shrewd guesses of what is likely to happen and act accordingly. Consider the advantage those German Jews who could see into the innermost reality of Hitler's Nazi movement enjoyed over the rest of their brethren. They were the ones who got out of Germany before it was too late.

The ability to make at least semi-accurate forecasts of the political future depends on the soundness of the theories used to interpret the relevant evidence. Bad theories are likely to lead to unreliable forecasts. That is why it is so important to get it right: because getting it wrong can sometimes mean the difference between life and death, as it did for those Jews in Germany who realized what was happening and got out while they still had a chance. How does one go about getting it right? What trick or method helps one guess the direction of political developments?

This is too difficult a question to answer in a mere essay. Indeed, several volumes would hardly be enough. The most I can do is give a few brief hints touching upon one or two of the more salient points involved in the question. One thing I must insist upon right from the start. Making shrewd political prognostications does not depend solely on brainpower. A man of genius can be a complete idiot when it comes to political prognostications; while, on the other side, a man of average brain power, provided he merely has some common sense and the ability to make qualitative judgments, may be very shrewd in his political guesses. Brainpower, in some instances, proves a stumbling block, as it tends to inflate egos and, through an excessive ability to rationalize, leads to self-deception and wishful thinking.

To appreciate how disastrous wishful thinking can be to political science, consider how the meteorologist goes about making weather forecasts. Unlike any number of political thinkers, he does not try to determine what ought to happen or what he wishes would happen, but what *will* happen. He may prefer sunshine to rain, stillness to wind, and warmth to cold, but if a cold windy storm is headed his way, he will not let his preferences interfere with his judgment of the fact. He knows that his job is to predict, as accurately as his science allows him, the weather. He is a scientist, not an advocate; he deals in facts, not wishes and feelings.

Yet it goes even deeper than this. Self-deception is the great vice of the ideologue. The ideologue may sincerely believe in his objectivity; but if he allows himself to be guided by his ideology, as he nearly always does, he will seriously compromise his judgment. Most of the communists in Germany in the late twenties and early thirties failed to recognize the danger posed by Adolf Hitler. The communists regarded Hitler as a mere outgrowth of capitalism. Hence they made no distinction between Social Democrats and the Nazi Party. Ernest Thälmann, the head of the German Communist Party, told the Riechstag in 1930 that fascism was already in power in Germany, because the head of the government was a Social Democrat. "Blinded by their absurd political analysis," writes historian Paul Johnson, "the Communists actually wanted a Hitler government, believing it would be a farcical affair, the prelude to their own seizure of power." [*Modern Times*, 282-3] Ideology and wishful thinking prevented the German communists from grasping the political reality of pre-Hitlerite Germany. They allowed the gospel according to

Marx to blind them to the danger posed by Hitler. Because of this foolishness, they unwittingly helped the Nazis seize power in 1933.

We find a similar kind of irresponsibility among many liberals and leftists in contemporary America, who cannot talk about anyone on the right without using such epithets as "ultra-conservative," "far right," "conservative evildoer," "McCarthyite," etc. The motive for this sort of exaggeration is, obviously, to discredit conservatism. But left-liberals should be careful lest their smears serve only to legitimize those who really are on the far right— i.e., the Birchers, the secessionists, the hard-core racists and other such ideological vermin. There are important differences between conservatives and other right-wingers like George W. Bush, Rush Limbaugh, and Bill Bennett on the one side and the conspiracy nuts and anti-Semites on the other. By confusing run-of-the-mill conservatives with those who really are on the *far* right, you undermine the ability of language to express important distinctions between various strands of opinion and ideology.

Being tied to any ideology, whether of the right or the left, is always a handicap in trying to forecast the political future. The ideologue is almost invariably more concerned with apologetics than with truth. His ideology means more to him than getting the facts right. Interpreting current events becomes a matter, not of trying to figure out how the political system really works and how it is likely to manifest itself in the future, but with demonstrating, through verbal legerdemain, that everything good that happens in the political world is the result of *his* ideology, while everything bad is caused by those who oppose his ideology.

The ideologue, in short, is more interested in what *ought* to happen than what *will* happen. Contrast this with the meteorologist, who never concerns himself with what ought to be, but only with what is likely to happen. The meteorologist says *There is a storm coming in tomorrow*, or *It will likely rain on Tuesday*—a far cry from saying *It ought to rain tomorrow*, or *It ought to rain on Tuesday*.

The separation of fact and value clears the mind of prejudices and enables it to make a rational assessment of all the relevant facts. Wishful thinking renders the mind incapable of rational analysis. If you want to know what will happen in any walk of life, the first thing you need to do is temporarily set aside your moral ideals. Only then can you think with a clear head.

Morality is not a problem for the meteorologist, because he understands that meteorological phenomena are beyond human control. The problem with politics is that, unlike the weather, human action can make a difference. Unfortunately, those who can make a difference in politics constitute a small minority. For most people, politics is, as we have seen, as uncontrollable as the weather. Therefore, those of us who are politically impotent really don't have any excuse. If we want to know what the political future might have in store for us, we have no choice but to study politics with the same sense of detached objectivity with which the meteorologist studies the weather. But first, we must learn how to liberate ourselves from the prejudices, the moral ideals, the ideological commitments that serve as obstacles to understanding political reality.

3. The Democratic Farce

The Florida Presidential election fiasco, which generated so much controversy in its day, is now nearly forgotten. Only a few unrepentant Leftists, bitter over George W. Bush's accession to the Presidential office, still gripe about it. Thus we find Eric Alterman, columnist for *The Nation*, speaking of the President's "proven political illegitimacy." Why does Mr. Alterman consider Bush's Presidency illegitimate? Because, he smugly assures us, "we know that Al Gore ... beat George Bush by roughly 537,000 votes nationally" and "also handily defeated him among legally cast votes in Florida." Even so, we find Bush, and not Mr. Gore in the White House. What does this say about the President's "proven political illegitimacy"? (2001)

Illegitimacy is obviously a subjective concept. Only those who strongly dislike Bush regard him as illegitimate. No one else cares whether Bush failed to win the popular vote or the so-called "legal" votes in Florida. Legitimacy is a state of mind. It has little if anything to do with technical questions regarding suffrages and vote counting.

What about all this talk we hear of the "sacredness" of democracy? "The fiasco [in Florida] provides a rare opportunity to rethink and improve our voting practices in a way that reflects our professed desire to have 'every vote count,'" opined Lani Guinier, again in *The Nation* (2000). Note the smugness of Guinier's conviction. She writes of our "professed desire" to make "every vote count." Whose "professed desire" is she referring to? The readers of *The Nation*, or everyone in general? I will assume she means all "reasonable" people. That is usually what people mean when they use "we," "our," or "us." After all, who could possibly be against making every vote count? Perhaps a few stray reactionaries (mostly fascists), but all decent men and women believe in the glorious creed of democracy, which can be summed up in Guinier's conviction, never questioned, never analyzed, never even fully comprehended, that every vote should count, regardless of the circumstances. A government "of the people, by the people, for the people" is the only "just" government.

This uncritical attitude towards democracy does little to shed light on the phenomenon itself. It is all fine and good to pontificate about the glories of democracy. But if we want to understand what democracy means in terms of facts, rather than in terms of mere rhetoric and emotion, we do well to look beyond all the sanctimony that shrouds the word and fix our gaze on the political reality of the thing itself. Democracy, as is obvious to anyone with eyes in their head to see, clearly cannot mean government of the people, by the people, for the people. In fact, there can be no greater distortion of the facts than to describe democracy with this phrase, for the simple reason that there is no such thing as "the people." Nations are made of individuals, not peoples. The term *people* is simply a vague description of many individuals. Because of its vagueness, it can be used as either the subject or object of a sentence without representing anything definite in reality. Lincoln's hackneyed phrase is little more than eloquent patter. As rhetoric, its value is immense; as science, its value is zero.

Those who confuse democracy with such phantom concepts as "General Will," "the people," "the public," the "rank and file," are merely spouting empty gibberish. No such entity exists. If it did exist, democracy would be superfluous. The *raison d'être* of democracy arises precisely because of the heterogeneous nature of the social order. The nation as a whole is not a unity, as democratic rhetoric suggests, but a disunity, made up of various factions and classes competing with one another for wealth and status. If this disunity did not exist, if the social order were completely harmonious, there would be no need for elections, ballot boxes, campaign speeches, national conventions, legislatures, parliaments, plebiscites, or any of the other vulgar trappings of democracy. If everyone in society agreed, elections would be unnecessary. Since there would be only one collective will, shared by everyone, it wouldn't matter who got elected. It would be far more efficient to select the government through a random lottery. An election, by its very nature, implies a disunity in the body politic. It introduces disagreement and faction into the very heart of society.

To understand democracy, you must first grasp the rationale of elections. What purpose do they serve in society? What are the benefits and hazards of holding them? Why are they important to a free society?

Right off the bat we can shoot down the most common misconception about elections. The purpose of democratic elections is not to determine the will of people, because no such thing exists. If the purpose of elections is not to determine or express the will of people, then what is its purpose?

To answer this question, we need to return to the problem of social heterogeneity. Consider the difficulty faced by every society, especially every "open society" characterized by widespread heterogeneity of beliefs and lifestyles. How does such a society go about making political decisions, when its populace is so divided? On the one side, we find the "far right"—the traditionalists, the nationalists, the fundamentalists. On the other side, we find the far Left—the radical professoriate, the chic artists, and other assorted intellectual riffraff. Between these extremes you have an entire spectrum of opinion, including bizarre combinations that borrow from both sides. It is clear that if everyone in society had to agree before any kind of "collective" action could be taken, public policy would be impossible. Before a democratic state can exist and function, it is necessary that the problem of social disagreement should be confronted.

Historically, five different solutions have evolved to deal with this problem: the cultural, the feudal, the monarchical, the totalitarian, and the democratic. The first one, the cultural, may exist in varying degrees in almost any society, but dominates only within primitive societies—i.e., in societies without a centralized state. In the absence of government, men are ruled by mores, taboos, and ancestor worship. Political organization doesn't enter into the social equation, despite the presence of chiefs and other "leaders." Since everything (or nearly everything) is determined by precedent, leaders have little room for self-initiative. They are not so much leaders as the first among followers.

Under this form of cultural totalitarianism, the problem of disagreement is solved by demanding that everyone respect the prevailing taboos. Those who show any initiative are punished, either through the petty persecution of the envious or, in more extreme cases, by ostracism.

Feudal society confronts disagreement with violence and decentralization. Within each fiefdom, a feudal baron rules through force. On a larger level, disagreements are handled either through violence or, when that proves inadequate, by acquiescing to the whims of local barons. Collective action on a grand scale becomes very difficult under such a system. National policy is nearly impossible, except on a few grand projects that most of the barons can agree on, like an invasion or a crusade. The individual cannot look to the state to protect him from the depredations of the feudal aristocracy, but must accept his position in society as his lord's vassal. Feudal societies tend toward lawlessness and violence. Disagreements are solved in favor of the strongest.

Monarchical societies attempt to solve the problem of disagreement through loyalty to a single person, the king. To be sure, reality diverges quite a bit from theory. Despite all the fine talk from monarchists about the divine right of kings and the absolute power of monarchy, kings never owed their power to divine right. Louis XIV was a powerful king because he had a standing army. Monarchy is largely based on force. Disagreements are settled through armed combat, which can easily escalate into civil war.

The rise of an elective, "democratic" method of settling political conflicts came about largely because of the bloody wars and revolutions that characterized the pre-democratic era in European history. Through a process of trial and error, societies discovered that representative institutions provide a better way of resolving political differences than internecine strife. The representative system allowed nations to make collective political decisions that most societal factions could live with. Compromise is essential to the democratic process. Each person in society accepts an outcome he regards as sub-optimal to avoid the bloodshed that would inevitably result if the political process were determined solely by force.

Democracy, then, is a political method that evolved to avoid sanguinary conflict arising from the fact that human beings can never agree about politics. In lieu of settling these inevitable differences through violence, society plays a game called democracy. We have elections, legislative bodies, presidents or prime ministers, and judges. In the helter-skelter of the political process, an outcome is reached that most of us can live with, even if none of us particularly care for it.

Traditional rationalizations of democracy fail to understand this simple truth. Consider the following description of democracy provided by the U.S. State Department: "Democracy is a system of self-government where the citizens are equal and political decisions are made by majority rule, but always with the protection of minority rights. In its purest form, democracy affords citizens the opportunity to participate directly in the decision-making process. This is called direct democracy. Given the size and complexity of today's societies, it is generally more practical for citizens to elect representatives who will govern and make decisions on their behalf. Representative democracy relies on regular, free, fair, and competitive elections to hold the government accountable to the people.

"In a democracy, the government exists to serve the people, not the other way around. Since democratic government derives its authority from the consent of the governed, the people have the capacity to change the government peacefully when they lose confidence in it. And they need not fear a bullet if they try." (1998, Gandal and Finn)

This description of democracy, while not entirely false, is clearly inadequate. Democracy, we are told, "relies on regular, free, fair, and competitive elections to hold the government accountable to the people." But is this how it works in America? Do we really have "fair and competitive" elections? (And what on earth does "fair" mean in this context? Fair to whom?) Does the government really exist to "serve the people"? (Which people? Who on earth are "the people," anyway?) And do these "people" (whoever they are) really have the capacity to change the government when they no longer have confidence in it?

Most of these assertions concerning democracy are, at best, exaggerations and, at worst, lies. The contention that democracy relies on regular and competitive elections to hold the government accountable is clearly an exaggeration. In real life, elections provide only partial accountability. Even in the most democratic of political systems, there still exists a wide latitude within which elected representatives can act. The Italian sociologist Vilfredo Pareto, after noting how sovereigns are often led by the nose by their advisers and ministers, observes that "His Majesty Demos" is "even less percipient.... The worthy Demos thinks he is following his own wishes, whereas in fact he is following the behests of his rulers. But this very often serves only the interests of his rulers for these, from the days of Aristophanes down to our own, have practised on a large scale the art of pulling the wool over the eyes of Demos." (Mind and Society, §2253)

Many examples could be provided by history, both ancient and modern, to prove that Pareto's view, cynical as some may find it, is more or less correct. An excellent example from more recent history involves the Congressional pay raise scandal of 1989—an event which, in its time, consumed the passions of many politically motivated Americans but which today is entirely forgotten. On the surface, it looks like a triumph for the democratic will of the electorate. If we look deeper into the whole incident, we discover that, far from asserting its "will," "His Majesty Demos" took yet another one in the backside. Here's what happened.

In 1989, a presidential commission proposed that Congress should get a whopping 52% pay increase, which would raise a Member of Congress's official income from $89,000 a year to $135,000 a year. As could be expected, the measure was not popular. That Congress should give itself a raise despite its gross failure to responsibly manage the nation's finances was more than most people could stomach. Congressional phone lines were jammed with complaints. Radio talk show hosts had a field day stirring up resentment against the nation's lawmakers. Opposition among the electorate was fierce and widespread. Nevertheless, Congress was determined to get its loot. As Jeffrey Birnbaum explained in *The Lobbyists*: "Congressional leaders carefully plotted to get the raise without having to take the perilous step of voting for it. Under the old rules of the presidential commission, the raise would automatically go into effect on Wednesday, February 8, which was just five days away, as long as Congress did not act to block it.... The Senate voted overwhelmingly against the hike. But that had been expected. The plan all along had been to delay a similar vote in the House, where leaders have more control over what legislation gets to the floor and when."

Despite the intensity of public opposition, the plan would have worked if House Speaker James Wright had not turned coward at the last moment and betrayed his colleagues. Yielding to pressures from his home district, the Texan scheduled a vote on the pay raise right before it could go into effect. "Many lawmakers," observed Birnbaum, "... considered this an act of betrayal. Many of them considered Wright's rash action as incredibly self-destructive." (1993, 23)

Wright had committed the cardinal sin of oligarchical leadership: in a moment of weakness he had betrayed the interests of his class to satisfy a mere whim of the electorate. A few months later Wright would pay for his sin by suffering the greatest punishment which Congress can mete out against its Speaker: he would be forced to resign.

In the meantime, the partisans of democracy could enjoy the illusion that the democratic system still worked. "See," they exalted after this great victory, "elected leaders can still be made to follow the wishes of the people, provided enough pressure is put on them." Alas, it would be a short-lived triumph. Though Demos had won the battle, in the long run, as usual, Demos would lose the war. In the following November, Congress eventually got its much desired pay raise. In 1991, the worthies in the Senate voted themselves a $35,500 raise! In the end, the politicians in Washington pretty much got what they wanted. In their unceasing war against the desires of their constituents, they suffered but one defeat, which they easily reversed a few years later.

This is not to imply that the government always gets what it wants and never pays heed to the desires of the majority. On the contrary, it pays very close attention to the desires of the electorate. The power of democratic governments does in fact rest partially on the "consent of the governed," but not in the sense meant by traditional democratic theory. Elections can help prevent gross abuses of power. They are less effective, however, against more subtle depredations of the public interest.

Most politically astute individuals are aware of this fact. Thus we find them constantly complaining about the "betrayal of democracy," as if whining about it will make it better. They can bellyache until their faces turn blue; it won't change a thing. Democracy by its very nature is corrupt—as are all forms of centralized power. When politicians "betray" democracy, they are merely acting out their roles in the democratic farce. It is a waste of time to wax indignant about it. Better to accept the reality and deal with it the best one can. Nor should we assume that we would all be better off if "true" democracy held sway. There are compelling reasons to believe that, even if democracy were possible, it would hardly be desirable.

One of the most tenacious myths concerning democracy is the conviction, held by many Americans, that the masses are an expository of wisdom, infallible in matters of statecraft. Nothing could be more mistaken.

This is a piece of gross sentimentality that has been refuted many times over. Consider Aristotle's view of democracy. He begins by noting that only a physician would be considered competent to judge matters of sickness and health. He goes on to suggest that this is true of "all professions and arts." Only the specialist, the expert is competent to judge matters involving his specialty. Aristotle then goes on to apply this principle to the elections of political leaders. "For a right election can only be made by those who have knowledge," Aristotle notes; "those who know geometry, for example, will choose a geometrician rightly, and those who know how to steer, a pilot; and, even if there be some occupations and arts in which private persons share in the ability to choose, they certainly cannot choose better than those who know. So that, according to this argument, neither the election of magistrates, nor the calling of them to account, should be entrusted to the many." (1999, 67)

Along these same lines, we find the biologist Thomas Henry Huxley essaying further arguments against democratic pretensions. "If I mistake not, one thing we need to learn is ... that voting power, as a means of giving effect to opinion, is more likely to prove a curse than a blessing to the voters, unless that opinion is the result of a sound judgment operating upon sound knowledge. Some experience of sea-life leads me to think that I should be very sorry to find myself on board a ship in which the voices of the cook and the loblolly boys counted for as much as those of the officers, upon a question of steering, or reefing topsails;

or where the 'great heart' of the crew was called upon to settle the ship's course. And there is no sea more dangerous than the ocean of practical politics—none in which there is more need of good pilotage and of a single, unfaltering purpose when the waves rise high." (1890)

How many people within the electorate are qualified to run a government? Very few. Then why should the masses be entrusted to run the state? Obviously, they shouldn't be so entrusted. In nearly all functions of government, a certain level of expertise is required if the task at hand is to be done at all. Not everyone is qualified to run a bureaucracy, collect taxes, distribute entitlements, pass legislation, and enforce the law of the land. Not everyone is qualified to lead government armies into battle; not everyone has the knowledge and foresight needed to make good judgments on issues of foreign policy; not everyone knows the law well enough to arbitrate legal proceedings.

An excellent illustration of this is provided by the sociologist Pitrim Sorokin, who lived through the Bolshevik Revolution and experienced first-hand the effects of trying to replace government officials with ordinary people. "In the first phase of the Soviet Revolution a common sailor from the Baltic fleet—a very ardent communist, but a person who was almost illiterate—was appointed dean of the law faculty of the University of Petrograd. A freshman was made the President, or rector, of that university. The president of the Supreme Economic Council, which controlled the entire economic life of Russia, could scarcely sign his name. Many persons were made 'red professors' in the university even though they lacked an elementary knowledge of their specialty. Persons ignorant of military strategy were appointed commanders of armies and divisions. On the other hand, first-class financiers were relegated to the position of paupers; the best scholars and scientists were thrown into prison or concentration camps and required to perform unskilled manual labor; poets by the grace of God were assigned clerical duties; and so forth.

"In consequence of this absurd allocation of functions the entire Soviet economy, army, diplomacy, science, arts, and social structure began to suffer. In order to alleviate the chaos, the vertical process had to be reversed. Accordingly, during the second phase of the revolution (after 1922) many an 'upstart' was demoted, and many a member of the former middle, upper, and professional classes was restored to his original position." (1942, 114-115)

If democracy really were majority rule, it would be an impossible system. Fortunately, it is no such thing. It is, as I have indicated before, a mere game, almost a kind of farce. Sentimentalists might take offense at this way of looking at it. Some might even go so far as to suggest that I am trying to criticize or impugn democracy. Those who entertain such thoughts are missing the point. Far from trying to undermine or attack democracy, I am merely seeking to save the democratic process from its own inept rationalization. If democracy really were majority rule, every honorable person would be duty-bound to oppose it. A system of government that placed power in the hands of ordinary men and women would be irresponsible. The majority is not fit to rule. Placing power in the hands of such people would be tantamount to committing national suicide.

Joseph Schumpeter was keenly aware of this defect in the common man. "Normally, the great political questions take their place in the psychic economy of the typical citizen with those leisure-hour interests that have not attained the rank of hobbies, and with the subjects of irresponsible conversation," Schumpeter observed. "These things seem so far off; they are not at all like a business proposition; dangers may not materialize at all and if they should they may not prove so very serious; one feels oneself to be moving in a fictitious world.

"This reduced sense of reality accounts not only for a reduced sense of responsibility but also for the absence of effective volition. One has one's phrases, of course, and one's wishes and daydreams and grumbles; especially one has one's likes and dislikes. But ordinarily they do not amount to what we call a will—the psychic counterpart of purposeful responsible action. In fact, for the private citizen musing over national affairs there is no scope for such a will and no task at which it could develop. He is a member of an unworkable committee, the committee of the whole nation, and this is why he expends less disciplined effort on mastering a political problem than he expends on a game of bridge." (1942, 261)

Democratic theory blindly ignores these all too obvious truths. It continues to believe in such gross improbabilities as the "wisdom of the common man" and the "right" to self-determination. Never mind that the facts do not accord with such notions. The common man may be very wise when it comes to his work, his hobbies and interests, and his family; but in politics, he lacks the experience necessary for developing reliable judgment.

Robert Michels, the great debunker of democratic theory, stressed the importance of hands-on experience in strengthening the power of political leaders in a democracy. "In proportion as they become initiated into the details of political life, as they become familiarized with the different aspects of the fiscal problem, and with questions of foreign policy, the leaders gain an importance which renders them indispensable.... This is perfectly natural, for the leaders cannot be replaced at a moment's notice, since all the other members of the party are absorbed in their everyday occupations and are strangers to the bureaucratic mechanism. This special competence, this expert knowledge, which the leader acquires in matters inaccessible, or almost inaccessible, to the mass, gives him a security of tenure which conflicts with the essential principles of democracy." (1915, 83-840)

When Michels speaks of the "principles of democracy," he means the principles of *theoretical* democracy. The conflict exists with the theory, not with democracy as it exists in the real world of fact. Democracy, as I have made clear, is not about expressing the "will of the people," but is a mechanism which enables a society made up of many different groups and individuals, few of whom can come to any kind of precise agreement, to make political decisions. Even if, however, it were possible to set up a government that really did express the "will of the people," society would still be ruled by a tiny elite. This is an unavoidable consequence of the division of labor that affects all social life in advanced civilizations. Under any form of government, whether democratic or autocratic, political authority must be to delegated to certain individuals. Here I don't necessarily mean elected officials, although they are the first that come to mind in a democracy. Bureaucrats also constitute a portion of the "ruling class," even though they are rarely elected. The bureaucracy constitutes the "permanent" government. It is here to stay, whether we like it or not. And its functions, even when lacking the efficiency found in competitive capitalism, are often indispensable for the survival of the nation. To give just one example, military logistics, which is so essential to modern warfare, would be impossible without bureaucracy.

The complexities involved in preparing an army for an invasion in a foreign land are staggering. Not only do the government authorities have to coordinate the transportation of the troops, they must also supply them with food and munitions, with parts and fuel for their vehicles, and with technical equipment such as computers and radios. None of these functions could be carried out without the expertise of government bureaucrats. To be sure, these bureaucrats make many mistakes. Stories of bureaucratic incompetence are notorious. But such stories don't prove that the job could be done better by non-experts. Try maintaining an army with a bureaucracy made up of inexperienced individuals drawn randomly from the masses and see how far you get.

In a democracy, political authority must be "delegated" to a handful of "experts." The necessity of this leads to what Michels called the "iron law of oligarchy." "Every party organization represents an oligarchical power grounded upon a democratic basis," explained Michels. "We find everywhere electors and elected. Also we find everywhere the power of the elected leaders over the electing masses is almost unlimited. The oligarchic structure of the building suffocates the basic democratic principle. That which *is* oppresses *that which ought to be*. For the masses this essential difference between the reality and the ideal remains a mystery.... The notion of the representation of popular interests, a notion to which the great majority of democrats, and in especial the working-class masses of the German-speaking lands, cleave with so much tenacity and confidence, is an illusion engendered by a false illumination.... The modern proletariat, enduringly influenced by glib-tongued persons intellectually superior to the mass, ends by believing that by flocking to the polls and entrusting its social and economic cause to a delegate, its direct participation in power will be assured." (1915, 401-402)

Many democratic ideologues are blind to these facts—perhaps intentionally so. They prefer to live in a world of fantasy, where democratic theory accords with political reality. To a certain degree, this is a good thing: it helps make practical democracy work. Men always have a tendency to expect too much out of human institutions. These unrealistic expectations, if left unrepressed, would inevitably lead to disappointment and outrage. If the practical kind of democracy described in this essay is ever going to work, it needs the illusions provided by theoretical democracy; which is to say, most people need to believe that democratic institutions more or less work as democratic theory prescribes. Otherwise, the masses would lose faith in the system and practical democracy, the democracy of farcical elections held merely to avoid violence, would collapse. Illusions are necessary for the majority of people, because without them they could never face up to and tolerate the limitations imposed on society by the human condition.

Not everyone can be blind to the obvious. A perceptive individual cannot help but notice the disparity between democratic theory and democratic practice. If everyone believes that democratic theory can and ought to prevail, the realization of its failure may occasion anger and resentment. Instead of accepting the fact that democratic theory can never be realizable in practice, the hunt begins for a scapegoat. The failure of democratic theory will be blamed on some group or ideological faction. It is the fault of big business or the liberal media or the radical right or the trilateral commission or the Jews. These groups, it will be maintained, have hatched a diabolical conspiracy against the will of the people. They need to be exposed and put down with force.

Against the indignation of conspiracy theorists, the truth labors in vain. People who are intent on blaming the failures of democracy on their favorite scapegoat are guilty of not one, but three separate errors. First, they erroneously assume that democratic theory represents an unquestionable ideal. As I have already explained, the ideal of majority rule is a false ideal. Even if the majority could rule, it would not be a good thing, because the majority is not fit to rule: it lacks the necessary expertise. The second error of the scapegoaters is to believe that democracy, in its idealistic, theoretical form, is a practicable system. Again, we have found this to be untrue. Michel's Iron Law of Oligarchy proves that theoretical democracy is an impossible system. The third and final error of the conspiracy theorists is their assumption that democracy's failure must be the handiwork of some individual or group that is working hard behind the scenes to thwart the will of the people. A flaw inherent in the human condition is here blamed on certain individuals, who are mercilessly condemned by the indignation of rabid ideologues.

Unfortunately, there is little that can be done about such scapegoating. As we all know, life is not fair. Not everyone can accept this. The unfairness of life must be blamed on this or that group. Hence the discovery of "them," that vague designation which the envy of small-minded people, embittered by their own failures in life, directs at the happy, the successful, and the uncomplaining. *They* have betrayed democracy. Who are *they? They* could be bankers, corporate directors, stock brokers, lawyers, politicians, the wealthy, Jews, white people, patriarchal males, etc. It goes without saying that all such scapegoating is a complete waste of time and resources. Why embitter oneself over matters which are beyond anyone's control? Why get bent out of shape over injustices that can never be redressed? Why this indignant quixotism, this tilting at windmills on behalf of that vaguest of vague abstractions, "social justice"? Why not simply accept things as they are, and make the best of it? But alas, it cannot be. Human beings perforce must torment not only themselves, but all society with their false and inane ideals. This, too, is part of the human condition, and we must bear it as best we can! It colors the great farce of life with the hue of tragedy. Thus we find the Left so embittered over democracy's failure to bring about economic equality that it must seek to do everything in its power to undermine the nation's morale, even in time of great danger. A similar type of vulgar resentment is found among right-wing conspiracy theorists, who would have us believe that all our problems stem from Jewish bankers and the Council on Foreign Relations.

Compromise is very difficult for men of militant temperament. Yet is precisely compromise that democracy, in the practical, real-world sense of the word, entails. We compromise with people whom we regard as mistaken or even crazy in order to live in peace. This is not always easy. Since the 1930s, conservatives in America have had to compromise with liberals—that is to say, with people who, despite their good intentions, have advocated one preposterous measure after another. To take but one example, consider the liberal view of crime during the fifties and sixties, summed up so eloquently in the title of psychiatrist Karl Menninger's book *The Crime of Punishment*. Crime, the liberals argued, is created by society: by deprivation, oppression, brutality, and injustice. Criminals are merely ordinary people victimized by unjust circumstances. The best way to deal with the problem of crime is not to punish the criminal (which is tantamount, according to this view, with "blaming the victim"), but to change society. Put an end to all the injustices of the capitalist system, and crime will diminish.

In the sixties, these liberal theories of crime were tested on a national level. The results proved conclusively that the theories were mistaken. Between 1960 and 1990, the total number of violent crimes in America increased by 550%. (1994, 22) So much for the sociological view of crime. Unfortunately, the millions of Americans who have been raped, robbed and murdered thanks to these policies have paid a huge price for these mistaken notions. If democracy means compromising with congenital idiots, what justification can we possibly find for it?

As with so many things in life, it comes down to tradeoffs. By putting up with the nonsense of the Left, we buy a little peace and tranquility. In politics, the alternative to compromise is violence. There are at least two sides to every issue, and one of them is always wrong. In a democracy, the side that is right has no choice but to compromise with the side that is wrong. To keep the peace, conservatives must put up with the lunacies of liberalism. The only alternative is armed conflict. Most people are willing to put up with a great deal of political and social mischief if only they can be allowed to live in peace, free from the horrors of internecine strife.

A century and a half-ago, the United States found itself divided over an issue that could not be settled through compromise. The consequence was the worst war in U.S. history. Sometimes democracy—government by compromise—simply cannot resolve the problems facing a nation. When men in power and influence set their hearts on policies that are self-destructive and refuse to compromise with the forces of moderation, democracy becomes less and less tenable. A crisis occurs. If compromise becomes impossible, democratic rule comes to an end. Either civil war or dictatorship becomes the fate of the nation.

4. Moral Externalities

Economics defines an *externality* as any cost or benefit not entirely borne by those responsible for it. A house with a front yard littered with broken-down old cars represents one example of an externality. The owner of the house bears some of the cost of his untidy yard in the reduced value of his property; but so do his neighbors, who through no fault of their own find the values of their homes taking a hit. Another example is pollution from a factory. The cost of the pollution is borne by the entire local community, whether they work or profit from the factory or not.

Economists often describe externalities in terms of costs and decision makers. As one economics textbook puts it: "An externality arises when the cost borne by the decision maker do not include all of the costs of his decision. Some are inflicted on people who were not involved in the decision. There are social costs of production that are not accounted for in private cost calculation." (1983, 426)

Externalities aren't always bad. An example of a good externality would be the neighbor who does a splendid job with the landscaping and upkeep of his home. Another example might be the Open Source movement, where programmers develop software then release it to the public without expecting monetary remuneration.

Economists, in keeping with their mania for the quantifiable, have generally confined their concept of externalities to matters dealing with cost or price. But the concept can be extended to matters far outside the sphere of economic accounting. There exist externalities in the moral sphere as well—externalities which, although their costs (or benefits) cannot be easily measured in terms of price or utility, nonetheless exercise a very real impact on our daily lives. To be sure, if, like the typical economist, we have eyes only for what can be quantified and are blind to the qualitative element of reality, then we will be incapable of noting these less effable, yet very real externalities. Even more to be pitied in this respect is the ideologue, whose attachment to some stale creed or dogma renders him incapable of grasping any aspect of reality that cannot be squeezed into the procrustean bed of his ideology. To escape from the tyranny of ideas—which is to say, the tyranny of rationalism—is the first step towards attaining what the ancients called *wisdom*. Ideas should describe and elucidate reality, instead of distorting or, even worse, *concealing* reality.

The subject of moral externalities—of burdens imposed on innocent bystanders because of the immorality of others—is a reality that has been ignored for too long. Although anyone with a lick of moral sense understands that immoral behavior has social consequences, far too often the subject is viewed in its grosser and more common manifestations, while the subtler problems that relate most directly to the issue of externalities are ignored. If a man drinks to excess or drives recklessly or commits adultery, most people will recognize that his actions affect others. That is why such behavior is regarded as immoral. Morality always exists in a social context. If a man's behavior only affects himself, then whether that behavior is "moral" or not has little relevance to the rest of us. Only behavior that affects others—whether positively or negatively—can be regarded as moral (or immoral) in any relevant sense of the word.

The concept of moral externalities has not, however, been evoked to describe the obvious moral consequences of human action. When a man cheats on his wife, the consequences to his spouse, the primary victim of his act, are obvious. No special concept need be devised to analyze such consequences. The notion of a moral externality, on the other hand, is somewhat more subtle, involving not only the immediate participants of a behavioral situation, but the secondary societal consequences as well—the outlying ripples in the pond of causation. A specific example will help bring the concept to life.

Imagine a neighborhood of two dozen families, all of whom are raising children, many of them boys, between the ages of five and fifteen. Now suppose that one of these families egregiously spoils their children, especially their male children, so that they develop into willful, savage, vicious, and utterly unmanageable brats. What is likely to be the result of this scenario? Isn't it possible that the spoiled children will corrupt some of the other children in the neighborhood, so that the efforts of parents to discipline their offspring are compromised because of the lax child-rearing practices of one family? Of course it's possible. Even one bad child can exercise inordinate influence on his peers simply because children are naturally attracted to an individual who does not face the same restrictions as they do. Antinomianism is cool among the young. It has charismatic appeal. All that is needed to make a bad child really influential over his peers is to have a few children begin following his example, thereby bringing into play the whole dynamic of peer pressure, until even good children must behave badly if only to keep themselves from being singled out and ostracized.

Now imagine that instead of one family spoiling their children, it is several families. The odds of moral corruption increase, until the neighborhood reaches the point where it becomes extremely difficult for even the strictest parents to prevent their children from being corrupted. We see this phenomenon at work today with our nation's youth. The corruption of hedonism, in the forms of drug use and sexual promiscuity, is rife among the teenage population. Almost a third of tenth graders have smoked marijuana in the last year; over half of twelfth graders have used illicit drugs (National Institute on Drug Abuse 2004); more than half of 17-year-olds have engaged in sexual activity. Not only teenagers, but society at large pays a large price for all this irresponsible hedonism. One out of every ten females aged 15 to 19 becomes pregnant every year. Nearly four out of every five of these pregnancies are unplanned. (Alan Guttmacher Institute 1999) Juvenile crime remains a huge problem. Nearly a third of teenagers aged 14 to 15 have admitted committing acts of vandalism. Twenty-eight percent of high school students report the presence of street gangs in their schools. Almost one in six teenagers has tried to run away from home at least once. (National Center for Juvenile Justice 1999, 67, 59, 79)

Classical economics makes a point of distinguishing between the immediate and the distant consequences of a specific action—between what is seen and not seen. "In the economic sphere an act, a habit, an institution, a law produces not only one effect, but a series of effects," wrote the French economist Frederic Bastiat. "Of these effects, the first alone is immediate; it appears simultaneously with its cause; *it is seen*. The other effects emerge only subsequently; *they are not seen*; we are fortunate if we *foresee* them." (1964, 1)

It becomes especially difficult to *foresee* the remote consequences of a specific law, policy, or social behavior when ideology, desire, or sordid economic interests have compromised one's objectivity. We see this very clearly in the case of homosexuality. According to the apologists of the "gay" lifestyle, an individual's private life is his own business. If the individual chooses to have sex with men, women, animals, vacuum cleaners—why should anyone care one way or another?

If the matter involved only consenting adults and no externalities of any sort, moral or otherwise, existed, there would be no reason for anyone to bother about the gay lifestyle. But is it really true that the effects of such behavior can *always* be confined to the individual's private life? In discussing such problems, we cannot choose the politically correct, feel-good approach. We have to face up to tough facts. In the case of homosexuality, externalities clearly exist, and that innocent people sometimes are forced to pay a price for the behavior of others.

In the state of California, it is unlawful for insurance companies to use HIV tests to determine eligibility for insurance. Nor can insurance companies select risks on the basis of sexual orientation. Such practices are regarded as "discriminatory" and "unfair." By forcing insurance companies to cover homosexuals, the state winds up driving up the cost of medical insurance for everyone else. A monogamous heterosexual couple struggling to raise a family must pay higher premiums so that promiscuous gay men can continue their sexually profligate lifestyles.

Here we have as good an example of a moral externality as we are likely to find. Homosexuals, as is well known (if rarely talked about), are considerably more promiscuous than heterosexuals. In a study of homosexuals in San Francisco immediately before the AIDS epidemic, seventy-five percent of gay men reported having sex with more than a hundred partners, while twenty-eight percent reported having sex with more than a thousand partners. (Pinker 1997, 473) As a consequence of these high rates of promiscuity, homosexuals, who make up one to two percent of the population, account for three to four percent of all gonorrhea cases, sixty percent of syphilis cases, and seventeen percent of hospital admissions (excluding STDs) in the United States. (International Organization of Heterosexual Rights 2003) Promiscuous homosexuality is an unhealthy, self-destructive lifestyle; yet thanks to these laws that prevent insurance companies from either charging higher premiums or denying coverage altogether, heterosexuals must help subsidize a lifestyle that flouts all traditional norms of decency and morality.

Because homosexuality imposes an *economic* cost on non-homosexuals, it could be argued that the externalities arising from the gay lifestyle should be regarded as economic in nature rather than moral. But since these costs originate in a behavior that, except for homosexual prostitution, is non-economic, it is best to regard them as moral externalities. They are costs imposed, not by individuals making economic decisions, but by individuals making personal decisions.

Not all moral externalities, to be sure, impose economic costs. Some impose what could be called "moral" costs—costs that compromise the quality of life rather than the value of economic goods. Such moral costs are not so easy to measure or describe. What, precisely, does the phrase *quality of life* mean? How does one distinguish a high quality of life from a low one?

Concepts such as this are best illustrated with examples. All things being equal, a man living in a run-down neighborhood full of thugs and street crime can hardly be said to enjoy as high a quality of life as the man who lives in a stable middle-class neighborhood where strong community values prevail. Many factors can affect an individual's quality of life. If most of his neighbors are afflicted with various moral defects, such as an inability to mind their own business or a wanton lack of consideration for others, this can also undermine the individual's quality of life. The example previously offered of the family that spoils and corrupts their children and then lets them loose to corrupt the rest of the kids in the neighborhood provides an even subtler instance of a moral externality. The point is that, even though an individual's quality of life cannot be quantified or measured in objective terms, it still exercises a very real effect on him.

Social interaction is a key element in a person's quality of life. The degree to which his interaction with others is congenial and mutually advantageous determines, to a large extent, the quality of his life. If the people around him are considerate, honest, dependable, respectful, and appealing, his life will be much the better for it. If, on the other hand, the people around him are self-absorbed, dishonest, rude, and unappealing, the quality of his life will likely be seriously compromised.

Although human nature can hardly be regarded as a kind of putty out of which society may shape whatever forms it pleases, the manner in which children are raised and educated can profoundly affect how they turn out as adults. The desires of the human heart remain fairly constant over time. Human beings all desire pleasure, status, and love, but how they satisfy these desires is hardly uniform from society to society or age to age. Every society evolves certain mores that govern how individuals seek to placate the elemental desires of the human heart. Child rearing plays a critical role in the type of character fostered and encouraged by a given society. There are two things in particular that are important in this respect: first, the ideals that a society ascribes to, the virtues it admires, the exemplary characters it sets up for imitation; and second, the means by which it seeks to achieve these ideals and virtues.

Anyone familiar with the history of Western social mores over the last two hundred years understands that a great sea change has occurred in societal conceptions of virtue. Although people still abhor murder, theft, cruelty, malicious avarice, and dishonesty, their attitudes towards other matters of conduct, especially those concerning sex and honor, have suffered a dramatic change. A recent movie adaptation of Shakespeare's *Hamlet* illustrates this only too well. The film, directed by Michael Almereyda, updates the play to present-day New York. Despite the immense cleverness by which a play originally set in Denmark during the Middle Ages is transferred to late twentieth century America, *Hamlet* just does not work in a modern setting. The sentiments of the characters—the social mores that serve as the background for the motives of so many of the characters in the play—simply do not make sense in a modern world. One simply cannot image any young man nowadays telling his sister, as Laertes does in Act I, to be careful lest her "chaste treasure" be open to the "unmaster'd importunity" of her boyfriend. We don't care about such matters any more. The obsession with honor, which forms so much of the emotional core of the play, is also foreign to modern sensibilities. Even Horatio's remark following Hamlet's death—"Now cracks a noble heart"—sounds odd to modern ears. What young man nowadays would ever use the adjective *noble* to describe a friend? The very idea of nobility, of greatness of character, has gone completely out of favor. "Students these days are, in general, nice," wrote the late Allan Bloom in *The Closing of the American Mind*. "They are not particularly moral or noble." (1987, 82)

This change in character was noticed more than sixty years ago by the philosopher George Santayana. "There can be no doubt of it: chilvary is now thoroughly dead," he wrote. "Our one preoccupation is to be safe. We don't know what we love, or if we do we don't dare mention it. We are willing to become anything, to be turned into any sort of worm, by the will of the majority." Santayana concludes with the following ominous observation: "Meantime our society has lost its own soul. The landscape of Christendom is being covered with lava; a great eruption and inundation of brute humanity threatens to overwhelm all the treasures that artful humanity has created. Brute humanity has the power to destroy polite humanity, because it retains the material equipment of modern industry which has recently grown upon man like a fresh hide, horns, and claws." (1951, 207-8)

The most conspicuous example of "brute humanity" in our own society finds its most chilling expression in youth culture. Young people today seek not to be good or noble, but merely to be "cool." The word *cool* is rather vague and can be used in a variety of contexts. Many young people use it to describe anything which provokes a sort of antinomian epiphany. A thing or experience is "cool" if it undermines adult or societal authority in a particularly outrageous and gratifying manner.

Over fifty years ago, Richard Weaver identified a new trait which he called "the spoil-child psychology." "The spoiled child has not been made to see the relationship between effort and reward," wrote Weaver. "He wants things, but he regards payment as an imposition or as an expression of malice by those who withhold for it. His solution ... is to abuse those who do not gratify them." (1948, 113)

Youth culture arises out of this spoiled-child psychology. It draws its sustenance from the hedonistic excesses of mass culture. Physical pleasures are ephemeral and uncertain. Indulgence dulls the appetite, thus paving the way for greater excess and despair. The extremes of youth culture should not surprise anyone who grasps the psychopathology of hedonism. Gangsta rap, white rage bands, destructive all-night parties, promiscuous sex, drug overdoses—all these are the inevitable consequence of unfettered hedonism. Letting children do as they please is merely another way of abusing them.

Youth culture, along with the sort of human beings it nurtures and inflicts upon the world, is the most important moral externality of the present age. The inability of our society, of our culture to develop the moral qualities of young people constitutes a serious failing for which we all pay a daily price. Consider as one example the ubiquity of cheating in our society, especially among the young. A *U.S. News and World Report* survey conducted in 1999 found that 84 percent of American students "felt the need to cheat to get ahead." (Kleiner and Lord 1999, 54-57, 61-64, 66) According to a Josephson Institute of Ethics survey of 8,600 American middle and high school students, 78 percent confessed to lying to their teachers and 71 percent admitted to cheating on at least one test. (2000) As a second illustration, consider the role that "rage" music plays in the lives of many young people nowadays. One heavy metal devotee confessed that he loved angry music "because it put him in a 'good mood,' by which he meant a mood conducive to smashing mailboxes with bricks." Another interviewee said hardcore metal put him in the mood to "go beat the crap out of someone." (O'Toole 1997)

It is not pleasant to live among people who are angry and resentful because reality refuses to cater to their desires. Such people, by their immaturity, their rudeness, their lack of consideration for others and their wanton irresponsibility, lower the quality of life for the rest of us.

Social manners have been deteriorating for decades. As long ago as the 1930s, we find traces of it, as F. Scott Fitzgerald noted in a letter to his daughter. "My generation of radicals and breakers-down never found anything to take the place of the old virtues of work and courage and the graces of courtesy and politeness," he wrote. (1964, 76) Describing contemporary manners, the historian Jacques Barzun wrote: "The word [manners] was seldom used and the practice highly variable. Business firms and airlines thanked their customers effusively, but civility between persons was scant, especially in cities." (2000, 782)

Not everyone is unhappy with the corruption of manners. There are those who regard manners with contempt, as outworn vestiges of elitism and snobbery. A liberal, democratic social order has no need for such artificial conventions. Such a view, however, misses the point. The case for manners has no where been more eloquently stated than by Edmund Burke in his *Letters on a Regicide Peace*: "Manners are of more importance than laws. Upon them, in great measure, the laws depend. The law touches us but here and there, and now and then. Manners are what vex or sooth, corrupt or purify, exalt or debase, barbarize or refine us, by a constant, steady, uniform, insensible operation, like that of the air we breathe in. They give their whole form and colour to our lives. According to their quality, they aid morals, they supply them, or they totally destroy them." (1796, 126)

If this gradual deterioration of social manners and personal conduct is indeed the legacy, or, at the very least, a symptom, of youth culture, what are we supposed to do about it? When confronted by an *economic* externality, we are usually told that the only remedy lies in government regulation. If corporations are spewing all manner of pernicious toxins into the air and water, laws or regulations must be passed to stop the pollution or to limit it within specific and reasonable parameters. Should the state intervene to regulate moral externalities in the same manner as it does for economic externalities?

In some respects, the state already does regulate, and sometimes even prohibits, certain types of moral externalities. An obvious example is prostitution. Except for a handful of counties in Nevada, prostitution is illegal everywhere in the United States. The externalities that arise from this activity should be fairly obvious. In the first place, the effect of prostitution on the moral tone of society must be considered. Commerce in sexuality is widely regarded as degrading, especially to women. It violates certain well established forms or manners that have evolved to regulate sexual relations.

A second objection to prostitution arises out of public health concerns. The typical prostitute, indulging, as her trade demands, in numerous sexual partners, is a ripe vessel for spreading sexually transmitted diseases. Since it is generally agreed by nearly everyone that the state is responsible for combating the spread of infectious diseases, state involvement in regulating or prohibiting prostitution becomes *de rigueur* right from the start. The only point at issue is the degree of involvement. Those who favor the legalization of prostitution contend that criminalizing the sex trade only serves to isolate prostitutes from state regulation. The state cannot, after all, regulate illegal activity. But if legalization led to a considerable increase in sex commerce, regulation might prove impractical.

The final and probably the most critical objection to prostitution arises from moral and economic externalities associated with sex trade. In the abstract, prostitution may appear fairly benign. After all, who is affected beyond the immediate participants? Prostitution, however, does not take place in the abstract. It is a very concrete activity that happens at a specific time and, most critically, at a specific place. That is precisely the problem with it. Although most people are willing to live and let live, they don't want prostitutes walking in front of their businesses or setting up bawdy houses in their neighborhoods. Prostitution is a magnet for crime. In Nevada, prostitution is only allowed in the countryside, away from the big metropolitan areas. There are very serious externalities associated with the sex business, and so most decent people, even those who believe in minding their own business, don't want to see it made legal.

Now if the state can interfere with prostitution, why can't it interfere with other palpable moral externalities, such as homosexual promiscuity or pornography? Here we have to be careful. The problem of externalities, whether of the economic or moral variety, cannot be solved simply by passing a few laws. What has the criminalization of prostitution accomplished when all is said and done? What has it achieved beyond harassing prostitutes and their customers? The activity goes on much as it would if it were legal, except that *some* local communities have the capacity to drive sexual commerce from their midst. I say "some" because, to be entirely honest, only communities with both the "collective" will and economic means to carry out that will can succeed in severely limiting, if not driving out altogether, the scourge of harlotry. Deprived areas, whether in the economic or moral sense of the word, have no such option. On the contrary, prostitution thrives in their midst, feeding off the moral and economic destitution of the local community.

The argument over economic externalities, when reduced to the barest essentials, becomes merely an argument between the claims of the state versus the claims of the individual. Those who make the greatest fuss about economic externalities are precisely those who are most eager to increase the role of the state in the economy; while those who seek to convince everyone that externalities pose no threat to society are precisely those who are agitating for deregulation and laissez-faire. Yet this is not the way to look at the matter at all. Both sides in the debate are guilty of assuming that externalities are confined to market related activity. This is not true. Government action can also lead to "externalities." The only difference between the externalities of government action and the externalities of the business world is that in the former case, the decision is made without reference to personal gain or loss in economic terms. Bureaucrats don't normally make economic decisions on the basis of profit and loss. That is why economists don't use the term *externalities* to describe the costs imposed by government action. However, this is little more than a question of semantics. Let us take another look at the text book definition of an externality: "An externality arises when the cost borne by the decision maker do not include all of the costs of his decision." Well, in the case of the state—or, rather, of the individuals acting as proxies of the state—there is no question of a cost borne by a decision maker, so in that sense, state action cannot lead to externalities. But clearly there are costs arising from government policies that are not included in the aim or purpose of the policy—costs, moreover, which are borne by innocent bystanders. These costs are analogous to the costs of externalities. The only difference is that the state is the main culprit in the business, rather than some private individual or corporation. It is fairly easy to blame an individual or even a corporation for the costs of externalities. It is not so easy to pin responsibility on the state, especially a democratic state which, in theory at least, is merely carrying out the "will of the people"—whatever *that* means!

As an example, consider the modern evolution of the welfare state. Before 1960, it was very difficult for a single mother to live on welfare. The incentives of the system pressured her to marry and get a job. After

1970, changes in the welfare system made it easier for single mothers to live on welfare. (Murray 1984, 154-164) The consequences of these changes are borne out not only by the enormous increase of single mothers on dole, but also, and more critically, in the percentage of illegitimate births, which rose almost by a factor of six between 1960 and 1991. Here we have what could be called a political externality: economic costs borne by taxpayers and moral costs borne by the community at large. Nor should we make light of these moral costs on the basis that it is nobody's business whether a child is raised in a two-parent home or by a single mother. Children from single-parent homes are two to three times more likely than children in two-parent homes to have emotional and behavior problems. (Bennett 1994, 46, 52)

Government action imposes costs on society at large. Even well intended laws can have bad consequences. Legislators would do better if, instead of passing more laws, more regulations, they would seek to pass better laws. Society requires simple, sensible laws that are as easy to follow as they are to enforce; laws that limit the costs of moral and political externalities as much as is humanly possible; laws that achieve, in short, more justice, more orderliness, more sanity with less state meddling. Before the state can achieve so much as a loose approximation of this ideal—and a loose approximation is the best that we could ever hope for—legislators must be guided by something other than ideology. The arrogance of the ideologue, who, armed with his rationalistic principles, thinks he can solve all the problems of society, is precisely the wrong way to go about it. Unfortunately, decisions in a democracy are rarely made in a spirit of caution and intellectual modesty. Political action is forged in the crucible of rank partisanship. If one side adopts a cautious approach, the other side will simply see this as an opportunity to gain an advantage. How else can we explain the torrents of law and regulation which inundate the justice system? Madness, not sensible intelligence or studied wisdom, rules our legislatures. The flotsam and jetsam of overbearing and ineffectual laws, clogging the arteries of the social order like so much cholesteric scum, can only lead to an arteriosclerosis of the economy, the state, and of society itself.

5. The Psychopathology of Leftist Thought

Since nearly all shades of political opinion have at least an element or smidgen of truth in them, it would seem to follow that they would also have at least an element or smidgen of relevance. After all, even the most perverse and wrong-headed ideology is likely to be right on at least one issue; and on that one issue it can potentially make a contribution, if ever so modest, to the national discourse. Yet in America—and, indeed, within the entire "civilized" West—we find ourselves confronted by an ideology boasting of millions of adherents that has virtually nothing to offer either to the art of statecraft or the development of social policy. By all objective standards of criticism and assessment, leftist political ideology is a colossal failure. The social policies it advocates are impractical and self-defeating, its criticism of the status quo unintelligent and overblown.

It wasn't always so. There was a time, not so very long ago, when the left did contribute, at least on a few issues, to the progress of civilization. The left was instrumental in ending the era of Jim Crow and other manifestations of institutional racism. It championed the working classes in the days when industrial workers barely earned $10 a week. It exposed the shady dealings and consumptuary excesses of the so-called "robber barons." It investigated political corruption and the abuses of business corporations, and in so doing helped bring about much needed reform in the private and public sectors. Despite an unfortunate predilection to champion lost causes and pursue false ideals, the left has made a genuine (though modest) contribution to the American Dream. But that all took place several generations ago, when America was, in some respects, very different from what it is today. With the passage of the Civil Rights Act, the left ceased to be relevant. It destroyed itself with its own success. All the curable social ills that it complained about have been treated. Any ills that remain were either incurable from the start or are merely the unintended side effects of too much left-liberal medicine. By the 1970s, leftist political ideology had lost its *raison d'être*. Unfortunately, no one on the left appears to have noticed this.

What does it mean to say that the left no longer has relevance? Namely this: that the characteristic positions of the left are so utterly lacking in sense or wisdom that they are entirely useless either as descriptions of facts or as guidelines to social policy. I realize that this is a rather extreme position to take. Isn't it grossly improbable to suggest that the left must be wrong about *everything*? Possibly. Granted, the left may now and again find itself on the right side, or close to the right side, of an issue. But even on these rare occasions when the left is right, or half-right, invariably it is right for the wrong reasons. Take the war in Iraq, for instance. Now let us suppose, for arguments sake, that the war in Iraq is a mistake. There are any number of reasons why this might be so. But whatever those reasons might be, you will almost never find them advanced by the denizens of the left. The left opposes the war for all the wrong reasons. Most of the arguments that the left advances against the war are little more than facile rationalizations of dubious passions. Consider, as one glaring illustration of this phenomenon, the leftist mantra that the war is wrong because "Bush lied." This cannot be taken as a serious objection to the war for the simple reason that it has nothing to do with the real reasons for the left's opposition to the conflict. The notion that Bush lied is a matter of faith for the left. They have never proven it beyond a reasonable doubt, because they really don't care whether he lied or not. If the evidence for Bush's veracity became so overwhelming that even the left had to accept it, that would not change their opposition to the war one jot. No leftist would come out and say, "Oh, it looks like Bush didn't lie after all. Therefore, I must support the war now." The left's opposition to the Iraq war has nothing to do with Bush's alleged mendacity. The left opposes the war because the war makes leftists feel uncomfortable. It calls into question some of the left's basic premises about human nature, particularly their quaint belief in the basis goodness of "oppressed" and "powerless" people. Hence Alice Walker's curious comment in relation to 9-11 and Osama Bin Laden, that "the only punishment that works is love." (Neuman 2001, 53) This could only be true if all human beings are intrinsically good. In that case, no evil could ever be ascribed to the internal motivation or character of a specific individual. Evil must have its roots in something external, in unjust circumstances or social oppression. Remove the injustice, abolish the oppression, and the evil will cease to exist.

The view that human beings are intrinsically good and that it is only institutions, such as globalist corporations, the Catholic Church, and the U.S. government, that make them do bad things, is hardly a view that can be embraced by an adult mind. It is the naive, petulant view of the spoiled child who stubbornly refuses to acknowledge the harsh realities of life. War and poverty, terrorism and crime, evil and stupidity are all very unpleasant to contemplate. The world would be a much better place if these things didn't exist. But these things most emphatically do exist; nor can any of the snake oil nostrums advocated by the left prevent or abolish their existence.

The essential irrelevance of the left stems, I suspect, from its psychological roots in a wanton failure to grow up. Leftist doctrine primarily emerges from an immature outlook on life. Specifically, it derives from what the social thinker Richard Weaver identified as the "spoiled child psychology." I have already, in another essay collected in this book (see "Moral Externalities," ch. 4), quoted Weaver's description of the spoiled child. Weaver's concept is so critical to understanding the unique pathologies of radical leftism that I will not hesitate to quote it again: "The spoiled child has not been made to see the relationship between effort and reward," wrote Weaver. "He wants things, but he regards payment as an imposition or as an expression of malice by those who withhold for it. His solution ... is to abuse those who do not gratify them." (1948, 113)

I have already sketched how the spoiled child psychology has contributed to the development of youth culture—a development

63

often viewed with sympathy by leftists. In this essay I will attempt to trace this psychology's influence on what is charitably described as "leftist thought." I say *charitably*, because there really doesn't seem to be much that can properly be described as "thought" within the leftist fold. One can observe among the Left, as Weaver noted about the pampered child, "a kind of irresponsibility of the mental process." Spoiled children, Weaver explained, "never have to feel that definition must be clear and deduction correct if they are to escape the sharp penalties of deprivation. Therefore the typical thinking of such people is fragmentary, discursive, and expressive of a sort of contempt for realities. Their conclusions are not 'earned' in the sense of being logically valid but are seized in the face of facts." (1948, 127)

This "contempt for realities" perfectly describes the body of ideas and precepts that passes for leftist doctrine. In response to the attacks on 9-11, George Lakoff described the "liberal and progressive" reaction as follows: "Understanding and restraint are what is needed. The model for our actions should be rescue workers and doctors—the healers—not bombers." And if anyone might get the wrong idea and think that Lakoff was merely indulging in a few vague sentiments, he further explicated his position by insisting that we must never allow ourselves "to be like" the terrorists. "We should not take innocent lives in bringing the perpetrators to justice. Massive bombing of Afghanistan—with the killing of innocents—will show that we are no better than they." (2004, 58)

Such notions are difficult to take seriously. A handful of terrorists kill three thousand Americans and Lakoff wants us to react with "understanding and restraint"! Our heroes should be rescue workers and doctors, not bombers (and by implication) soldiers! What kind of foolishness is this? Does Lakoff have no appreciation for what it takes to survive in the world? When someone is trying to kill you, restraint and "understanding" are not what is called for. Even sillier is Lakoff's insistence that we should not take innocent lives in our quest for "justice." What if that's not possible? Terrorists are known, for example, of using innocent civilians as "shields." If we can't stop terrorists without putting the lives of innocent civilians at risk, does this mean that we should just give up and let the terrorists continue to carry out their nefarious plans of wiping us out? Lakoff's position is not very well thought out. It makes assumptions that are implausible and then criticizes the Bush administration on the very basis of these palpably absurd presuppositions.

The poor quality of Lakoff's thought is further evinced by how he frames the differences between the left and the right on the issue of terrorism. The right, he claims, desires "retribution and vengeance," while the left only wants "justice." Again, this is little more than a headlong collapse into fatuity. It entirely misses the point. What most sensible people want in regard to the terrorists is to stop them from killing us. Retribution and vengeance, justice and understanding are of little concern. What is important is survival: preventing the enemy from achieving his stated goal of wiping us out. Somehow, this obvious bit of common sense finds no place in Lakoff's head. His leftist ideals have lobotomized his mind, turning him into little more than an ineffectual spouter of flatulent nonsense. This is a shame, because Lakoff, at least in his scientific work, often demonstrates a sharp and penetrating intelligence. It is only when he turns his attention to politics and foreign affairs that he begins voicing opinions so lacking in sense and wisdom that one begins to fear for his sanity.

Lakoff's contempt for realities pales in comparison with the contempt manifested by Noam Chomsky, regarded in some circles as the world's preeminent intellectual. Chomsky operates on the simple premise that nearly everything that America ever does is wrong. And not just wrong in a minor key sort of way, but in wrong in a criminal and even genocidal way. America, Chomsky would have us believe, is the biggest terrorist of all. ("I choose to live in what I think is the greatest country in the world, which is committing horrendous terrorist acts and should stop," Chomsky has asserted.) On the war in Afghanistan, Chomsky claimed that "plans are being made and programs implemented on the assumption that they may lead to the death of several million people in the next couple of weeks. Very casually, with no comment, no particular thought about it, that's just kind of normal, here, and in a good part of Europe." Chomsky has also blamed Israel and the United States for intentionally imposing "suffering and starvation on Palestinian civilians because they voted the wrong way." He denies that Israel even has a right to exist. "The whole question of recognizing the right of a state to exist was invented solely for Israel," he claims. "People, on the other hand, have a right to exist. So the people who live on the land—Israelis and Palestinians—have a right to live in security and peace." But this is an artful dodge. Having a right to exist is meaningless without the power to enforce that right. Without an Israeli state, the Jews in Israel would likely be dispossessed and slaughtered by the Palestinians. Chomsky, apparently, could care less about these inconvenient realities. He simply cannot tolerate any civilized country using force to defend itself from third world barbarians. (Chomsky 2007)

I could go on in this manner, quoting this or that leftist to demonstrate the left's bristling contempt for reality. Leftist economics, with its inexplicable preference for the impractical and utopian ideals of socialism over the time-tested achievements of free markets; leftist personal morality, with its irresponsible sexual hedonism which helped precipitate the AIDS epidemic (Horowitz 1998, 155-178); and leftist identity politics, which, in the words of the leftist fellow traveler Richard Roarty, is "a vision of an America in which the white patriarchs have stopped voting and have left all the voting to be done by members of previously victimized groups, people who have somehow come into possession of more foresight and imagination than the selfish suburbanites" (Horowitz 1999, 237); all these various nooks and crannies of leftist pathology could be minutely examined to show the left's apathy toward fact and reality. But what would be the point of so much tedious analysis when the conclusion is so obvious and, in any case, has already been established many times over by other writers? The sheer contempt for facts and logic is plainly evident within the leftist fold. The only real question is: what accounts for this contempt? Why is the left waging this childish, futile war against reality?

This question brings us right back to our starting point: Weaver's spoiled child psychology. The main reason for ascribing the origins of leftist ideology to a psychology of childish resentment stems from the sheer irrationality of the positions which the typical leftist instinctively embraces and champions. Whether it's the left's opposition to the war on terror, its sympathy with Palestinians and other Muslims who wish to wipe out Israel, its pathological hatred for corporate capitalism, or the greater concern it evinces for criminals over victims—such views cannot plausibly be explained because of innocent error. The individuals who originally devised them could hardly have been well-intentioned idiots. Idiots perhaps they were and are; but well-intentioned? Not likely. Something darker and more disturbing is at work here. There must be a method to the madness, if only we could see our way to the core of it.

The spoiled child psychology is precisely the sort of leprosy of the soul best fitted to explain the psychopathology of leftist ideology. In any case, there are no better explanations of this disagreeable phenomenon, no rival theories that offer a superior account of the many strange, senseless, and counterintuitive convictions embraced and propagated by the left.

The most prominent sentiment animating leftist political passions is a deep and abiding dissatisfaction with the social, political, and economic institutions of the West, particularly in their American variants. What accounts for this dissatisfaction? Why is the left so down on America? If we consult the reasons provided by prominent leftists, we soon find ourselves in a thicket of hyperbolic assertions and false ideals. All the complaints, the whining, the bitter accusations, the paroxysms of moral indignation—in short, all the gesticulations of horror and disgust which the left indulges in to express its disapproval of America— can be reduced, ultimately, to one pithy phrase: *the left disapproves of America because America is not perfect*. Such is America's great crime. To be sure, that is not how the left chooses to express the matter. The left will gripe and moan about homelessness, poverty, inequality, racism, sexism, homophobia, etc. But to criticize and despise America for these imperfections demonstrates the left's fundamental superficiality. What powerful, multi-racial, multi-ethic nation has ever been less racist, less sexist, less homophobic than America? What nation has ever enjoyed greater wealth and greater economic opportunity? Did the Roman Empire, with its brutal slave system and sadistic jurisprudence, come closer to achieving left-wing ideals? What about the Old Regime of France? Or the British Empire? Or the Soviet Union? Or China or India or any other great nation whose history confronts us in the annals of the human race? In terms of left-wing ideals, America is as good as it gets. If the left should argue that Western Europe comes closer to its ideals than America, such an argument simply has no relevance. Since the nations of Western Europe would not even exist as independent democracies were it not for American power, there is no point in holding them up as left-wing ideals. Before we can take any ideal seriously, we have to be sure that that ideal is self-sufficient, that it can survive in the world on its own resources. Leftist ideals, whether achieved in America, Western Europe, or Canada, depend on American power for their existence. So why does the left continue to berate and belittle America? Why do they resent American power—the very power which they depend upon to work their mischief in the world?

When you get right down to it, it is not poverty or inequality or racism or sexism or the homophobia or any of the other left-wing bugbears that have disillusioned the left with America. These things are merely pretexts or excuses for left-wing rage. What really annoys and exasperates the left is not the ills of corporate capitalism or the nefarious social policies of the radical right, but the fact that we live in an imperfect world that imposes onerous burdens and responsibilities on every man, woman and child. Fundamentally, what the left cannot abide is the somber realities of the human condition!

Here we find striking evidence of the spoiled child psychology. The spoiled child resents few things more than the burden of adult responsibilities. Such responsibilities are seen not merely as an imposition, but even as a crime. And wherever a crime is committed, there must be a criminal—the person responsible for the crime. In the juvenile mind of the leftist, usually Mom and Dad are blamed for the crime—or the political or social equivalent thereof. Leftists hate America because, in their minds, America is the political and social equivalent of Mom and Dad, and it is Mom and Dad whom they blame for a world that refuses to cater to their infantile expectations. Because the world isn't perfect, because it refuses to pamper and sooth and flatter the leftist's tender, mollycoddled ego, he blames America. It is America's fault that life is tough and reality humiliating. Like the petulant child, the leftist lusts for vengeance against his country. Hence the eagerness with which he embraces policies that weaken and undermine the nation. Perhaps he really doesn't want destroy or abolish America. He just wants to punish America and make it suffer like he has suffered.

For those who suspect that I am being unfair to leftists by ascribing to them the base sentiments of the typical spoiled-child, I will repeat that I am merely trying to explain the grotesqueries of leftist ideology. These people make very curious pronouncements. It is difficult to take any of them at face value. The pettiness, the resentment, the sheer viciousness of the left, particularly in any venue where it is given free rein, is difficult to evade. Look at the outrages committed by leftists in the universities, where dubious speech codes are used as a pretext to harass and persecute anyone the left despises. When a law professor explained the term "servitude" by noting the "ex-slaves" in his class, he was subjected to weeks of persecution, despite his willingness to apologize to those he might have offended. (D'Souza 1991, 201) An English Professor voted against a motion advancing less traditional course work for an English Ph.D. program and was subjected to months of petty persecution by his colleagues. (Collier 1993, 97-111) Examples like this could be added by the hundreds. Anyone who has faced the small-minded wrath of University leftists knows exactly what I am talking about. The indignation and the accompanying harassment and persecution are so out of proportion to the initial "offense" that it becomes obvious at a glance that these leftists *want* to be offended, that they actively seek out anything they can interpret as offensive to feed their need to inflict vengeance on some hapless scapegoat. An inoffensive liberal professor refers to some black students as ex-slaves and immediately it becomes one of the great crimes against humanity. Although the professor readily and eagerly apologizes, that is of no account. Your worm-eaten leftist has no use for apologies. They do not serve his darker purposes. An apology doesn't satiate his lust for revenge, his incurable desire to make others suffer what he has suffered. For that is really what it is all about: to make others suffer, particular others better constituted than himself.

While not all leftists are consumed by a lust for vengeance, the objects of their sympathy and disdain demonstrate a peculiar psychopathology. What, for instance, should we make of the left's hostility toward the so-called "religious right"? As far as I can gather, the phrase "religious right" refers to politically active individuals who believe in the traditional moral values of Christianity. Those values include belief in parental authority and discipline ("spare the rod and spoil the child") and opposition to sexual hedonism. Where does the left stand on these issues? They tend to favor policies which either promote sexuality or attenuate the unpleasant side effects of imprudent sexual indulgence. Hence the left favors abortion on demand, gay liberation, condoms in schools, and sex education. The left tends to oppose corporal punishment and other forms of strict discipline. Some leftists take a rather dim view of the whole concept of parental authority. "Humiliations, spankings and beatings, slaps in the face, betrayal, sexual exploitation, derision, neglect, etc. are all forms of mistreatment, because they injure the integrity and dignity of a child, even if their consequences are not visible right away," writes the leftist psychotherapist Alice Miller on her website (2007). Note Miller's conflation of humiliation, spanking, and "slaps in the face" with "sexual exploitation" and "neglect," as if disciplining a child by spanking is equivalent to sexually abusing the youngster. Miller contends that most parents are subject to a ghastly compulsion which forces them to mistreat their children in all sorts of subtle yet deeply subversive ways. By demanding that their children control their desires and submit to the authority of moral law parents commit what Miller calls "soul-murder." "Until the general public becomes aware that countless children are subjected to soul-murder every day society as a whole must suffer as a result," Miller warns. (Mack 1994, 32-33) Predictably, this point of view has been eagerly embraced by left-leaning psychoanalysts in America. By expanding the conception of abuse to include any exercise of parental authority whatsoever, these leftist psychotherapists seek to abolish parental discipline altogether, even going so far as to make it illegal. According to Dana Mack, an affiliate scholar at the Institute for American Values, "Parents have actually been convicted of such 'crimes' as restricting television viewing, or taking a child out of school for reasons unacceptable to school authorities." (1994, 35) In California, Assemblywoman Sally Lieber, a leftist Democrat, has introduced legislation to outlaw spanking toddlers. "Under current law, parents can beat their children to a reasonable degree," Lieber explained. "I just think that that's plain wrong and we ought to ban any sort of physical attack on children who are not old enough to defend themselves." (Yi 2007)

Given the left's strong distaste for discipline and restraint, particularly on sexual matters, is it any wonder that they should so despise and abhor the religious right? It is hardly any wonder at all. What demands an explanation is the left's animus against discipline and restraint. Why does the left frown on discipline, on punishment, on anything that smacks too strongly of delayed or frustrated gratification? The spoiled-child psychology explains all this in a single bold stroke. The spoiled-child doesn't want to be disciplined or restrained or frustrated or punished. He wishes to do as he pleases without suffering any consequences. In short, he desires a license for irresponsibility.

This liberation from responsibility is what motivates the left's sentimental attachment to socialist utopias. What, after all, is socialism all about? *From each according to their ability, to each according to their need.* Such is the classic statement of socialism. The operative word here is *need*, an obvious synonym for *desire* and *want*. Socialism is a system where those with the most needs, wants, and desires, rather than those who have contributed most to the system, get the lion's share. Appeasing the insatiable needs of the so-called "oppressed," *that* is what socialism amounts to in the end. In short, the spoiled child's paradise, where need trumps hard work and sacrifice.

Of course, leftists are careful not to put it in this way. They instead blather on about the evils of corporations and the Republican Party. Yet this is of little consequence. When people lust after impossible ideals, their real motives quickly become obscured by moral posturing and facile rationalization. Leftists have no clue about their underlying psychopathology. They are so taken in by their own rationalizations that they don't even understand the futility of their jejune ideals. Hence the profound error of taking leftist ideology at face value. The arguments leftists bring forth to defend their convictions are little more than window dressing, a diversion to hide what is really going on. If you want to get to the root of leftist ideology, you have to peel away all the layers of rationalizations and poke your finger into whatever you find hidden beneath. I have suggested that, more often than not, your inquiries will yield some form or another of the spoiled-child psychology. Extensive research would be required before we could estimate the degree to which this conjecture accords with reality.

Part 2: Economics

6. Machiavellian Economics

The Enron debacle gave the pundits and the politicians an opportunity to vent their ideological passions. Senator Ernest Hollings called the corporate scandal a "cancer" that's "got to stop." Politicians on Capitol Hill did their utmost to express outrage and indignation at the behavior of those Enron executives who, realizing that their incompetence had bankrupted the company, devised a confidence scheme to pass all the losses to the company's hapless employees and shareholders. It's a "great tragedy" repeated one Senator at the conclusion of another round of dreary Enron hearings.

Such histrionic breast-beating has its place, no doubt; but it is of little use for attaining a rational understanding of the issue at hand. To grasp the deeper meaning of the Enron mess the intrepid investigator must place all his moral indignation to the side and proceed with the calm and deliberate detachment of an anatomist dissecting a corpse. Nor can the discerning analyst become so obsessed with his subject that he forgets his larger purpose. The individual corpse, in and of itself, means little, if anything, to the anatomist. He seeks something of considerably greater significance: the principles of anatomy, to which the corpse is a mere instrument or illustration. The same logic applies to the dissection of a case like Enron. The significance of the Enron debacle has little to do with the specific crimes of its corporate managers: those are of interest only to criminal investigators and shallow journalists. Enron draws its significance from its larger implications concerning how American corporations, in an age of rapid debt expansion, conduct their finances. The real question at the heart of the Enron debacle is not *How could anything so horrible happen?* but *How many more corporations are guilty of similar financial chicaneries, and to what extent is all this related to the problem of excessive debt in an age of unbridled credit expansion?*

The investigator, when tackling a question of this sort, must place all his prejudices to the side and go about his business as impartially as human nature will allow. His goal must be to reach the truth of the matter, come what may. He should never confuse what did or might happen with what should or ought to have happened. These are entirely different questions that lead to entirely different answers. The moralist, in his obsession to determine what ought to be, often ends up ignoring the simple fact that he can control only one person: himself. How others behave is beyond his control. He can attempt to influence them through persuasion or moral denunciation. But it is not clear that this will lead to anything substantial. The behavior of other human beings is as much an independent reality removed from our volition as is any fact of brute nature. Men cannot be governed by slogans. Society, as a whole, has a momentum of its own that defies the attempt by professional busybodies and moralists to change or redirect it. Human beings are not blank slates upon which we can write what we please. There are deeper powers in each of them that push them this way and that. If the analyst can grasp the mere outlines of these powers—and that is about as much as anyone can hope to see of them—then perhaps some understanding of this strange beast, *Homo sapiens*, can be attained.

Those who attempt to grasp the subtleties of political, economic, and social phenomenon by subjecting them to ideological interpretations will almost certainly go astray in their conclusions. If the investigator's first priority is to prove his own prejudices and his second to convert others to his point of view, how can anyone trust him? The entire scientific enterprise, whether in the "natural" or "social" sciences, can only succeed on the basis of trust. Those of us who are not scientists, who don't have expertise in a given field of research, are not able to judge. We haven't done any of the research. We don't know the relevant facts. It's the scientist's job to do the research and know the facts. But if the putative scientist is more interested in establishing his own presuppositions and converting other people to his views, how can he fulfill his side of the bargain? The spread of knowledge, especially scientific knowledge, rests on the argument from authority, which, although technically a fallacy of logic, is nonetheless necessary in a society that requires an extensive division of labor merely to get things done. We cannot all be scientists, devoting the lion's share of our spare time to checking the investigations and experiments of the thousands of full-time researchers who infest our universities and think tanks. That is why scientists ought to avoid ideological agendas. A scientist, especially if, as is the case with social scientists, his research involves facts about controversial political and social subjects, must remain above the ideological fray, allowing the facts to speak for themselves, rather than for some surreptitious ideological agenda.

Achieving genuine objectivity in social science is not easy. It requires a certain kind of temperament and self-discipline, the rare ability to examine social phenomenon with the detachment of the entomologist dissecting a cockroach. Just as the entomologist is little concerned with devising a better cockroach, so the social scientist, when he is in the midst of his research, must care little for "improving" society or bettering the condition of his fellow man. At the very least, he must lay his philanthropic impulses aside while he goes about his business of discovering important truths about the social order. The ideologue inevitably winds up painting a rosier picture of society than the facts warrant. An uncompromising, truculent realism is the first priority of the intrepid social scientist.

That very few social scientists live up to these ideals is lamentable but true. Nietzsche's remarks about the mendacity of philosophers also describe far too many scholars, especially in the humanities and the social sciences. "They are all advocates who resent that name, and for the most part even wily spokesmen for their prejudices which they baptize 'truths,'" Nietzsche wrote. "They all pose as if they had discovered their real opinions through self-development of a cold, pure, divinely unconcerned dialectic (as opposed to the mystics of every rank, who are more honest and doltish—and talk of 'inspiration'); while at the bottom it is an assumption, a hunch, indeed a kind of 'inspiration'—most often a desire of the heart that has been filtered and made abstract—that they defend with reasons they have sought after the fact." (1968a, 202)

This phenomenon is so widespread that it hardly requires documentation. Most books written by scholars today are works of advocacy. Most come from a left-liberal perspective, but some come from the center and a few from the right. These books include some valuable contributions, some real scholarship. But the non-expert can never really trust these works, because of the difficulties of distinguishing genuine scholarship from mere propaganda.

Although there were several important attempts in the pre-modern world to study society impartially, free from ideological bias, we don't find any great successes along this line until Machiavelli. Why Machiavelli should have been the first consistently non-ideological social and political theorist is not altogether clear. He certainly had no self-consciousness about it. He regarded himself as a great patriot who merely used his objectivity to better serve his country. He once wrote: "I love my fatherland more than my own soul." (Grazia 1989, 347)

Machiavelli believed that the best way he could help his country was by seeing things as they really are, rather than as he or anyone else might wish them to be. Although a republican at heart, when it became clear to him that republicanism could not save Italy from the depredations of foreign invasion, he became a tentative monarchist, and wrote his most famous work, *The Prince*. Machiavelli always strove to be a realist. He never allowed his personal inclinations to blind himself to the facts.

Machiavelli's revolutionary method of analyzing politics has for centuries been condemned for divorcing politics from ethics. This charge, as James Burnham has pointed out, is confused. "Machiavelli divorced politics from ethics only in the same sense that every science must divorce itself from ethics. Scientific descriptions and theories must be based upon the facts, the evidence, not upon the supposed demands of some ethical system. If this is what is meant by the statement that Machiavelli divorced politics from ethics, if the statement sums up his refusal to pervert and distort political science by doctoring its results in order to bring them into line with 'moral principles'—his own or any others—then the charge is certainly true." (1943, 44)

Machiavelli stressed knowing the facts *before* one passes moral judgment. If you put the moral judgment first, thinking that somehow the facts will fashion themselves to fit your values, you will never understand the truth of the matter. Facts always come first, despite what the passionate moralist may think or argue. No values can be attained, no morality defended, when we live in ignorance and despair of the true causes of our sins and sorrows.

In the centuries following his death, Machiavelli's reputation suffered most at the hands of the ruling class. When the Catholic Church instituted the notorious Index, it honored Machiavelli by choosing him as one of first writers condemned. Two centuries later, one of the most powerful kings of the eighteenth century, Frederick the Great of Prussia, actually wrote a book entitled *Anti-Machiavel*.

It is understandable that the great and the powerful would find Machiavelli detestable. Machiavelli understood their ways better than anyone, and they resented finding themselves described so perfectly. "If any man will read over my book ... with impartiality and ordinary charity," Machiavelli wrote of *Il Principe* to a friend, "he will easily perceive that it is not my intention to recommend that government or those men described to the world, much less to teach men how to trample upon good men, and all that is sacred and venerable upon earth, laws, religion, honesty, and what not. If I have been a little too punctual in describing these monsters in all their lineaments and colours, I hope mankind will know them, the better to avoid them, my treatise being both a *satire* against them, and a true *character* of them."

Toward the end of the nineteenth century, Machiavelli's realist methodology was adopted by a number of prominent social scientists, including Max Weber, Vilfredo Pareto, William G. Sumner, Robert Michels and Gaetano Mosca. To these men do we owe a genuinely realistic theory of politics and society. Curiously, although Weber, Sumner, and Pareto all began as economists, none of them ever got around to devising a fully developed theory of economics. Of this group, Pareto did the most work in this area. In *Les Systèmes Socialistes* and the *Manuel d'Economie Politique*, we find many brilliant observations, but no unified vision. Pareto expended all his theoretical energy in devising a mathematical "equilibrium" theory. Unfortunately, this theory is valid only if we assume a "static" economy. Since modern capitalism is, by its very nature, excessively dynamic, Pareto's theoretical economics falls considerably short of the reality it attempts to describe.

The attempt to describe economics realistically, following Machiavelli's scientific methodology, finds its greatest exponent in the work of Joseph Schumpeter. No economist understood capitalist reality better than Schumpeter. Although he entertained an excessive admiration for the theoretical economics of Walras and Pareto, Schumpeter never allowed his admiration of pure theory to compromise his grasp of economic and social facts. While most pro-capitalist economists continued to believe that the market succeeded because of competition, only Schumpeter understood that the free market could never thrive on competition alone. An element of monopoly was also needed to enable businesses to earn a profit and raise capital. Schumpeter was also one of the very few economists who understood the role of credit creation and modern finance in the development and implementation of economic innovation. Whereas most economists view credit creation from some sort of ethical perspective, Schumpeter saw it for what it is: a flawed but necessary means of raising capital for economic innovation.

Although Schumpeter's achievement is great, he did not quite succeed in bequeathing to posterity a fully developed system of "Machiavellian economics." He really had no interest in such an undertaking. He saw himself, not as a Machiavellian, but merely as a theorist trying to solve specific economic problems. A fully realistic theory of economics would emerge, he thought, in time. In the meantime, the groundwork had to be laid. Greater work had to be done on the empirical side of things. Theory needed better integration with fact. Walras' equilibrium theory needed to be extended and enriched with a correlative dynamic theory. Schumpeter, finding himself confronted with all these problems, really did not know where to begin, and instead contented himself with doing only partial work on some of them. In his final years, he gave up theoretical work altogether and spent most of his time writing a history of economic thought.

Since Schumpeter, economics has sunk into a pitiful condition. Most of the work done by so-called professional economists in our universities is either excessively empirical and statistical or confoundedly mathematical. Economists only see what their prejudices allow them to see. If they happen to be anti-capitalist, they have very sharp eyes for the seamier side of capitalist reality. If, on the other hand, they are pro-capitalist, then they only notice the positive side of the ledger. A fully Machiavellian vision of economics is no where to be found. Here and there, one might find a feeble approach to it; but a complete, uncompromising exemplification of it does not exist.

The task of developing a thoroughly realistic economics, though difficult, is not impossible. A great deal of the research has already been done on economic problems. The facts are readily available to anyone who wishes to take the trouble to study them. It is simply a matter of analyzing these facts scientifically and drawing the requisite conclusions. I have done a bit of work along these lines myself. Although I can hardly boast of having developed a full-fledged theory, I have stumbled upon a few basic ideas or principles that could be useful in constructing more adequate theories. I have found eleven principles that are critical in the development of any realistic theory of economics. They are listed as follows:

1. The Scarcity Principle. Scarcity is the rule in economic affairs. All economic goods are limited; human desires, on the other hand, remain unlimited and insatiable.

2. The Uncertainty Principle. All human actions are conducted on the basis of incomplete knowledge. Risk and uncertainty are two critical factors affecting economic decision-making and the development of economic institutions.

3. The Profit Principle. The first consideration of nearly every business in a free market is to keep the budget out of the red. When a business enterprise fails at this task, it inevitably goes out of business.

4. The Nation-State Principle. Markets always exist within a legal framework set by nation-states in competition with other nation-states.

5. The "Mixed Economy" Principle. All economies are in some sense "mixed," that is, there are no "pure" economic (or political) systems in the real world. Political and economic factors are always commingled. The notion that economics can be separate from politics is empirically unsupportable. In the real world, there exists no clearly defined separation between economics and politics. This separation is purely conceptual in nature and should never be taken literally, as if it corresponded to an actual fact. It is a tool of analysis rather than a description of reality.

6. **The Spoliation Principle.** Some degree of economic spoliation always occurs in society. There is no such thing as an economy that does not feature some form of "expropriation." For every sheep there exists a wolf, ready to gorge himself on the delectable flesh of the lamb.

7. **The Status Principle.** Economic actors tend to be more concerned with status than with money, which is rarely pursued for its own sake, but only as an indispensable means to achieve "status."

8. **The Inequality Principle.** There always has been and always will be inequality of income.

9. **The Monopoly Principle.** Competition in a free market must contain an element of monopoly to be effective. Pure competition would be as disastrous as pure monopoly.

10. **Markets spontaneously coordinate the division of knowledge and labor.** The extraordinary ability of the market to make the best use of the knowledge of each market participant is largely what provides capitalism its immense productive advantage over socialism.

11. **The Principle of the Elitist Foundation of Progress.** All progress, including all economic progress, is dependent on a handful of (often) "antisocial" innovators—individuals who, by discovering new and more productive ways of getting important tasks done, wind up destroying traditional methods.

There are, to be sure, other important principles necessary for an adequate comprehension of economic reality; but these eleven will make a good start. I will proceed by explaining each principle in more detail and showing how various economists, under the sway of ideological passion, end up violating or ignoring them.

* * *

1. The Scarcity Principle. Academic economists are right on this one. Their introductory textbooks nearly always define economics as the science of scarcity and choice. "Economics is the study of how scarce resources are allocated among competing ends," is how one textbook puts it. (Skousen 1991, 14) What this means in plain English is, to quote Milton Friedman's famous words, "there is no such thing as a free lunch." In fact, not even "free" things are free, in the sense of imposing no costs. To consume one "free" item means that you cannot consume another—at least not simultaneously! This fact imposes a cost on the consumption of the free item. Since not all values can be attained simultaneously, attaining (or consuming) any economic value entails a cost of some sort, no matter how infinitesimal.

2. The Uncertainty Principle. Although no one denies the importance of this principle, economists often fail to understand some of its deeper implications. A good example involves the issue of oligopoly under capitalism. Why are so many industries dominated by two or three immense corporations? Wherefore all this economic concentration, this epidemic of mergers which has afflicted capitalism since the Industrial Revolution? Most economists believe it came about because of what are called "economies of scale." It is widely believed that production at a larger scale leads to lower costs. In other words, an automobile factory that makes 100 cars a day will be more productive than a factory which produces only ten cars a day. There are many reasons for this, including opportunities for greater specialization and the reduction of overhead expenses. However, economic concentration would take place even without economies of scale. Economic concentration constitutes one the best hedges against uncertainty.

All business activity involves taking incalculable risks. No business can know for certain how much it should produce or what it should charge for its wares. Nor can any investor ever accurately predict how much he can gain from a specific investment. Uncertainty is an all-pervasive fact of economics. "It is a world of change in which we live, and a world of uncertainty," wrote Frank Knight, the economist who best understood the influence of uncertainty on business life. "We live only by knowing *something* about the future; while the problems of life, or of conduct at least, arise from the fact that we know so little. This is true of business as of other spheres of activity. The essence of the situation is action according to *opinion*, of greater or less foundation and value, neither ignorance nor complete and perfect information, but partial knowledge. If we are to understand the workings of the economic system we must examine the ... significance of uncertainty." (1921, 199)

According to Knight, "one of the important causes of the phenomenal growth in the average size of industrial establishments" is the attempt by businesses to "group" or diversify its risk by extending its scale of operations. "In so far as a single businessman, by borrowing capital or otherwise, can extend the scope of his exercise of judgment over a greater number of decisions or estimates, there is a greater probability that bad guesses will be offset by good ones and that a degree of constancy and dependability in the total results will be achieved. In so far uncertainty is eliminated and the desideratum of rational activity realized." (1921, 252)

A large business organization deals with risk in much the same way as an investment broker: it diversifies its risk by sticking its thumbs in as many pies as possible. If a company like Ford loses loads of money trying to market a sports car, it can make up the difference from its profits in the van and truck markets. If a mega corporation like Time-Warner loses money at CNN, it can make up the difference with sales of music on the Internet. The more a company diversifies its operations, the greater the chance that it can avoid bankruptcy as a result of any single calamity in one market or another.

It should be obvious that, because of the prevailing role of uncertainty in human life, businesses in a free market will always seek to insure themselves against uncertainty through expansion and mergers. This is a fact of economic life.

There exist several other very important consequences of the influence of uncertainty on economic life. Economic concentration is not the only means used by businesses to deal with the inherent risks of capitalist enterprise. Various legal expedients are resorted to as well, the most famous being the development of the limited liability corporation. But even more critical is the use of political methods to create a more "secure" economic environment. Businessmen have eagerly sought to use the power of the state to help control uncertainty.

3. The Profit Principle. There exists much confusion on this issue, especially among critics of capitalism. Even though the first consideration of most businesses is to make a profit, this does not mean that businessman under capitalism only care about making money, and that the ultimate end of all capitalist enterprise is to become filthy rich. Entrepreneurs and capitalists care about other things besides money. Money, for them, is simply a means, not an end. Economic enterprises must make money to stay in business. If a business makes no profits, its position against its competitors becomes increasingly tenuous. It will inevitably experience great difficulties in competing against profitable companies. It also becomes vulnerable to any kind of downturn in the economy.

Such are the difficulties faced by a company that merely breaks even. But it is even worse for the enterprise that runs up debts. Firms must make money or they die. It is as simple as that. A company with no concern for the bottom line does not have a future. Profits are the lifeblood of business. Without them, no business can survive.

The importance of profits is well illustrated by the Great Depression. As any historically literate person knows, the depression lasted for almost an entire decade—the longest such period of economic decline in American history. Why did it last so long? Was the Stock Market crash of 1929 really so devastating that it took the economy nearly ten years to recover?

No, of course not. The economy should have recovered in at least half the time. As a matter of fact, it did start recovering in the mid-thirties, only to suffer another major setback in 1937. Economic historian Benjamin Anderson described this setback as follows:

"The break in the Stock Market was one of the most violent in our whole history. The decline in the curve for industrial production, 1937-1938, was the most violent decline in an eight- or nine-month period that our history records. The break amounted to 34%... The extreme down swing between the peak of 1929 and the low of 1932 in volume of business was greater, but at no stage of that decline was anything like so rapid a downward movement revealed." (1949, 438)

We hear ever so much about the Stock Market crash of 1929, along with all the economic disasters which followed—but hardly a word of this second crash of 1937. In the thirties, America experienced what would nowadays be called a "double-dip depression." The U.S. economy went through two business crises, one massive and prolonged, the other short but very precipitous. Everyone remembers the first, possibly because it took place under a conservative Administration and historians tend to be liberal. But the second is every bit as important and should not be forgotten by those who wish to understand the effect that bad government policies can have on the economy.

What caused the 1937 business crisis? The evidence suggests that the second catastrophe was caused by the New Deal—specifically, by the New Deal's repeated attacks against business profitability. Again, to quote Anderson:

"What then, were the explanations of the Stock Market crash and the business crisis? With respect to business, there is one outstanding fact. Business expands when profits are improving. Business contracts when profits decline or when there is a serious threat to profits. Now, profits are what is left of gross income after costs are subtracted, and the labor factor in costs is overwhelmingly important. In the years 1936 and 1937 labor income was running well over 70% of the total national income, whereas profit income did not exceed 15.3%

"A 10% increase in aggregate labor income at the expense of aggregate profit income would thus mean cutting profit income approximately in half, which would lead to violent business reaction."

Anderson blames the increase in labor costs on "trade union activity" inspired by the Wagner Act. Starting in 1936, the C.I.O, under the leadership of John L. Lewis, triggered a series of "immense strikes," "sit down" strikes, and the occupation of factories and plants. "Unionization was rapidly accomplished and wages were rapidly raised." This caused "a rise in wages unmatched by a corresponding rise in the productivity of labor."

Anderson cites one other critical factor responsible for crippling the profitability of business in the mid-thirties; high taxes, including the infamous "Undistributed Profits Tax" of 1936, which taxed corporate savings, making it very difficult for businesses to set aside funds for investment. Steeply progressive income taxes and high taxes on capital gains hit individual investors especially hard. "These rates, applied to profits made in the Stock Market, meant that men of substantial means simply could not engage in many Stock Market transactions," wrote Anderson. "If they were successful, the Government took most of the profits. If they had losses, they took them themselves." (1949, 444, 445, 450)

Anderson makes an important point. Opponents of capitalism are always decrying the "exorbitant" profits of business, while ignoring altogether the losses. The enormous profits attract the attention of everyone, especially the envious. But no one bothers his head about the losses. The losses are forgotten, along with the businesses that are ruined by them.

No economy can remain strong and vibrant unless at least some businesses are making a healthy profit. If this means that a handful of businesses will make "exorbitant" profits, then so be it. That is the price one pays for living in a wealthy country. If we really need to redistribute wealth and appease the envious, the best way to accomplish this goal would be to institute luxury taxes and sumptuary laws against wealthy consumers. The attempt to achieve "social justice" through high taxation merely puts the economy as a whole at risk, thus hurting nearly everyone, poor and rich alike. In order to increase jobs and worker productivity, businesses have to make a profit. Replacing worn out machines, funding research and development, trying new methods of production cost money. Where are businesses supposed to get the money to pay these costs if not from profits? If you reduce profits, you reduce capital investment and progress. Who benefits from that?

4. The Nation-State Principle. Among the most zealous champions of the free market there exists a coterie of anarchists who defend an ideology known as "anarcho-capitalism," which argues that government is completely unnecessary. Legislation, law enforcement, defense of homeland, protection against infectious diseases, maintenance of roads and canals can all be accomplished, contend these anarcho-capitalists, by the market. All kinds of rationalizations are brought forth to "prove" that the market can replace the state and that everyone would be better off if government ceased to exist. Ideologues who don't share these views are quick to offer "refutations," allegedly "proving" that anarcho-capitalism would lead to a Hobbesian war of all against all or the dominance of big business or some other unpleasant outcome.

All such arguments, however, whether for or against the anarcho-capitalist imbecilities, miss the point entirely. Anarcho-capitalism is not bad because it would lead to deplorable consequences. As a matter of fact, it would lead to no consequences at all, because no such system will ever be exemplified in the real world. Its advocates can argue for it until they are blue in the face: it won't matter one jot. Social systems are not brought about by mere patter. Politics is not a matter of argument or persuasion. Societies always contain a significant number of predatory individuals who, through intimidation and fraud, seek to take advantage of others. To protect themselves, weaker individuals must find some individual or group who will defend them against such predators. If the state fails in this task, these weaker individuals will seek protection from some other source—from a marauding aristocrat or a trade union, a local politician or a Mafioso boss. Whoever provides protection to the weak becomes a kind of *de facto* state. The only kind of anarchy that can ever exist is of the feudal variety, in which a collection of disorganized *de facto* states compete for "clients." This form of pluralistic statism can never be brought about by intention or design. No government or democracy or social order would ever choose to become feudalistic of its own free will. Feudal anarchy occurs only after a very serious breakdown in the social order. The feudal anarchy that afflicted Europe during the so-called "Dark Ages" came about because of the complete collapse of mercantile trade in Western Europe. The Moslems had taken control of the Mediterranean and blocked the shipping routes into Western Europe. Barbarian incursions cut off trade in the North. Western Europe was forced to live off its own resources, with disastrous consequences to the economy. Without trade, cities shriveled to virtually nothing and political centralization became impossible. (Pirenne 1925, 22-25)

The rise of the modern nation-state was an essential factor in the development of free market capitalism. This is a point not well understood by those who have an ideological axe to grind. Free market zealots tend to regard the nation-state as essentially hostile to capitalism. They argue that the nation-state burdened early capitalism with over-regulation, monopoly, ruinous taxation and senseless wars. There is much truth in this view. Many state policies are in fact harmful to the development of industrial capitalism. But other state policies are absolutely necessary. The state must provide the legal framework necessary for the development of unambiguous property ownership. Without this legal framework, it becomes very hard to use property as a source of capital. The primary reason capitalism succeeded in the West while floundering in other parts of the world is that the West discovered how to use property as a source of capital. In the Third World, most people have no clear rights to the property they control. As a result, they find it very difficult to capitalize their property for business uses. The Institute for Liberty and Democracy has estimated that the poor of the Third World own real estate worth 9.3 trillion dollars, which is twice as much as the total amount of U.S. money in circulation. But this 9.3 trillion is close to useless. Since the ownership rights over this wealth is not clearly defined, it cannot be used to fund new business enterprises. It remains, in the trenchant words of economist Hernando de Soto, mere "dead capital."

To bring capital to life, a legal framework provided by the state is necessary. This legal framework hardly exists in the Third World, where "extralegality," as de Soto puts it, "is the norm." (2000, 35, 6, 30-32) A market without a legal framework is a market in a state of anarchy. Those anarcho-capitalists who think the market can function without the state should look closely at the extralegal markets in the Third World. Here we find the closest approximation to the anarcho-capitalist ideal that is ever likely to be exemplified in reality. Yet what have these markets accomplished? Very little. They are tremendously under-capitalized. They exist in the midst of some of the worst poverty in the world. The market, by itself, is incapable of developing a workable legal framework that can transform property from dead capital into living, fungible assets.

A critical component of a functional, market-based legal system is that it enables property to be represented in writing: in titles, securities, contracts, and other documents. These representations, before they can serve as the basis of a full-fledged capitalist economic order, require systematic integration. "The reason capitalism has triumphed in the West and sputtered in the rest of the world is because most of the assets in Western nations have been integrated into one formal representational system," notes De Soto. "This integration did not happen casually. Over decades in the nineteenth century, politicians, legislators, and judges pulled together the scattered facts and rules that had governed property throughout cities, villages, buildings, and farms and integrated them into one system. This 'pulling together' of property representations, a revolutionary moment in the history of developed nations, deposited all the information and rules governing the accumulated wealth of their citizens into one knowledge base." (2000, 52)

It should be understood that, without a state, this integration of property representation systems could not have taken place. In the nineteenth century, people were too scattered and too disputatious to get together and enforce a common representative standard on their own. Only a centralized government could accomplish such a task. One standard had to be imposed on all, even if no single locality were completely satisfied with it. The American Articles of Confederation failed because they could not impose the economic uniformity necessary to develop a strong and flourishing national economy. The American constitution, which laid the groundwork for a strong central government, helped create the conditions out of which American capitalism arose. America would never have become the world's greatest economic nation were it not for the Constitution.

The need for a legal framework is not the sole reason capitalism can only exist and flourish under the auspices of the nation-state. The state also plays an instrumental role in helping businesses grapple with the problem of uncertainty. I have already mentioned how uncertainty leads to the development of massive corporations. This development also depends on the formation of legal rules regulating business organization. Corporations depend on legal privileges that provide limited liability to shareholders, thus reducing the risk of investing in new and daring enterprises. Many other examples could be cited demonstrating how the state, by reducing uncertainty, creates the environment necessary for the capitalist engine to function. Even something as simple as maintaining law and order is absolutely critical to capitalist enterprise. Investors must feel that they are safe in both their persons and their property before they will feel comfortable investing their assets in risky ventures. No rational person will make the sacrifices involved in saving and investing their wealth if they fear that some criminal can take it all away at the drop of a hat.

Although the nation-state is necessary to the development of capitalism, this does not mean that all states have or will conduct themselves in a manner beneficial to the capitalist order. Many states pursue policies that harm capitalist development and make economic progress next to impossible. This is why so many pro-capitalist ideologues regard the state as a menace. They see examples all around them of governments sabotaging the free market and assume that the state, by its very nature, is hostile to the capitalist order. But this is an error of judgment. Even though many states pursue policies detrimental to capitalism does not mean that capitalism would be better off if there were no states at all. Capitalism requires a secure environment in which property rights are enforced and integrated under a standardized system. Only a strong, centralized state can provide this necessary framework. A "minimal" state (i.e., a weak state) would only find itself prey to aggressive foreign nations and domestic troublemakers. Power always exists in concentrated forms. A free market can only flourish when a state, representing one form of concentrated power, acts in its favor and protects it from other, less friendly concentrations. Capitalism without a state is virtually a contradiction in terms, a solecism of social reality. Wherever you find capitalism you will also find a state.

An important corollary of the Nation-State Principle is what could be called the underlying mercantilist core or substratum of the international market. Thanks to the classical economists, mercantilism, the predominant economic philosophy before the Industrial Revolution, became thoroughly discredited. Nevertheless, it would be a mistake to dismiss mercantilism in its entirety. Amongst all the chaff of error, there existed a few kernels of hard truth that cannot be ignored. Nations and peoples do in fact compete, not merely in the sense that they contend on the world market, but in the larger sense that they contend for political advantage and prestige on the world's stage. If a nation wants to enjoy at least some degree of security against foreign aggression, it must take its place among the world's leading powers. This requires subordinating economic policy to political and military concerns.

All the great statesmen of world history have understood this. They have all realized that, despite the economic benefits of free trade, the nation's military and political standing must come first. Developing and protecting the nation's industrial base must always be the first priority of the statesman who has his country's interests at heart.

Most economists since Adam Smith have argued that state policies aimed at protecting industrial technology and preventing huge trade deficits are counterproductive. According to Ricardo's law of "comparative advantage," a nation is better off specializing in what it does best. If that means making wine instead of manufacturing automobiles, then that is precisely what should be done. Never mind that countries devoted predominantly to agricultural production remain mere backwaters, defenseless against industrial powers with imperial ambitions.

The economic historian David S. Landes, commenting on Ricardo's theory, pithily wrote: "The statesmen who guided the destinies of European nations did not have access to this logic; and if they had, they would have paid it little mind. They linked industrial advance to power." (Landes, 233)

The classical economists believed that free trade leads to greater economic efficiency. In the main, they appear to have been right. However, they were never so naive as to raise free trade to the status of a sacred cow. Thus Adam Smith regarded the defense of the country as one of the "two cases in which it will be advantageous to lay some burden upon foreign [trade] for the encouragement of domestic industry." "The defense of Great Britain, for example, depends very much upon the number of its sailors and shipping," Smith wrote. "The act of navigation, therefore, very properly endeavors to give the sailors and shipping of Great Britain the monopoly of trade of their own country, in some cases by absolute burdens upon the shipping of foreign countries." Smith had no doubt that the act of navigation was "not favorable to foreign commerce, or to the growth of that opulence which can arise from it." But "as defense ... is of much more importance than opulence, the act of navigation is, perhaps, the wisest of all the commercial regulations of England." (Landes, 406-408)

A nation's survival depends on more than just the defense of its territories. Decadent mores can be another serious problem. When large segments of a nation's populace develop various feelings, attitudes, and habits unfavorable to the strength and progress of the nation, it would appear the duty of any statesman who truly cares about his country to take whatever measures possible to save the nation. Leaders are not supposed to be passive, standing by and doing nothing while everything falls to pieces around them. If the statesman chooses patriotism over nihilism, honor over ignominy, life over death, then his line of conduct is set: he does whatever he can to prevent his country from committing suicide. There may in fact be little he can do; but that is no excuse for doing nothing at all.

One form of decadence involves an infatuation for accumulating debt, especially foreign debt. The nation, as a whole, prefers to spend rather than save. When it can no longer raise credit within its own borders, it looks to other countries to supply the deficit. The consequence is a massive trade deficit.

Free market ideologues claim that there is nothing wrong with these trade deficits. They simply represent what consumers want. If consumers in America prefer to spend their money and go into debt to the producers of Japan and China, why should we interfere? "What matters to the economy is not the difference between imports and exports but the extent to which Americans are free to benefit from the efficiencies, opportunities and consumer choice created in an economy open to world trade," writes one such ideologue, Daniel T. Griswold of the Cato Institute. "In the final analysis, nations do not trade with each other; people do. Every international transaction that Americans engage in will, by definition, leave both parties to the transaction believing they are better off than before—otherwise the transaction would not occur. By this measure, the 'balance of trade' is always positive, benefiting the nation as a whole."

But this is only true if Americans trade responsibly. Contrary to Mr. Griswold's ideology, transactions do not always leave both parties better off than before. People make bad trades all the time. Sports franchises are notorious for bad trades. The Boston Red Sox traded

Babe Ruth to the New York Yankees for cash. The Red Sox suffered greatly for the imbecility of that trade.

If an entire nation behaves foolishly and makes unwise trades, accumulates debts, and runs up massive trade deficits, it is not behaving in a manner conducive to its long-range survival. It is committing economic suicide. In the sixteenth century, Spain entered on a course of reckless consumption. The consequence? Bankruptcy, dishonor, and precipitous decline. "By the time the great bullion inflow had ended in the mid-seventeenth century, the Spanish crown was deep in debt, with bankruptcies in 1557, 1575, and 1597," writes David Landes. "The country entered upon a long decline. Reading this story, one might draw a moral: Easy money is bad for you. It represents short-run gain that will be paid for in immediate distortions and later regrets." (Landes, 173)

Once a nation begins accumulating massive trade deficits, is there anything it can do to prevent or postpone the inevitable day of reckoning? Probably not. In earlier ages, raising tariffs on imports, by reducing consumption on foreign goods, would stem the flood of foreign investment and raise interest rates, thereby discouraging consumption and encouraging savings. Such a tactic is no longer feasible in the globalist economy of the twenty-first century. We have become too dependent on the efficiencies inherent in a global free market. Turning back could trigger a worldwide economic catastrophe.

While free-market ideologues might rejoice in this predicament, the very fragility of the global free market system is itself a cause of concern. Globalism depends on security, particularly security of trade. A terrorist attack involving weapons of mass destruction could effectively shut down the world's ports. If target nations were forced to examine every crate shipped into their ports, trade would slow to the merest trickle. The long list of Globalism's enemies includes Islamic terrorists, backed by terrorist states like Syria and Iran. It appears doubtful that these terrorists will never get their hands on weapons of mass destruction. When they do so, the era of Globalism may find itself coming to an end.

5. The "Mixed Economy" Principle. Ideologues are often fond of categorizing certain types of action as "political" and other types as "economic," as if each were mutually exclusive. In reality, human action is rarely either political or economic, but often partakes of both categories. Business always involves an element of politics, and politics frequently merges into business.

There are two common misconceptions propagated by ideological thinkers on this issue. We owe the first to free market ideologues, who are fond of arguing that the mixed economy occurs only because the government is allowed to interfere with business. If a strict policy of "laissez-faire" were enacted, these ideologues argue, the result would be a "pure" form of market capitalism, unsullied by the contamination of politics. It is the intervention of government in the market that causes all the economic woes of society. "Government control of the economy, no matter in whose behalf, has been the source of all the evils in our industrial capitalism—and the solution is laissez-faire capitalism, *i.e.,* the abolition of any and all forms of government intervention in production and trade, the separation of State and Economics, in the same way and for the same reasons as the separation of Church and State." (Rand 1967, 109)

Just as with the case of market anarchism, we are confronted with an argument that completely misses the point. The notion that government intervention into the economy can somehow be abolished is on par with the view that salt can be abolished from the sea. Political policy is not determined by ideological principles. On the contrary, it is largely the product of competing interests. In a democracy, these interests play a game known as an election to determine which interests will have the largest say in the determination of public policy. In an oligarchy, political elites compete among themselves for the privilege of directing the nation. Under a dictatorship, the dictator and his cronies make the decisions. In all three of these cases, public policy emerges, not from ideology, but from demagogy, intrigue, and/or brute force. Under almost any political system, the ruling elite will find itself to a certain degree carried on by the force of events. No single individual, not even a dictator, can do whatever he pleases. There are always other powerful interests that have to be placated in order for the government to maintain political stability. In a democracy, the tendency is for the various ideological factions to come to some sort of ad hoc compromise; because short of that, no policy can be implemented at all, and the government collapses, plunging the nation into internecine strife. Merely to keep a democratic government up and running requires give and take among the various political factions competing for power on the national stage.

With all this in mind, it should be clear why the ideology of laissez-faire could never serve as the basis of public policy. No dictatorship or oligarchy would ever accept such a system, because that would clearly go against the political interests of the ruling elite. A democratic government would never accept laissez-faire, because it would be impossible to get it passed over the objections of rival political and economic interests. Democracies can only exist when all the major political factions feel that they are getting at least something out of the democratic process. If one ideology were to triumph completely over the others, democracy would break down and society would relapse into violence. Compromise is necessary for the preservation of democratic government. When compromise becomes impossible, the only way for political factions to settle their differences is through armed combat. Societies can be governed only by force and/or consensus. Force is obviously antithetic to laissez-faire; but so is consensus, which can only be attained through compromise.

Ironically, advocates of laissez-faire are fond of blaming the factionalism of democratic rule on government intervention. "A mixed economy is rule by pressure groups," complains one such advocate. "It is an amoral, institutionalized civil war of special interests and lobbies, all fighting to seize a momentary control of the legislative machinery, to extort some special privilege at one another's expense." (Rand 1967, 207) Again, we are confronted with an irrelevant argument. The fact is, all societies, of whatever nature or description, are characterized by a "rule by pressure groups." Factionalism always exists. That is simply the nature of human society. Individuals compete not merely for resources, but, as we shall later see, for status as well. Out of these conflicts a concerted policy of laissez-faire can never emerge. It is a dead ideology, advocated by a mere handful of insignificant ideologues whose disdain for the political process is simply a cover for their political impotence.

Most human beings are not obsessed with a specific ideology. They are pragmatists eager to make their way in the world and get things done. This is especially true of businessmen, who tend to be among societies most shameless pragmatists. They have to be. Economic competition forces them to adopt whatever measures lead to success in business, regardless of moral considerations. If business *A* flourishes through cutting corners or flooding the airwaves with disingenuous advertising, then their principle competitor, business *B*, must do likewise, if only to avoid being driven out of business.

It is an axiom of business that no potential source of capital and profit can be ignored. One such source of capital and profit is the state, and businessmen have rarely shrunk from tapping into this fertile source of revenue. This, again, may appear ironical in the light of the laissez-faire ideology, which is usually promoted in the interest of business. However, actual businessmen, even while occasionally paying lip service to this ideology, act in a very different manner. When possible, they have always sought special dispensations from the state, either in the form of tariffs, rebates, low interest loans, and expansionary monetary policies. They were even responsible for much of the landmark business regulation that was passed during the first two decades of the twentieth century. As historian Gabriel Kolko has noted, "The dominant fact of American political life at the beginning of [the twentieth] century was that big business led the struggle for the federal regulation of the economy." (1963, 57-58) A survey conducted in 1911 found that American business supported federal incorporation laws by a majority of four to one, a licensing law by nearly two to one, and a trade commission by nearly three to one. (Lustig 1982)

Why would American businessmen favor government regulation? There are a variety of reasons, but perhaps the most important one relates to the issue of uncertainty brought up earlier. Businessmen around the turn of the century held a different view about economic competition than is prevalent today, especially among free market zealots. They did not regard competition as altogether beneficial. They saw it as potentially ruinous to sound business enterprise. As an American Tobacco Company executive candidly argued in 1912: "Unrestricted competition had been tried out to a conclusion, with the result that the industrial fabric of the nation was confronted with an almost tragic condition of impending bankruptcy. Unrestricted competition had proved a deceptive mirage, and its victims were struggling on every hand to find some means of escape from the perils of the environment. In this trying situation, it was perfectly natural that the idea of rational co-operation in lieu of cut-throat competition should suggest itself." (Kolko 1963, 13-14)

It would be easy to regard these sentiments as mere rationalizations of monopoly power. Obviously, businessmen working for established firms would prefer to limit the competition they face, because that makes things easier for them. But the issue goes far deeper than naked self-interest and greed. Remember what was said earlier about uncertainty and its role in economic decision-making. Uncertainty is a huge problem in economic life. Businessmen have to spend a great deal of time and effort trying to minimize it.

Now the existence of competition increases the amount of uncertainty confronting private enterprise. The millions of dollars and thousands of man hours invested in a given business can end up going for nothing because some competitor, through aggressive pricing and ruthless wage practices, manages to offer a cheaper product to consumers. Imagine how difficult it would be to raise the enormous amount of capital required to fund a business like Chrysler or Boeing if, at a drop of a hat, that enterprise could be ruined by a foreign competitor who is subsidized by his national government. Wouldn't an investor, before putting his life savings at risk, want assurance that there existed at least some form of protection against this sort of "ruinous competition"? Wouldn't it be advisable that at least some of the risks involved in starting a business, especially a capital-intensive business, be minimized to encourage greater investment in the economy as a whole?

In asking these questions, I am not trying to take one side or the other, but merely attempting to explain the motivational complexes involved in the development of political capitalism. It may very well be, as the free market zealots insist, that what businessmen regard as ruinous competition is merely the process by which the market weeds out less efficient business organizations. Certainly, competition does have that effect. But it may have other effects that work in the other direction. A plausible case could be made that, in its extreme form, competition may undermine its efficiency advantages by increasing the risks involved in investment. This is not to underestimate or disparage the many positive effects of competition. These are absolutely critical. Nor would I deny the risks of monopoly and economic concentration on the other side. The efficiency of political capitalism, of a market limited by protectionism and other restrictions, depends on whether protected businesses abuse or take advantage of their privileges. Since there exists no guarantee one way or the other, in many instances political capitalism will in fact lead to loss of resources and demoralizing corruption, just as its opponents insist. All that I am suggesting is that it does not *always* lead to loss in total output.

If the statistical record of American economic history can be trusted, we must conclude that political capitalism has worked astonishingly well in this country. The United States has enjoyed consistently high rates of economic growth during the last century and a half. Until recently, Japan also enjoyed much success with political capitalism as well. Only in the Third World has this political system of economics proved a conspicuous failure. The reasons for this are many, but most of them can be reduced to socio-cultural factors over which no one, including the state, has any control. What is needed for political capitalism to be successful is a class of entrepreneurial geniuses eager to take advantage of the special privileges offered by government policies. If this class does not exist, or if it is completely stymied by bad or poorly enforced laws, political capitalism will merely lead to inefficiency and plunder.

Another uncertainty-hazard facing investors and businessmen involves the obverse side of government regulation, the side most emphasized by those who oppose regulations of all kinds. Obviously, not all forms of regulation benefit business. Indeed, business regulation can be far more ruinous than the most severe and unmitigated competition. The rational businessman/investor will be as eager to control government regulation as he is to limit ruinous competition. Here we have the second motivational element in the development of political capitalism. Big business not only sought to use the state to limit competition; it also sought to protect its interests from over zealous business regulation. In any democracy, there will always exist anti-business forces. Disgruntled workers, envious intellectuals, sensitive "artistic" types, and humanitarian busybodies will all tend to oppose business enterprise as a matter of principle. Some may oppose business enterprise because they imagine that a different arrangement of society would be morally superior. Others will oppose it because of failures in their own economic enterprises, due either to incompetence or the unscrupulous practices of their competitors. And finally, there are those who have a genuine claim to being "victims" of the system—i.e., individuals who have suffered either an unjust dismissal at their place of work or have been defrauded or ill-treated in their role as consumers. Whatever the reason, whether trivial or genuine, it is obvious that in any capitalist society there will exist a significant number of people who will detest business activity and who will be eager to control, regulate, punish or abolish the free enterprise system.

Hostility to capitalism will inevitably lead to political agitation and the attempt to regulate corporations on behalf of the "public good." Such measures are often very harmful to business interests. They create unexpected problems that can lead to catastrophic loss of revenues, thus creating new sources of anxiety and uncertainty. The businessman might find himself ruined, not by competition or fickle consumer demand, but by some new business regulation fostered by political agitators who regard capitalism with disdain. In an effort to protect themselves from harmful economic regulation, businessmen have often sought to place themselves at the forefront of economic reform, so that when the inevitable regulations are passed, they can make sure the resulting measures do not prove detrimental to their interests. As Kolko writes of businessmen during the so-called "progressive" era in American politics: "In proposing the federal regulation of business, advocates of the new Hamiltonianism were quite aware of the advantages such regulations would have in shielding them from a hostile public.... There was a 'world-wide movement of general dissatisfaction and of social unrest,' Joseph T. Talbert, vice-president of the National City Bank of New York, told a group of his associates in the spring of 1912. 'It would seem, therefore, to be the duty of all who influence public opinion, and have the power to lead and mould it, to seek not so much to check the movement as to direct its course in such manner that the blindly instinctive impulses of human nature may not destroy the economical organizations of capital.'" [178]

The principle at work here is very simple. Suppose there exists some movement to increase corporate taxes or close tax loopholes for the rich or pass draconian federal regulations against the economic interests of speculators. In that case, big business, high finance, and various trade associations will get together and sponsor a bill that purports to deal with the grievances fueling the movement. In some sense, this is what the Federal Reserve Act amounted to. Few in the world of banking and finance were entirely pleased with the idea of the Federal Reserve. But they knew that reform was needed. The banking system, as it stood at the end of the nineteenth and beginning of the twentieth centuries, was in dreadful condition. It was becoming increasingly difficult for institutions of high finance to get things done. A rising economic and political superpower requires a centralized banking system, as Alexander Hamilton persuasively argued in the eighteenth century. If America wanted to become rich, prosperous, and capable of defending itself in a world infested with aggressive, warlike nations, it would need a federal bank that could help raise the enormous credits required for the development of modern industry. It would also need a bank for defensive purposes, to help fund government deficits in wartime. Great Britain had become the world's greatest power on the strength of the Bank of England. Before America could achieve its destiny as the twentieth century's greatest economic and political power, it would need a central bank of its own.

The banking community, fearing that bank reform would be carried out either by demagogic inflationists or clueless politicians, decided to push for what would eventually become the Federal Reserve Act. In 1912, Congress inaugurated an investigation into the abuses of the banking system and, as Kolko puts, "frightened the nation with its awesome, if inconclusive, statistics on the power of Wall Street over the nation's economy." The "ogre of Wall Street was resurrected by the newspapers, who quite ignored the fact that the biggest advocates of banking reform were the bankers themselves." (1963, 220) These hearings, despite their anti-business tone, paved the way for the passing of the Federal Reserve Act, a piece of legislation which, for the most part, was in harmony with the interests of Finance Capitalism.

Opponents of the Federal Reserve and of the American banking system have often attempted to give a conspiratorial interpretation to these events, with the implication that the entire process was all very sinister and contrary to the interests of ordinary Americans. Such conspiratorial musings are entirely beside the point. The Federal Reserve System, despite its many flaws, is far preferable to what the conspiracy theorists would put in its place. What the anti-banking forces have always wanted was a "democratic" bank—that is, a bank subject to the manipulations of demagogues, most of whom would probably turn out to be dangerous cranks, often harboring inflationist agendas. Under capitalism, it will not do to have a bank controlled by "the people." Since most people are debtors, any such bank would likely pursue policies that favored debtors and harmed creditors. This would debauch the whole credit system and send the nation reeling into poverty and disgrace. While most criticisms of the Federal Reserve, whether by conspiracy theorists or laissez-faire ideologues, are often more true than false, it is not clear that a viable alternative exists. If you grasp how capitalism works in the real world, rather than in the fantasy world of ideological theory, you will understand, as Alexander Hamilton, America's greatest financial genius, understood, that a centralized banking system which enables entrepreneurs to use credit creation to divert capital from traditional methods of production to new, innovative methods, becomes a necessity of the modern, industrial economy. Economics and politics are fundamentally about tradeoffs, about choosing between the lesser of two evils, that is, between bad and worse. The Federal Reserve undoubtedly has much that can be said against it; but any alternative system would likely prove even worse.

6. The Spoliation Principle. The American essayist and social commentator Albert Jay Nock once suggested that there are only two methods "whereby man's needs and desires can be satisfied," the "political" and the "economic." This is something of an exaggeration, since, as I have already noted in this essay, the distinction between the political and economic spheres is greatly blurred in real life, and exists only for analysis rather than accurate description. But in stressing the use of political means to acquire the wealth of others, Nock was clearly on to something. Pareto gave an even more accurate rendering of Nock's principle when he noted that "the efforts of men are utilized in two different ways: they are directed to the production and transformation of economic goods, or else to the appropriation of goods produced by others." (1909, IX, 17) The mixed economy is, among other things, a spoliation economy. Businessmen resort to "political" means of raising capital in the hope of earning greater profits.

It is ironic that socialists have placed so much emphasis on capitalist spoliation, since socialism is considerably more vulnerable on this score. Capitalism remains the least "exploitive" of all economic systems, if by "exploitive" we mean expropriation of wealth from others. Socialism, communism, mercantilism, feudalism, fascism all give the state an immense role in the economy—a significantly greater role than does capitalism. Under certain extreme forms of socialism, the state controls the entire economy. Politicization of the market can go no farther than that. And where you have politicization, there will you find spoliation.

Left-wing critics of capitalism will eagerly point out that under capitalism, spoliation takes place whether the state interferes or not. The institution of private property, especially private property in the means of production, supposedly enables expropriation on a grand scale. Here, however, it is important to note that this kind of "expropriation" does not constitute a clear case of spoliation. What is "expropriated" under capitalism is what the Marxists call "surplus value"—a terribly vague and unscientific expression based on the fallacious labor theory of value. Manual labor does not constitute the full "value" of a product. The value of economic goods is determined on the demand side. Profits accrue to those enterprises that can sell their goods on the open market for more than it costs to produce them. A critical factor in achieving this end is worker productivity. The more productive the labor force, the lower the costs of producing consumer goods; and the lower the cost, the greater the opportunity for profits. But who contributes most to worker productivity? Is it the workers or the entrepreneurs?

Through the entire course of civilized human history, the masses of people have worked very hard. It is only recently that working people have had much to show for their effort. Why is labor considerably more productive under capitalism than under previous systems? Since it is obviously not a question of how hard people work, some other factor must be involved. Marx would have said it was capital. This is partly true, but it is not the whole truth. What is critical in the development of labor productivity is the discovery of better ways of using capital. As Schumpeter put it: "Different methods of employment, and not saving and increases in the available quantity of labor, have changed the face of the economic world." (1934, 68) And who is responsible for these "different methods of employment"? Surely it is not the laborers themselves, who passively do what they are told. The instigators of economic progress, those most responsible for the tremendous spike in labor productivity during the last two hundred years, are the entrepreneurs, the businessmen, the visionary capitalists who redirected existing capital from old to new methods of production.

If we were to combine this insight with the faulty logic behind Marx's labor theory of value, we would be forced to conclude that the many wage increases that laborers have enjoyed since the commencement of the Industrial Revolution have been expropriated from the entrepreneurs, the true "creators" of economic value. After all, laborers don't work any harder today than they did two hundred years ago, when they made much less. Then why do they deserve to make so much more? Their labor is clearly not responsible for the great increase in worker productivity. Why then should they be so amply rewarded? If it is simply a matter of "fairness," shouldn't the entrepreneurs receive all the increases in wealth brought about by capitalist innovation and progress?

Fortunately for manual laborers, it is not simply a matter of "fairness." Indeed, these questions really shouldn't be settled in terms of "fairness," which is a vague and subjective conception. If we become obsessed with what is fair, we will lose sight of relevant realities, as Marx lost sight of the role of the entrepreneur in economic progress because of his obsession with proving that the capitalist process leads to the expropriation of surplus value from the proletariat. Although Marx pretended to be "scientific" and morally "neutral," his labor theory of value, the cornerstone of his entire polemic against capitalism, is a purely subjective concept: its premises assume Marx's conclusions.

Note that my use of the concept *spoliation* is completely free from subjective influences. I am not trying to put a moral spin on it one way or the other. I do not seek to make any judgment whether spoliation is "right" or "wrong," "good" or "evil." The moral judgments I will leave to others. In the meantime, we will try to understand the *reality* of spoliation, so that we can grasp the phenomenon itself and its role in modern economic life.

Spoliation is the appropriation of goods owned by others. Appropriation involves taking property from others without their permission. Spoliation is not a legal concept. The question of legality often has little to do with it. If Peter takes property from Paul, it matters little if the taking is "legal." Indeed, the development of "legal" spoliation is often of critical importance in civilized societies. Pareto went so far as to regard it as a hallmark of progress. "It may be said," he wrote, "that of the two procedures by which the property of others can be appropriated, i.e., directly by violence or fraud or indirectly by the help of public powers, the second is much less harmful to social well-being than the first. It is a refinement and improvement on fraud and violence, just as the rearing of domestic animals is a refinement and improvement on hunting wild animals." (1966, 139)

The term "appropriation" suffers from a certain degree of scientific vagueness. Circumstances exist where it is debatable whether a transfer of property from one individual really qualifies as "appropriation." In the real world, ownership is not always a clear-cut issue. Disputes concerning division of property in a divorce case offer a classic example of the ambiguities involved in questions of ownership. Civil cases often deal with such problems. There exists no scientific solution to these disputes. The courts solve them arbitrarily and rarely to anyone's satisfaction. Because of the difficulties involved in these borderline cases, we will content ourselves with obvious examples of appropriation, such as tariffs, credit creation, land grants, and subsidies. These represent the most palpable and clear-cut examples of spoliation in an advanced capitalist economy. Tariffs "appropriate" money from consumers to producers, from importers to exporters, from unprotected to protected businesses. Credit creation "appropriates" money from creditors to debtors, from savers to spenders, from established firms to innovative enterprises. Land grants and subsidies appropriate money from taxpayers and government bondholders to the beneficiaries of the grants (e.g., the railroads in the nineteenth century). All this is fairly obvious and will not be disputed by anyone free from the mendacious influences of ideology.

In my essay, "Notes Towards a Theory of the Business Cycle," I suggested that credit creation is one of the means by which capital is transferred from established businesses following traditional means of producing goods to innovative businesses attempting new methods of production. If this conjecture corresponds to reality, it would lead to some rather paradoxical conclusions. New and more efficient methods of production make up the essential factor in economic progress. But new methods require capital. Where is this capital to come from? Since new methods are more likely to be followed by newer, capital impoverished firms, it is highly probable, as Schumpeter suggested a hundred years ago, that one of the best sources of investment capital for the funding of new, innovative methods of production is credit creation. This scandalous hypothesis, which Schumpeter brilliantly defended in his *Theory of Economic Development*, suggests that spoliation, under special circumstances, may actually increase the productivity and wealth of society.

Here we must be very careful. The fact that credit creation *sometimes* leads to great productivity or wealth neither justifies the practice nor assures that it *always* will have this positive effect. The ethical problems associated with credit creation and expansionary monetary policies are beyond the scope of this essay. But since credit expansion involves spoliation, the plunder of money *from* creditors and savers *to* spenders and borrowers, it is unclear whether the practice can be justified on the basis of traditional moral principles, especially in light of the Biblical stricture, "Thou shalt not steal" (Exodus 20:15). At the same time, this is a practice that has been used in the Capitalist nations for over a hundred and fifty years with great success. It has helped entrepreneurs raise millions of dollars in capital that otherwise might never have been brought into existence. In the U.S. alone it has played a huge role in the development and progress of the nation's techno-industrial base.

It is no less clear that credit creation, whatever its "positive" effects in diverting capital to entrepreneurial innovation, also has been the prime mover of the business cycle and the main cause of economic crises. It caused the Great Depression of the 1930s and the hyperinflation of Weimar Germany, two economic catastrophes that paved the way for Hitler and the slaughterfest of World War II. When Third World nations have attempted monetary expansion through credit creation, the consequences have always been unfortunate. Even here in America (circa 2008), credit expansion has brought the economy to an impossible position, where it seems to be tottering uneasily on the edge of an abyss, with universal bankruptcy on one side of the chasm and hyperinflation and the collapse of the dollar on the other. Any time a nation's central bank, along with its leading financial institutions, choose to traipse down the primrose path of easy credit and ballooning corporate and consumer debt, the risk of serious economic calamity is always present. The U.S. has thus far managed to avoid catastrophe largely because the world's monetary system is based on the dollar. But this process of irresponsible debt accumulation cannot go on forever. At some point, economic fundamentals must reassert themselves. No nation can expand credit indefinitely and expect to pay no consequences for such wanton fiscal irresponsibility.

At the same time, if the financial leaders of a nation choose to play it safe and abstain from credit creation, they may find their country falling behind other nations who choose not to be so cautious. In other words, the unwillingness of a nation to expand banking credit to fund entrepreneurial innovation can lead to a drop in its economic standing among nations. Since, as I mentioned before, there will always exist competition between nations, any state that chooses to handicap itself by eschewing credit creation may find itself at the mercy of its less scrupulous rivals. Of course, those states that follow a reckless policy of monetary expansion may also be harmed as well. Either way, there are risks. In any case, we should not be so naive as to believe that the "moral" option is necessarily the "practical" one, if by "practical" we mean the survival of the homeland.

Other forms of spoliation have similar characteristics to credit creation in that they generally lead to the destruction of wealth but may, under special circumstances, actually facilitate production. Tariffs represent another apposite example. In the nineteenth century, American tariffs effectively transferred capital from the hands of farmers and planters into the hands of entrepreneurs and industrialists. This transfer of wealth facilitated the economic development of American industry, paving the way for the high standard of living Americans enjoy today. Industrial development requires huge amounts of capital. It is naive to think, as some free market ideologues have argued, that entrepreneurs can raise all the capital they need merely from the loan market or by issuing stocks or bonds. What they need, along with capital financed from loans and stock offerings, is capital financed from profits. This is where most of capital comes from in American industry. Profits are what drive a capitalist economy. Without profits, as we learned earlier, economic progress is close to impossible.

According to economic theory, a competitive market tends to eliminate profits over time. That is how a free market, under conditions of laissez-faire, works. "The primary attitude of competition, universally recognized and evident at a glance, is the 'tendency' to eliminate profit or loss, and bring the value of economic goods to equality with their cost," noted Frank Knight in *Risk, Uncertainty, and Profit.* (1921, 18) There is little reason not to believe that, in the main, this is true. The competitive system does tend to reduce, if not eliminate, business profit. There are, of course, exceptions to this (mostly as a result of barriers to entry in certain capital intensive industries). But where entry is inexpensive and the market is free and competition intense, there will be little room for profit.

To the extent that an industrial economy approximates the theoretical ideal of perfect competition, to that extent does there exist the aforementioned long-term tendency toward zero profits. While such a tendency might gratify the hearts of socialist ideologues who regard all capitalist profits as "expropriation," it would be disastrous for the economy as a whole. In order for capitalism to work, this tendency of the competitive system must to some degree be attenuated. The alternative would be an economy exemplified by "ruinous" competition, low profits, and (possibly) serious capital shortages.

Businessmen are well aware of the problem. That is why they have turned to protectionism and other methods of political spoliation. They need profits to fund their innovations. And, as Schumpeter recognized, "protection increases the rate of profit."

Schumpeter is one of the only major economists in the past century to question the mainstream view that tariffs are always bad. Here, briefly, is Schumpeter's explanation of how tariffs can increase profits: "Whatever we may think about this from other standpoints, in a rapidly progressing country [protectionism] will have the effect of accelerating the pace of that progress by propelling investment and making it easier to face risks.... In so far as protection reduces losses, keeps markets from being disorganized by foreign distress sales and so on, another argument [can be made for it.] Also, independently of either booms or depressions, the fiscal interest in profit margins is an important consideration." (1951, 173)

What about the free trade argument of classical economics, advanced by nearly every important economist since Adam Smith? Doesn't protectionism favor big business at the expense of consumers? Doesn't it involve what amounts to outright spoliation? Must it not lead to the destruction of wealth? If we examine the matter simply from the standpoint of economics alone, without reference to politics, culture, or society, we would have to answer all these questions in the affirmative. Protectionism, if viewed simply from an economic point of view, undoubtedly leads to plunder and the destruction of wealth. The economic journalist Frederic Bastiat gave the classic argument against protectionism in his article about a "negative railroad." "I have said that as long as one cares only for the interest of the producer, it is impossible to avoid running counter to the general interest," Bastiat wrote. "I find a remarkable illustration of this in a Bordeaux newspaper. M. Simiot raises the following question: Should there be a break in the tracks at Bordeaux on the railroad from Paris to Spain? He answers the question in the affirmative and offers a number of reasons, of which I propose to examine only this: There should be a break in the railroad from Paris to Bayonne at Bordeaux; for, if goods and passengers are forced to stop at that city, this will be profitable for boatmen, porters, owners of hotels, etc."

And Bastiat continues: "But if Bordeaux has a right to profit from a break in the tracks, and if this profit is consistent with the public interest, then Angoulême, Poitiers, Tours, Orléans, and, in fact, all the intermediate points, including Ruffec, Châtellerault, etc., etc., ought also to demand breaks in the tracks, on the ground of the general interest—in the interest, that is, of domestic industry—for the more there are of these breaks in the line, the greater will be the amount paid for storage, porters, and cartage at every point along the way. By this means, we shall end by having a railroad composed of a whole series of breaks in the tracks, i.e., a *negative railroad.*

"Whatever the protectionists may say, it is no less certain that the *basic principle of restriction* is the same as the *basic principle of breaks in the tracks*: the sacrifice of the consumer to the producer, of the end to the means." (1964B, 94-95)

This is a very strong argument. If protectionism is so wonderful, so fruitful, so advantageous to the development of industry, why should we limit its practice to national borders? Why shouldn't tariffs and protective duties also be instituted between provinces and states, counties and even cities and neighborhoods? It should be obvious to even the most untutored and illogical mind that protectionism between the individual states of America would be a most disastrous and wasteful policy. But if protectionism can't work between California and New York, why would any sane person believe it would work between America and Japan?

This argument, although certainly persuasive, is not as conclusive as it may appear at first blush. There is a flaw in it that requires a bit of subtlety to recognize. The argument examines the question solely from an economic point of view. But, as we know from the Mixed-Economy Principle, there are non-economic factors that enter a question of this type. The purely economic act does not exist. There are always other factors that affect the degree to which any economic policy, including protectionism, is "good" or "bad" in terms of productivity.

Vilfredo Pareto, who, early in his career, had been a follower of Bastiat and a fervent advocate of free trade, adopted a far more nuanced view in his later years. Although he continued to maintain that protectionism destroys wealth, he came to understand that it had other effects which, under special circumstances, might make up for the wealth lost in spoliation. "We find that protection transfers a certain amount of wealth from a part, A, of the population to a part B, through the destruction of a certain amount of wealth, q, the amount representing the costs of the operation," Pareto wrote. "If, as a result of this new distribution of wealth, the production of wealth does not increase by a quantity greater than q, the operation is economically detrimental to a population as a whole; if it increases by a quantity greater than q, the operation is economically beneficial. The latter case is not to be barred *a priori*; for the element A contains the indolent, the lazy, and people, in general, who make little use of economic combinations; whereas the

110

element *B* comprises the people who are economically wide-awake and are always ready for energetic enterprise—people who know how to make effective use of economic combinations." (1916, §2208)

This is a very important insight. It explains how spoliation on a grand scale can exist side-by-side with tremendous economic growth. The great industrialists of the nineteenth and early twentieth centuries are often referred to as "the robber barons." At the close of his great muckraking tome, *History of the Great American Fortunes*, Gustavus Myers wrote: "Be it known that the frauds and plundering here described, great and continuous as they have been, are far from being the complete story; for every one fraudulent transaction accidentally coming to public notice, scores of such transactions have unquestionably gone down into the sewers of time, unvisited by a ray of daylight." (1909, 694) Although Myers, in the course of his long and exhausting history, is guilty here and there of over-interpreting the facts to make them fit his thesis, there is no denying the shady dealings, the fraud, the outright plunder committed by many of the leading industrialists of the "robber baron" era. Even today, with lobbyists from nearly every major corporation choking the halls of Congress, it is undeniable that spoliation still takes place in the form of special privileges, tax breaks, and government contracts. This seamier side of capitalism is a fact of life; there is no getting around it. Those who, motivated by a libertarian or free-market ideology, wish to evade these unpleasant facts merely demonstrate how little they care about the truth.

But it is not only free market ideologues who deserve reproach. Those who, motivated by socialist and anti-capitalist ideologies, seek to condemn market capitalism precisely on account of these very same "robber barons" are missing another critical truth. The fact remains that, despite all their skullduggeries, their plunderings, lootings, graft, and corruption, the great industrialists are responsible for building the country. While it is undoubtedly true that some of them practiced theft on a grand scale, at the same time, it is no less true that they used the proceeds of this plunder to capitalize the economy. In other words, what they took, they gave back many times fold.

Socialists and other adepts of "social justice" will vehemently deny this. They will insist that the workers did everything—or at least should be credited for everything. For reasons cited earlier, we must reject this plunge into mawkish sentimentality. The workers undoubtedly did their part—and most valiantly at that, living, all the while, under horrible conditions, in noisome, disease ridden tenements and working ten hours a day, six days a week. But all their toil would have gone for nothing if it had not been for the entrepreneurs who figured out how to put these long hours of ceaseless toil to the best and most efficient use. Capitalism is all about combining capital and innovation to increase labor productivity to benefit, not merely the capitalist, but the working man as well, who has gained immeasurably, in terms of comfort and wealth, from the capitalist engine of production.

A glance at the relevant facts will provide further evidence for this thesis. The last three decades of the nineteenth century represent the very acme of capitalist spoliation. Nearly everyone agrees on this point. Advocates of laissez-faire can cite the land grants, the tariffs, and the political corruption. Socialists can point to the shameless plundering of public lands and assets, the intimidation of labor, the outright fraud committed by or on behalf of the reigning plutocracy. In whatever light we judge the facts, we can't deny them: these things took place. The railroads received millions of dollars worth of land from the government. Politicians were bought and sold like commodities on the open market. Protectionism reigned supreme. And yet the country not only prospered, it grew by leaps and bounds. Gross national product nearly quadrupled in the thirty years between 1870 and 1900. Wages rose by 53 percent. (Buchanan 1998, 167) Within a few short decades, America became the world's leading industrial power. How else can we explain these anomalous facts except by embracing Pareto's paradoxical thesis? How can you have great wealth creation existing side-by-side with great spoliation unless a significant portion of the spoliation is being funneled back into the economy as investment in new, more efficient methods of production? If someone can come up with a better explanation, he is welcome to make the attempt.

Again, to repeat what was stated earlier: none of this in any way is meant as a defense or justification of the capitalist system. I will leave such polemical considerations to those best suited to that sort of ranting. My interest is solely in getting to the truth of the matter. It may be that, on moral considerations alone, the capitalist system should be "abolished," despite the consequences that might result. All that I desire is for these consequences to be faced realistically and not in terms of wishful thinking. Those who believe that capitalism is wrong and should be replaced by something else need to understand that there may exist very serious ramifications from attempting such a reform, that it may lead to untold sufferings and disasters. Economic policy should not be a plaything of our wishes. The only moral imperative of the economist qua economist is to see things as they are, despite his personal and political preferences. If capitalism turns out to be the worst possible system, "except for all the others," then we need to face up to that truth and not be crybabies about it. As Thomas Carlyle sternly warned, "No Ostrich, intent on gross terrene provender, and sticking its head into Fallacies, but will be awakened one day,—in a terrible *à-posteriori* manner, if not otherwise!"

7. The Status Principle. Economists do themselves an ill turn if they confine their studies merely to "economic" truths. One extremely important truth that they have ignored too often involves the issue of status or preeminence. "People everywhere strive for a ghostly substance called authority, cachet, dignity, dominance, eminence, esteem, face, position, preeminence, prestige, rank, regard, repute, respect, standing, stature, or status," writes cognitive scientist Stephen Pinker. "People go hungry, risk their lives, and exhaust their wealth in pursuit of bits of ribbon and metal. The economist Thorstein Veblen noticed that people sacrificed so many necessities of life to impress one another that they appear to be responding to a 'higher, spiritual need.'" (1997, 493)

Socialists have often criticized capitalism because of the intensity of market competition. They argue that society would be much better off if people cooperated more and competed less. But this sentiment is based on a denial of status and the competition for status. As the political theorist Gaetano Mosca put it: "If we consider ... the inner ferment that goes on within the body of every society, we see at once that the struggle for preeminence is far more conspicuous there than the struggle for existence. Competition between individuals of every social unit is focused upon higher position, wealth, authority, control of the means and instruments that enable a person to direct many human activities, many human wills, as he sees fit." (1939, 30)

People want to be regarded as the best, they want to finish first, they want others to look up to them and respect them. Under capitalism, people achieve status by competing in the market. Now market competition is influenced by the principle of consumer sovereignty. "The customer is always right," goes the adage of business. Businesses must sell their products; that is to say, they must satisfy their consumers. If customers aren't satisfied, they'll spend their dollars elsewhere. Capitalism, in short, funnels this instinct for status or preeminence into a competition to satisfy the needs of paying consumers. Granted, this funneling effect does not in all respects work perfectly, but it does manage to channel potentially destructive instincts into a somewhat beneficial direction. Under other systems, and particularly under socialism, the drive for preeminence becomes channeled almost exclusively in a political direction. Those who wish to achieve preeminence seek to dominate within the political realm, which is governed, not by dollars and cents, but by prisons and torture chambers. This is one of the major reasons why socialism, when attempted on a grand scale, turns out to be an unmitigated horror. Whether it's the Soviet Union, the People's Republic of China, North Korea, or Cuba, any attempt to found a truly socialist nation (rather than just a very large welfare state), creates a political elite characterized by a ruthlessness and barbarity unknown among the plutocratic democracies of the West.

To repeat what I said earlier: in politics and economics, the choice is never between good and better, but only between bad and worse. Capitalism obviously has many flaws. Any candid person who does not have an ideological stake in the system will readily admit so. Most other systems appear to be significantly worse, at least in terms of consumption levels and the misuse of power.

Since we are on the subject of criticism against the capitalist system, we might as well touch upon another popular slander of the system. Capitalism has long been accused of turning people into sordid moneygrubbers. America, where capitalism has achieved its greatest triumphs, is often regarded as a mere shopkeeper's paradise, fit only for those bent on making piles of filthy lucre. Even Alexis de Tocqueville, otherwise so penetrating an observer of American mores, believed that "the love of money" was "at the bottom of all that the Americas do." H. L. Mencken, another penetrating observer of American mores, disagreed with Tocqueville's assessment. "The character that actually marks off the American is not money-hunger at all," Mencken argued; "it is what might be called, at the risk of misunderstanding, social aspiration. That is to say, [the American] is forever trying to improve his position, to break down some barrier of caste, to secure the acceptance of his betters. Money, of course, usually helps him in this endeavor, and so he values it—but not for its own sake, not as a thing in itself. On the contrary, he is always willing to pay it out lavishly for what he wants. Nothing is too expensive if it helps him to make a better showing in the world, to raise himself above what he has been." (1991, 22)

This observation about the relation between money and status is instrumental to understanding the significance of economic competition in a capitalist society. It is not money grubbing or "materialism" that motivates individuals under capitalism: it is "social aspiration," status, preeminence—call it what you will. It is, in short, the same thing that motivates people in all societies. What distinguishes one society from another is not the degree of competition or rivalry between individuals, but only the form that this competition takes, the rules that govern the games people play to decide who's boss. In tribal societies, it is usually the strongest man who becomes preeminent. As Pinker notes, "The word for 'leader' in most foraging societies is 'big man,' and in fact the leaders usually *are* big men." (1997, 495) In feudal societies, the great knights, with their suits of armor and heavy swords, dripping in blood, became the most feared and respected members of the social order. Under socialism, preeminence falls to those with political pull—bureaucratic administrators, military officers, and operatives in the secret police.

Whatever can be said for or against economic competition under a "free" market, at least it's not a zero sum game. If conditions are right and capitalism is "successful," the consequence is that most people, from the capitalists on down to the humblest of manual workers, receive a material benefit. In capitalist America, the lower middle-class enjoys a higher standard of living, in terms of material comfort, than did the feudal barons of the Middle Ages. Capitalist production is not a zero-sum game because it can be increased in absolute terms, so that there is more wealth to go around. To be sure, not everyone will enjoy the fruits of capitalist production. A small minority of shiftless and/or dysfunctional individuals, along with "crazy" persons and the congenitally unlucky, will miss-out. But all in all, nearly everyone will have more than they would under other systems. If we judge merely by the standard of wealth and material comfort, then we have no choice but to conclude that capitalism has been enormously beneficial to mankind.

If material comfort were the only aim of human nature, there would be no justifiable reason for opposing capitalism. It would, however, be an error to regard men as mere hedonic stimulus-response machines. Human beings want other things besides clothes and jewelry, computers and VCRs, automobiles and houses. "Man shall not live by bread alone," says the gospel. Very true: he also hungers for preeminence. But unlike wealth, there is only a limited amount of preeminence to go around. In order for Peter to become top dog, Paul must be content with being something less than top dog. In this sense, the competition for preeminence *is* a zero sum game. In fact, it is worse than that: it is a game that almost everyone loses. Only a handful of elites can assume a position of dominance in society. While most people are content with occupying a humble position in the sempiternal pecking order, not every loser in the competition for status is gracious about it. Many problems facing society are a direct consequence of resentful non-elites, of failures in the competition for preeminence who believe that the game has been unfairly rigged against them and who are eager to compete under an entirely different set of rules.

Here, in a nutshell, is the genesis of the revolutionary mindset. It matters little that the revolutionaries themselves come up with other reasons to justify their resentment. The fact remains that if their attempts to climb the social ladder had not been so ignominiously frustrated, they would not be agitating for political revolution. "It is on such soil," wrote Friedrich Nietzsche, "that every weed, every poisonous plant grows, always so small, so hidden, so false, so saccharine. Here the worms of vengefulness and rancor swarm; here the air stinks of secrets and concealment; here the web of the most malicious of all conspiracies is being spun constantly—the conspiracy of the suffering against the well-constituted and victorious, here the aspect of the victorious is *hated*. And what mendaciousness is employed to disguise that this hatred is hatred! What a display of grand words and postures, what an art of 'honest' calumny! These failures: what noble eloquence flows from their lips!... There is among them an abundance of the vengeful disguised as judges, who constantly bear the word 'justice' in their mouths like poisonous spittle, always with pursed lips, always ready to spit upon all who are not discontented but go their way in good spirits.... The will of the weak to represent *some* form of superiority, their instinct for devious paths to tyranny over the healthy—where can it not be discovered, this will to power of the weakest!"

And Nietzsche continues, driving home his point in the most graphic language: "They are all men of *resentiment*, physiologically unfortunate and worm-eaten, a whole tremulous realm of subterranean revenge, inexhaustible and insatiable in outbursts against the fortunate and happy and in masquerades of revenge and pretexts for revenge." (1968a, 558-560) Shakespeare captured this twisted spirit of ambitious, status-seeking *resentiment* when he put in the mouth of Richard III the following memorable lines:

Then, since this earth affords no joy to me
But to command, to check, to o'erbear such
As are of better person than myself,
I'll make my heaven to dream upon the crown;
And, whiles I live, to account this world but hell,
Until my mis-shap'd trunk that bears this head
Be round impaled with a glorious crown.

The historian Jacob Burckhardt, a colleague of Nietzsche's at the University of Basel, also noted this phenomenon of history, especially as it related to the competition for status and the concomitant rise of antisocial forces. "It is part of the wretchedness of life on earth," he wrote, "that even the individual believes that he can only attain a full consciousness of his own value if he compares himself with others and, in certain circumstances, actually makes others feel it. The state, law, religion, and morality are hard put to it to keep this bent within bounds, that is, to prevent its finding public expression." (1979, 216)

How does this phenomenon of status and *resentiment* relate to economics? It relates in the following way. In the first place, once the importance of status competition is clearly understood, economists can no longer subscribe to the naive theory, propagated by classical economists like Say and Bastiat and by laissez-faire ideologues like Ayn Rand, that there exists, under a free market, a harmony of interests whereby no one ever gains at the expense of anyone else. If the principles of classical economics were perfectly true and people only cared about material interests, this view might hold true. Men's interests, however, go well beyond the desire for mere creature comforts. There is one thing men want more than wealth—namely, status; and in pursuit of this one thing, they are capable of going to great lengths, including turning society upside down, as they have done in France, Russia, China, North Korea, Cambodia, and many other places notorious, not for peace and plenty, but for starvation, brutal oppression, gulags, and ignominious death.

The lesson to be gained from these hard facts is that capitalism, despite whatever successes it may enjoy in the material realm, will always have its enemies. There will always exist people for whom a high standard of living is not enough. They want more than large houses, big cars, and a television in every room. They want what only a few people can have; they want *preeminence*—which means: the ability not merely to have others *recognize* their "superiority," but also to make these others *feel* it. In other words, to command, check and overbear such as are better than themselves.

As long as a capitalism flourishes somewhere in the world, there will exist worm-eaten ideologues fuming against it. Within capitalist countries, entire factions, supported by major political parties, will do everything in their power to sabotage and stifle free enterprise. On the world stage, nations will declare themselves enemies of capitalism and seek to destroy it. The rulers of such nations may be religious fanatics who despise the rationalism and secularism that flourishes so readily in a capitalist economic order, or they may simply be jealous of the wealth and power generated by a healthy capitalist system. Whatever their motivations, they will scheme and agitate and stir up senseless wars merely to put an end to the free market.

Status-competition is hardly confined to individuals: it exists between nations as well. Once the individual has made himself master of the state, he is unlikely to stop there. As soon as he becomes preeminent among his own people, he begins to look abroad in search of other

118

peoples to dominate. The psychology behind this is well illustrated by Plutarch in his history of Pyrrhus, the king of Epirus who reigned a few hundred years before Christ. "There was one Cineas, a Thessalian, considered to be a man of very good sense. This person, seeing Pyrrhus eagerly preparing for Italy, led him one day when he was at leisure into the following reasonings: 'The Romans, sir, are reported to be great warriors and conquerors of many warlike nations; if God permits us to overcome them, how should we use our victory?' 'You ask,' said Pyrrhus, 'a thing evident of itself. The Romans once conquered, there is neither Greek nor barbarian city that will resist us, but we shall presently be masters of all Italy, the extent and resources and strength of which anyone should rather profess to be ignorant of, than yourself.' Cineas, after a little pause, 'And having subdued Italy, what shall we do next?' Pyrrhus not yet discovering his intention, 'Sicily,' he replied, 'next holds out her arms to receive us, a wealthy and populous island, and easy to be gained; for since Agathocles left it, only faction and anarchy, and the licentious violence of the demagogues prevail.' 'You speak,' said Cineas, 'what is perfectly probable, but will the possession of Sicily put an end to the war?' 'God grant us,' answered Pyrrhus, 'victory and success in that, and we will use these as forerunners of greater things; who could forbear from Libya and Carthage then within reach, which Agathocles, even when forced to fly from Syracuse, and passing the sea only with a few ships, had all but surprised? These conquests once perfected, will any assert that of the enemies who now pretend to despise us, anyone will dare to make further resistance?' 'None,' replied Cineas, 'for then it is manifest we may with such mighty forces regain Macedon, and make all absolute conquest of Greece; and when all these are in our power, what shall we do then?' Said Pyrrhus, smiling, 'we will live at our ease, my dear friend, and drink all day, and divert ourselves with pleasant conversation.' When Cineas had led Pyrrhus with his argument to this point: 'And what hinders us now, sir, if we have a mind to be merry, and entertain one another, since we have at hand without trouble all those necessary things, to which through much blood and great labor, and infinite hazards and mischief done to ourselves and to others, we design at last to arrive?' Such reasonings rather troubled Pyrrhus with the thought of the happiness he was quitting, than any way altered his purpose, being unable to abandon the hopes of what he so much desired." (1864, 476-477)

Political dangers threaten capitalism from within and without. Neither the wealth of capitalism nor the alleged "harmony" of interests promoted by the free market will prevent these threats from working their mischief. Conflict is endemic to life. Capitalism, whatever its merits as an engine of production and a breeding ground for entrepreneurial innovation and material progress, cannot hope to escape the realities of human nature merely on its strengths as a system of political economy. We now know that the fall of the Berlin Wall did not necessarily mean that capitalism had won. The enemies of free markets and economic freedom simply changed their main points of attack, becoming environmentalists or anti-globalists or Islamic fundamentalists or Russian nationalists. Little changed except the rationalizations brought forth to justify anti-capitalist agitation.

From these facts we can draw a very important conclusion. Capitalism, by its very nature, is an unstable system. It is not, as some of its critics have suggested, unstable due to economic reasons. The trade cycle is not the reason for capitalism's instability. Oscillations in economic output have little if anything to do with the issue of stability. Economically, capitalism is as stable as the rock of Gibraltar. Capitalism acquires most of its instability from social and political factors. Capitalism is unstable because it has no way of dealing with those ambitious, status-seeking individuals who fail to attain the level of preeminence they desire in society. Previous societies, whose ruling elites gained prestige through violence, handled such troublemakers by putting them down with force. This is not seen as an option in most capitalist societies, because it goes against cherished traditions regarding the "rights" of people to speak freely and criticize the system. The ruling elites in capitalist societies prefer to govern on the basis of consent rather than force. Governing by force requires giving power to those who are good at violence. Plutocratic elites tend not to be very good at using force. They are businessmen, not soldiers. Concern for their own preeminence in society inclines them against calling for the suppression of anti-capitalist agitation, whether at home or abroad. When a plutocracy becomes too dependent on military elites for its power, it soon loses power altogether and ceases to be a plutocracy.

Of course, all these observations are made at a very high level of generalization. There may exist periods or situations in which none of these generalizations apply. Capitalist societies are capable of awesome displays of military power. Their ability to innovate, to mass-produce, and to manage resource allocation in the field can grant them huge advantages over their enemies. At home, plutocrats can be ruthless. In the nineteenth century, labor unions were put down by force. The capitalist did not shun using the arm of the state to intimidate those he regarded as troublemakers. Even so, he was unable to keep down the labor movement indefinitely and in the thirties, he found himself at their mercy.

It should also be remembered that all social systems, regardless of their economic character, are, in the long-range scheme of things, intrinsically unstable. It is only a question of more or less. Sparta, a military oligarchy, enjoyed eight centuries of rule. But eventually, the weaknesses in its system ended its hegemony. It happens to every society, to every system. No society, no system is perfect. Some systems, however, appear less stable than others. Historically, capitalism—along with market-orientated societies in general—has to be ranked among the less stable systems.

8. The Inequality Principle. The Left has long been obsessed with equality, with tearing down "privilege" and giving everyone a chance to partake in the wealth of society. The socialist philosopher Ted Honderich tells us that, in the name of the "Principle of Equality," the "goal or end of a society must be to make well-off those who are badly-off." (2005) Honderich suggests several methods by which this ideal can be attained, including the transfer of goods to the "badly off" from the "well-off." Like all political thinkers afflicted with the curse of ideology, Honderich appears to believe that society can be changed simply be enunciating certain principles in a book or on a website. Nothing could be further from the truth. The obstacles to redistributing income confront the crusading socialist at every turn. To begin with, those who have money will naturally oppose any attempt to take their income and hand it to the less fortunate. Societies, we must remember, are always governed by a ruling class or elite. This is true even in so-called "democratic" societies. Always, a mere handful of people will make most of the political decisions affecting society. "Among the constant facts and tendencies that are to be found in all political organisms, one is so obvious that it is apparent to the most casual eye," wrote Gaetano Mosca. "In all societies—from societies that are very meagerly developed and have barely attained the dawnings of civilization, down to the most advanced and powerful societies— two classes of people appear—a class that rules and a class that is ruled. The first class, always the less numerous, performs all political functions, monopolizes power and enjoys the advantages that power brings, whereas the second class, the more numerous, is directed and controlled by the first, in a manner that is more or less legal, now more or less arbitrary and violent." (1939, 50)

It is important to note that this is an observation, not a prescription. Mosca is not stating a preference. He does not necessarily favor rule by elites. He is merely stating a fact, proven by common observation. In any organization, whether political or social in nature, someone has to fulfill the administrative function. A nation can no more be governed by "the people" then an ocean liner at sea can be steered by the passengers. Administrative, judicial, and legislative functions all require special expertise. Not everyone is qualified to be a Supreme Court judge or a Secretary of State or a four star general. These positions require unique talents possessed only by a select group of people. The ability to get elected to office is in itself a special talent. Not everyone can raise the hordes of cash necessary to make a successful run at the Senate or the Presidency. Although elected officials are supposed to "represent" the people, since no unanimity of opinion exists among the population at large, politicians have a wide latitude of action available to them. Even in those circumstances where the electorate opposes a certain policy, it is not difficult to evade the so-called "will" of the majority simply by concealing one's true agenda under beautiful phrases. Let us suppose a politician desires to pass legislation that will benefit the oil companies that generously supported his election campaign. Nothing is easier. The politician can merely call the oil-friendly legislation an "energy reform bill," and insist that he seeks merely to conserve energy and help consumers. Little do his constituents, most of whom know next to nothing about economics or energy policy, understand that a bill to conserve oil resources will merely drive up the price of gas and oil, allowing the oil companies to reap huge profits. Despite all the sanctimonious patter we hear about the United States being a country of the people for the people by the people, the fact remains that politicians, bureaucrats, business leaders, and well-organized special interest groups have a much greater say in the conduct of domestic and foreign policy than does the average Joe.

From these facts we can conclude that inequality is part and parcel of the very fabric of political society. No nation can exist without a ruling elite. Pure democracy is impossible, a solecism within the grammar of social reality. Yet this is not the only source of inequality which the hapless sentimental egalitarian, intent on "social justice" and "equality," must reckon with. There is another problem, well described by Pareto in his *Manual of Political Economy*: "Human society is not homogeneous," Pareto wrote; "it is made up of elements which differ more or less, not only according to the very obvious characteristics such as sex, age, physical strength, health, etc., but also according to less observable, but no less important, characteristics such as intellectual qualities, morals, diligence, courage, etc.... Just as one distinguishes the rich and poor in society even though income increases gradually from the lowest to the highest, one can distinguish the elite in a society, the part which is *aristocratic*, in the etymological sense, and a common part.... The notion of this elite is dependent on the qualities which one seeks in it. There can be an aristocracy of saints, an aristocracy of brigands, an aristocracy of scholars, an aristocracy of thieves, etc." (1909, 90)

The fact that some people are "superior" to others in certain qualities, especially in the qualities necessary to succeed in the competition of life, means that certain individuals will always end up securing more wealth and power for themselves than their "inferior" competitors. This is a fact proven again and again in the annals of every civilization on record. Only Stone Age savages have escaped this law of society.

The social, economic, or political "game" that people play in order to determine their economic status differs from society to society. In feudal societies, military prowess was among the qualities most esteemed and rewarded. In capitalist societies, business and investment skills reap the greatest financial rewards. In socialist societies, political skills prove the most critical. But whether society is democratic or oligarchic, capitalist or socialist, feudal or imperial, those who are most generously endowed with the skills necessary to get ahead in society will acquire for themselves an unequal portion of the national income. To the victors go the spoils. Since life always involves a competition for preeminence, there will always be winners and losers. This is the harsh reality of the human condition. All the senseless talk we hear from the Left about equality and social justice won't change this fact one iota.

We need consider just one other fact to complete our picture. Since, as I have established, inequality of property is embedded in the very nature of society, so that every society, even socialist societies, are plagued by it, it follows that any attempt to bring about "equality," whether through persuasion or force, will have to reckon with a powerful contingent of property owners who will not surrender their wealth without a fight. Let us keep in mind the role that wealth plays in status. People want wealth, not simply because they need it to satisfy physical wants and desires, but (far more critically) because wealth is an indicator of status. Now there exists a sociological law that goes something as follows: human beings will generally do everything in their power to maintain their present level of preeminence in society, since any drop is regarded by most people as a deep humiliation, to be avoided at all costs. Moreover, *how* they fight is even more critical than the fact that they *will* fight. Social and political elites generally seek to maintain the rules, laws and institutions that helped make them become elites in the first place. Winners usually favor the existing rules of the game. They will resist any effort to institute new rules.

Sincere egalitarians believe that, by making society more "cooperative," they can abolish the brutal competition for preeminence once and for all. But this is sentimental balderdash. While cooperation is an important element of human society, the notion that any social order can be perfectly cooperative is absurd. There exists far too much diversity in opinion and values for any such utopia to exist. The ruling elite would oppose it with every ounce of their considerable strength and ingenuity. If (per impossible) it had any chance of succeeding, the elites would simply pretend to support it, with the intent of monopolizing the critical positions in the state so that they could make certain that they would remain on top. Even in an egalitarian social order, where everybody is supposedly equal, some would still be more equal than others—just as Orwell wryly predicted. The desire for preeminence is simply a part of human nature. It, along with the inequality which it begets, is embedded in the very fabric of the human condition. It cannot be abolished or done away with by social fiat.

I can do no better, in concluding this section, then to quote Gaetano Mosca's final assessment of the egalitarian-socialist ideal. "The conclusion of the [socialist] doctrine as a whole ... seems to us utterly fantastic—namely, that once collectivism [i.e., cooperativism] is established, it will be the beginning of an era of universal equality and justice, during which the state will no longer be the organ of a class and the exploiter and the exploited will be no more. We shall not stop to refute that utopia once again. This whole work is a refutation of it. One should note, however, that that view is a natural and necessary consequence of the optimistic conception of human nature which originated in the eighteenth century and which has not yet completed, though it is coming pretty close to completing, its historical cycle. According to that idea, man is born good, and society, or, better, social institutions, make him bad. If, therefore, we change institutions, the seed of Adam will be, as it were, freed of a choking ring of iron, and be able to express all their natural goodness. Evidently, if one is going to reason in that fashion one will go on and reason that private property is the prime and sole cause of human selfishness. Aristotle argued much more soundly, in his day, that selfishness is the prime and sole cause that makes private property inevitable. Combating the communistic theories of Plato, that Stagirite declares that private property is indispensable if the individual is expected to produce and therefore provide for his own needs and the needs of his family and city. The justification that St. Thomas offers for private property in the *Summa* is almost identical. We do not believe there could be a better one, as long as the human being loves himself and his own family more than he loves a stranger." (1939, 447-448)

9. The Monopoly Principle. Capitalism has often been criticized for fostering and abetting oppressive monopolies. "Private capital tends to become concentrated in a few hands," complained Albert Einstein, resulting in "an oligarchy of private capital the enormous power of which cannot be effectively checked." Monopolies, mainstream economists tell us, are "inefficient." They promote waste and stifle "innovation." A monopolistic company like Microsoft, because it constitutes a threat to "competition" and the free market, must be penalized, broken-up, and chopped into little pieces. Never mind that Microsoft became the dominant provider of computer operating systems because consumers choose Windows over Mac OS, IBM's OS/2, BeOS, NeXT, Linux and other competing products. Because of Microsoft's dominant position in the market, it can effectively "force" consumers to choose Windows, even if they would be better off with a competing product.

Monopolies are almost universally regarded as a public menace. Laws have been erected to put them down whenever and wherever they have sprung up. Socialists insist that we will never rid ourselves of the curse of monopoly until we abandon capitalism altogether.

All this is little more than ideological axe-grinding taken to unpalatable lengths. Before we give way to histrionic ethical posturing and vast displays of moral fervor, perhaps we should make an effort to understand what these monopolies are all about, how they arise, and their precise benefits and costs.

When discussing the phenomenon of monopoly, it is useful to distinguish between two types of forces: the political and the economic. In the real world (as we discovered under the "Mixed-Economy Principle") there are no purely political or economic forces: all, or nearly all, are mixed to some degree. But for the sake of analysis, let us make an effort to distinguish the economic from the political. The economic forces deal primarily with the market: with the production and consumption of economic goods. Political forces, on the other hand, deal with government, law, legislation, and "representative" institutions. Economic actions tend to be those that are made on the basis of consensus, whether via contract or trade. Political actions may be consensual, but at the bottom there always exists the threat of force, whether "democratic" or "autocratic" in origin.

If we examine the phenomenon of monopoly, we will find that many of the worst monopolies are political in nature—founded, at bottom, on state backed force. The most comprehensive monopolies are those founded on law, i.e., through special privileges, charters, grants, etc. "We must remember that in the great majority of cases it was the state itself which through its legislative, administrative and judicial activities first created conditions favorable to the formation of monopolies," the German economist Wilhelm Röpke testifies. "There are in fact not many monopolies in the world which would exist without privileges having been consciously or unconsciously granted by the state, or without some sort of legislative or administrative measure, legal decision or financial policy having been responsible for it… That the state acted as midwife is quite clear in those cases where a monopoly was expressly granted a special charter, a procedure which is particularly characteristic of the early history of European monopolies.… It is very useful to recall that in monopolism's early days and right up to the nineteenth century, certain legal rights were established by granting individual privileges which today … have lost their character of being exceptional and have become a matter of course, so much so that most people have completely forgotten that these rights were originally based on privileges granted by the state and, in spite of their everyday legal aspect, are still that. We are thinking particularly of the legal status of patents and corporations which have proved to be of such importance for the development of modern monopolism." (1942, 230-231)

This is not to say that monopolies can never arise without the help of the state. Free market ideologues who make such contentions are clearly more interested in espousing a cause than they are in learning the truth. Nonetheless, if we look at markets over the long term, there exists a very definite economic tendency working against the establishment of permanent monopoly. Monopolies that make huge profits *ipso facto* provoke competition. Even if, due to special circumstances, it is impossible for anyone to compete in the monopolized market, nearly all economic goods have substitutes that serve as a kind of proxy competition. If Joe's Airlines cornered the market on passenger airline service, there would still exist competition in the form of substitute methods of travel, including trains, busses, automobiles, and cruise ships. No monopoly can ever be perfect. If you corner the market on gold with the idea of gouging your customers, you will find consumers switching their allegiance to silver and diamonds. These substances are not perfect substitutes for gold, but in a pinch, they will do.

Ideological opponents of capitalism are under the illusion that the market is inherently monopolistic, that under conditions of economic freedom, ruthless capitalists will always drive their competitors out of business until nearly every industry becomes controlled by a single monopoly. There is even a widespread belief that the fierce competition of American capitalism during the nineteenth century produced just this result. This is not what really happened. The least regulated era in American capitalism was also the most competitive, just as classical economic theory would have predicted. Gabriel Kolko's testimony on this point is invaluable. "Despite the large number of mergers, and the growth in the absolute size of many corporations, the dominant tendency in the American economy at the beginning of this century was toward growing competition," Kolko states. "Competition was unacceptable to many key business and financial interests, and the merger movement was, to a large extent, a reflection of voluntary, unsuccessful business efforts to bring irresistible competitive trends under control. Although profit was always a consideration, rationalization of the market was frequently a necessary prerequisite for maintaining long-term profits. As new competitors sprang up, and as economic power was diffused throughout an expanding nation, it became apparent to many important businessmen that only the national government could 'rationalize' the economy. Although specific conditions varied from industry to industry, internal problems that could be solved only by political means were the common denominator in those industries whose leaders advocated greater federal regulation. Ironically, contrary to the consensus of historians, it was not the existence of monopoly that caused the federal government to intervene in the economy, but the lack of it." (1963, 4-5)

This is pretty much in line with what I argued earlier under the uncertainty principle. Established businesses desire regulation because it introduces stability into markets. This reduces the terrible toll of uncertainty and creates opportunities for sustained profits. The lifeblood of capitalism, as we discovered earlier, is profits, which not only keep businesses solvent, but also constitute a critical source of working capital.

Now, as has already been mentioned, under a system of "perfect" competition, there would be no profits. If free entry exists in every industry, sustained profits would be impossible. As soon as a business organization began taking in more revenues then it expended in costs, other businesses, eager to cash in on a thriving market, would immediately enter the industry and, in effect, reduce the profit level to zero. But this would have a catastrophic effect on business activity. Capitalist enterprises desperately require profits, not because they are greedy or because capitalists worship mammon, but because profits are necessary, first of all, as a bulwark against the business cycle, and secondly, as a source of capital expenditure for growth and innovation.

Capitalism, then, in order to thrive as a system of production, must enable at least some companies to be profitable. If these profits cannot be sustained under a regimen of unmitigated competition, other methods have to be devised to create opportunities for sustained profits. Whether this means tariffs, patents, trademarks, special licenses or bureaucratic regulation, such measures form an essential part of the capitalist system. They are not "exogenous" to the system, as the partisans of laissez-faire naively believe. Capitalism is not just an economic system. It is a political and a cultural system as well. It cannot exist or flourish without certain political and cultural elements upon which it depends. It requires an entrepreneurial class, a sophisticated banking system, and a large degree of economic freedom. What it does not require is perfect laissez-faire. Some degree of interference, some degree of regulation, may actually increase the overall productivity of capitalism.

There exists no technique or set of principles that would tell us precisely how much regulation is needed for maximum output. The tendency for governments is to provide too much regulation rather than too little. This is one of the reasons why regulation usually hinders rather than assists production. Especially harmful are those regulations that allow government officials to interfere in the production process. Bureaucrats are rarely better at making economic decisions than businessmen. The regulations that most benefit capitalist production tend to be in the form of legal codes providing general guidelines for what is and what is not permitted. Regulations over the quality of meat, for example, or for the maintenance and safety of airplanes, can benefit capitalist production by reducing the uncertainty of consumers and transferring at least a portion of the responsibility for the inevitable mistakes that happen in every industry to government officials. The airline industry does not have to worry about going out of business when one of its planes crashes, because consumers believe that government regulators will determine how the crash happened and will take steps to make sure it doesn't happen again. Hence, through these regulations, an environment is created that is conducive to profitable commercial activity.

These regulations, when they are not completely wasteful and destructive, also have an additional effect which, under certain circumstances, might prove beneficial. Business regulations generally increase the costs of doing business. This, in turn, constitutes an additional barrier for entry into the market. New firms must not only raise the capital necessary to get a business off the ground, they must also lay aside a certain amount of money to pay for the paperwork mandated by government officials. The effect of this is to limit or mitigate the competitiveness of markets. Ideally, this limitation or mitigation of competition will be just enough to allow some companies to earn sustainable profits without eliminating competition altogether. What capitalist markets require is a balance between competition and profit-making. There must be enough competition to allow innovation and the rise of new entrepreneurial talent, and enough profit to pay for fresh outlays of capital. The economy that comes closest to achieving this delicate balance will be the economy that out-competes its rivals.

Because of the tendency of governments to over-regulate, the danger is mostly on the side of state-assisted monopoly and excessive interference in the market, rather than on the side of freedom of trade and competition. There are always plenty of advocates for regulation and special privileges. There are few who advocate more competition and greater economic freedom. Most economies around the world, whether capitalist or not, tend to be grossly over-regulated. Some businesses, especially established businesses, benefit from such an arrangement; but over-regulation does tend to lead to greater centralization of industry and, *ipso facto*, a reduction of the competitive level.

Theoretically, this over-regulation might yield gains by increasing stability within markets, for the reasons stated above; but this is not what usually happens. Over-regulated economies tend to be inflicted with hyperactive legislatures that are constantly passing new regulations and changing the regulative landscape in favor of this or that special economic interest. Constant changes in the legal framework of economic regulation are harmful to the stability of markets, because such changes introduce a new element of uncertainty. Suddenly businesses not only have to worry about constant changes in consumer demand and the price of the factors of production; they must also concern themselves with what the government is likely to do next. Regulations are most effective when they are few in number, unambiguous, and addressed to solve real problems in the economic sphere.

Just as we divided the forces behind the establishment of monopoly into economic and political, we could also distinguish between monopolies that harm and monopolies that benefit productive efficiency. According to classical and (for the most part) contemporary mainstream economics, there is no such thing as a "beneficial" monopoly—not at least in terms of economic efficiency and productive capacity. Monopolies, these theories argue, inevitably lead to monopoly "restriction" of supply and, *ipso facto*, "excess capacity."

The economist Joseph Schumpeter gained a certain measure of notoriety for his conviction that monopolies are not always detrimental to economic production. In *Capitalism, Socialism, and Democracy*, Schumpeter challenged the prevailing theory of monopoly and suggested a very different theory. "The theory of simple and discriminating monopoly," Schumpeter wrote, "teaches that, excepting a limiting case, monopoly price is higher and monopoly output smaller than competitive price and competitive output. This is true provided that the method and organization of production—and everything else—are exactly the same in both cases. Actually however there are superior methods available to the monopolist which either are not available at all to a crowd of competitors or are not available to them so readily: for there are advantages which, though not strictly unattainable on the competitive level of enterprise, are as a matter of fact secured only on the monopoly level, for instance, because monopolization may increase the sphere of influence of the better, and decrease the sphere of influence of the inferior, brains, or because the monopoly enjoys a disproportionately higher financial standing. Whenever this is so, then that proposition is no longer true. In other words, this element of the case for competition may fail completely because monopoly prices are not necessarily higher or monopoly outputs smaller than competitive prices and outputs would be at the levels of productive and organizational efficiency that are within the reach of the type of firm compatible with the competitive hypothesis."

And Schumpeter continues: "There cannot be any reasonable doubt that under the conditions of our epoch such superiority is as a matter of fact the outstanding feature of the typical large-scale unit of control, though mere size is neither necessary nor sufficient for it. These units not only arise in the process of creative destruction and function in a way entirely different from the static schema [i.e., from the competitive model of academic economics], but in many cases of decisive importance they provide the necessary form for the achievement. They largely create what they exploit. Hence the usual conclusion about their influence on long-run output would be invalid even if they were genuine monopolies in the technical sense of the term.

"Motivation is quite immaterial. Even if the opportunity to set monopolist prices were the sole object, the pressure of the improved methods or of a huge apparatus would in general tend to shift the point of the monopolist's optimum toward or beyond the competitive cost price in the above sense, thus doing the work—partly, wholly, or more than wholly—of the competitive mechanism, *even if restriction is practiced and excess capacity is in evidence all along.*" (1942, 100-102)

Schumpeter's theory is an attempt to explain what, in light of the neo-classical theory of monopoly, would appear as an immense anomaly. In the last century, the U.S. economy has become considerably more "monopolistic"; and yet, instead of becoming less productive, the American economy has persisted as the largest and most productive economy in the world. In the 1980s, following Ronald Reagan's election as President, the U.S. relaxed strictures against corporate mergers. The result was a frenzy of economic concentration. But did this damage U.S. productivity? No, not in the least. The American economy, after languishing for an entire decade in stagflationist doldrums, suddenly found a new lease on life. It would appear that a new theory is needed to explain these hard facts relating to economic concentration.

In making a case for a new theory, I am not suggesting that the neo-classical theory must be tossed aside altogether. It should be obvious not merely from the history of mercantilism, but also from what we know of economic concentration in communist and Third World nations, that monopolies can be very harmful. But they are clearly not harmful in every instance. If we want our theories to describe reality as adequately as possible, we need to revise the neo-classical theory so that it better fits the reality we find here in the United States. Economic concentration and monopoly can increase economic efficiency by, among other things, raising the nation's net supply of capital and, as Schumpeter puts it, increasing the "sphere of influence" of those who are more intelligent and better fitted for making use of that scarce economic resource known as capital.

10. Markets spontaneously coordinate the division of knowledge and labor. Few people nowadays doubt that market economies are more efficient and productive than "command" or socialist economies. Why is this so? Obviously, incentives have something to do with it. The market economy does a better job of rewarding people for their ingenuity and effort than does socialism. But even more critical to the success of the free market is how it uses and coordinates the knowledge of market participants.

In society, the economic knowledge of each individual, although limited, is unique. Only the individual knows his own economic valuations. Since such information is vital to businesses offering goods and services, how can the valuations of consumers be communicated to producers? History demonstrates that by far the most efficient method of communicating and distributing vital economic knowledge is through market prices. As the economist Friedrich Hayek puts it, market prices are "a kind of machinery for registering change, or a system of telecommunications which enables individual producers to watch merely the movement of a few pointers, as an engineer might watch the hands of a few dials, in order to adjust their activities to changes of which they may never know more than is reflected in the price movement." (1948, 87)

Critical to the efficient distribution of knowledge in a market is the institution of private property. Economic assets owned in common are incapable of generating accurate economic values. Hence, if oil were common property, it would be impossible to determine the value of this commodity in the context of the valuations of the members of society. If everyone could use oil without paying for it, the supply of oil would quickly be exhausted. Nor would its distribution be efficient. In a market where economic resources exist in the form of private property, distribution is directed by economic value, which is determined by what people are willing to give up in exchange for the desired economic good. If you want oil, you must be willing to surrender something that other people value. Since people don't value so-called common property in the same way they value their own property, private property becomes necessary to generate the requisite values needed for the functioning of the market. These values represent knowledge: they indicate not only what people want, but also what they are willing to give up to get what they want. No other institution is capable of distributing the knowledge of economic values as efficiently as market capitalism.

11. The Principle of the Elitist Foundation of Progress. Herman Weyl, an important physicist and follower of Einstein, was fond of suggesting that if ten or twelve specified individuals were to die suddenly, knowledge of contemporary physics would be lost forever. Perhaps this was an exaggeration. But the general point behind the observation is true nonetheless. The progress of the human race, whether in science, culture, economics, or politics depends on a small elite of innovators. Without the ingenious discoveries of this elite, the human race would still be scavenging in the bushes for food and chasing wild animals with spears. It is only the exceptional geniuses, the innovators and pathbreakers, the discoverers and thinkers, the men of great force and energy and vision who have led the world out of the Stone Age into the twenty-first century. "Universal history, the history of what man has accomplished in this world, is at bottom the history of the Great Men who have worked here," wrote Thomas Carlyle in *On Heroes and Hero-Worship.* "They were the leaders of men, these great ones; the modellers, patterns, and in a wide sense creators, of whatsoever the general mass of men contrive to do or attain; all things that we see standing accomplished in the world are properly the outer material result, the practical realisation and embodiment, of Thoughts that dwelt in the Great Men sent into the world: the soul of the whole world's history, it may justly be considered, were the history of these."

There exists a widespread reluctance, especially in the democratic West, to acknowledge the truth of this. Any suggestion that "progress" is largely the handiwork of a select elite is regarded as a kind of slander against the common man. Isn't the progress of civilization the work of anonymous toiling men and women, forgotten by the history books and scorned by snobbish men of letters? And how can anyone suggest that an elite of so-called innovators or geniuses is in some sense more valuable than the rest of humanity? Aren't such views merely an attempt to justify the oppression of the many by the few?

In discussing such issues, we must not allow ourselves to be carried away by the predominant egalitarian sentimentality of the day. The question whether civilization is largely the handiwork of a select elite or of mankind in general has nothing to do with the intrinsic worth of specific individuals or with the political status of the common man in society. It is simply a fact that some people are more creative than others, and that this creativity makes a huge difference for the progress of mankind. Now whether these creative innovators are entitled to special privileges by virtue of their special talents is an entirely separate question that has nothing to do with the point at issue. Creative people don't need privileges; they simply need to be "left alone" so they can develop their talents. Nor are such individuals necessarily more "valuable" as human beings than anyone else. They are merely "superior" in terms of their creativity and ambition, in their ability to think of new ways of getting things done. In many other ways, they may be vastly "inferior" to the average non-creative person. Especially in terms of personal morality, creative individuals often leave much to be desired. Their greater intelligence and their indispensability allows them to get away with things that would prove ruinous to ordinary human beings.

The critic and political journalist H. L. Mencken was a very shrewd and disillusioned observer of the human scene. Throughout his life, he was impressed and even a bit flabbergasted by the vacuity of thought evinced by most human beings. It never ceased to amaze him that an individual could go through life without once entertaining a single original thought. Late in life, he made the following observation concerning the masses of people and their relation to human progress: "The existence of most human beings is of absolutely no significance to history or to human progress," Mencken wrote. "They live and die as anonymously and as nearly uselessly as so many bullfrogs or houseflies. They are, at best, undifferentiated slaves upon an endless assembly line, and at worst they are robots who leave their mark upon time only by occasionally falling into the machinery, and so incommoding their betters. The familiar contention that they at least have some hand in *maintaining* civilization—that if they do nothing to promote it they at all events do not retard it—this contention is plainly not valid. If all human beings were like them civilization would not be maintained at all: it would go back steadily, and perhaps quickly. This is proved by a glance at Appalachia, the domain of 'the only pure Anglo-Saxons' left in the United States. The culture prevailing among these backward folk is precisely the same today as it was when the great movement into the West began, and they were thrown off from the stream of more intelligent and enterprising pioneers. Save for the infiltration of a few cultural traits from outside, they live now exactly as their ancestors lived then.... If they have yielded to improvement in this or that particular, it has always been against their will and in spite of their resistance."

From these observations, Mencken concluded that "the torch of civilization is carried ... by a small minority of restless and enterprising men. The members of this minority work in countless ways, and there is an immense variation in the nature and value of their several activities... What they always aim at, whether by design or only instinctively, is the improvement of human life on this earth. One of them may do no more than devise a new and better rat trap, or a new way to make beans, or a new phrase, but some other, on some near tomorrow, may synthesize edible proteins or square the circle. Out of this class come not only all the men who enrich civilization, but also all those who safeguard it. They are the guardians of what it has gained in the past as well as the begetters of all it gains today and will gain hereafter. Left to the great herd it would deteriorate inevitably, as it has deteriorated in the past whenever the supply of impatient and original men has fallen off. This is the true secret of the rise and fall of cultures. They rise so long as they produce a sufficiency of superior individuals, and they begin to fall the moment the average man approximates their best." (1956, 39-40)

Mencken's "elitism" today would be considered well beyond the pale. Even so-called "conservatives" would squirm uncomfortably if confronted by it. However, in the light of obvious facts available from history, this "elitist" view of society comes closer to the truth than most Americans are willing to admit. As evidence, consider several illustrations drawn from history. First, let us examine Portugal between the fifteenth and seventeenth centuries.

In the fifteenth century, the Portuguese were in the forefront of navigational technique. They were the first European nation to sail around the treacherous Cape of Good Hope (called in those days the Cape of Storms), a tremendous achievement given the limited technology of the time. In the sixteenth century, Portugal began to regress. In a few decades they went from the forefront in navigational theory to the rear. How did this happen? How could a country, within the course of a few decades, suffer so precipitous a decline in their standing among seafaring nations?

The main culprit appears to have been the persecution of Jews. For most of the fifteenth century, Portugal had shown tolerance toward its Jewish population. In 1497, this attitude suffered a dramatic change. Pressure from the Roman Catholic Church led to a campaign of forced conversions for the nation's 70,000 Jews. In 1506, Lisbon witnessed its first pogrom, in which 2,000 Jews were indiscriminately slaughtered. This oppression had disastrous results for the Portugal's intellectual life. Most of the leading savants in Portugal, including its best astronomers, were Jewish. These men left in droves during the early years of the sixteenth century. "By 1513, Portugal wanted for astronomers," wrote historian David Landes; "by the 1520s, scientific leadership had gone. The country tried to create a new Christian astronomical and mathematical tradition but failed." (1999, 134-135)

If a nation persecutes its best scientists, its leading astronomers, its greatest intellects, it will decline very quickly, as Portugal declined in the fifteenth century. Most of the best minds in Portugal during the fourteenth and fifteenth centuries happened to be Jewish. With the persecution of the Jews, Portugal destroyed its intellectual elite and condemned itself to centuries as a cultural and intellectual backwater. Even as late as 1900, 78 percent of the population of Portugal was illiterate. Leadership is absolutely critical to progress. If an "elite" group of leaders is found wanting, the results can be catastrophic for the average man.

Spain suffered a similar diminution of its intellectual life, leading to an even more spectacular decline. In the sixteenth century, Spain was Europe's leading power. By the end of the seventeenth century, it was a pathetic backwater. The same could be said of the rest of southern Europe. Landes describes the process of Spain's and southern Europe's decline as follows: "In the centuries before the Reformation, southern Europe was a center of learning and intellectual inquiry.... The Protestant Reformation, however, changed the rules. It gave a big boost to literacy, spawned dissents and heresies, and promoted the skepticism and refusal of authority that is at the heart of the scientific endeavor. The Catholic countries, instead of meeting this challenge, responded by closure and censure.... Persecution led to an interminable 'witch hunt,' complete with paid snitches, prying neighbors, and a racist blood mania. Judaizing conversos were caught by the telltale vestiges of Mosaic practice: refusal of pork, fresh linen on Friday, an overheard prayer, irregular church attendance, a misplaced word.... So Iberia and indeed Mediterranean Europe as a whole missed the train of the so-called scientific revolution." (1999, 179-180)

Egalitarians could interpret these facts as a testament to the disastrous effects of policies aimed at "thought-control," rather than as evidence for the importance of elites. But thought-control is harmful precisely because it bears hardest on those most capable of thought—that is to say, on the intellectual-scientific elite. If a nation destroys its great men either by silencing them, driving them out of the country, or making it impossible for them to develop their talents, that nation will decline.

Keep in mind as well that many of the Jews persecuted by Spain and Portugal wound up in England or the Netherlands, two countries which, despite their relatively small populations, accomplished great things in the sixteenth and seventeenth centuries. The English benefited most from the persecutions of Catholic countries against enterprising Jews and Protestants, many of whom wound up in the land of hope and glory, where they made important contributions to the development of British industry. It is not surprising that England should have quickly established itself as the world's leading power. Thanks to the influx of talent from abroad and the cultivation of brains at home, it could boast of more first-rate minds than any nation. In the eighteenth century, other European governments began paying Englishmen to come and help them set up industry. (1999, 281)

The recruitment of outstanding talent is, of course, a mainstay of modern business. Nowadays we even have "headhunters" who search for individuals with special skills. Talent in business is worth a lot of money. In sports, we find the same obsession. Sports franchises are not interested in common men: they desire the most talented, the most outstanding players they can get their hands on, because the team with the best players usually wins. All this is common sense. Yet when stated in its abstract form and applied to society generally, it draws howls of protests and charges of "elitism" from Leftists, who cannot abide the fact that some people contribute a great deal more to the progress of a nation than others.

To extend our inquiry a bit further, imagine what English Elizabethan literature would be like without Shakespeare, Marlowe, and Spencer; or Greek philosophy without Democritus, Socrates, Plato, and Aristotle; or Italian Renaissance political theory without Machiavelli and Guccinardi; or German romantic music without Wagner, Brahms, and Schumann; or English empirical philosophy without Locke, Berkeley, and Hume. Any intellectual movement that has accomplished anything worth remembering in history has always been the work of a handful of men. To assume, as many die-hard egalitarians assume, that these men are replaceable, that others would have stepped forward to fill the breach if they had died prematurely or been snuffed out by persecution, is to assume what is neither provable nor probable.

There is, however, another side of the question which requires consideration. As I noted earlier, superiority in intelligence, creativity, and leadership does not in any way insure superiority in morals or character. Greatness in scientific, literary, political or economic achievement often goes hand-in-hand with moral depravity. As the German novelist Thomas Mann has suggested, there exists something demonic in the nature of genius, something cold and ruthless, selfish and amoral. We see this clearly in the biographies of great artists, composers, poets, philosophers, and even scientists. Nearly all these great men were in some manner or form "abnormal." Even the ones who more or less followed traditional moral practices were strange in other ways. Spinoza, as far as anyone knows, never did anything immoral or base in his entire life, yet he nevertheless demonstrated an almost pathological indifference to the fashions of society. Milton was also an eminently upright man—but impossible to live with, as his first two wives discovered. The same could be said for Beethoven, a great moral idealist, but a difficult man to be around. Machiavelli and Friedrich Nietzsche, on the other hand, were very pleasant and kindhearted fellows, but consider what they wrote. Machiavelli sings the praises of Caesar Borgia, the Italian poisoner and ruthless tyrant, while Nietzsche condemns the gentle gospel of Christ. Whenever we are in the presence of exceptional ability, we often find what can only be described as a kind of quasi-demonic excess. The genius is not like the rest of us. It is as if all the energy of his mind has flowed into completing the great task that he was sent into the world to accomplish, leaving the moral centers of his brain impoverished.

Camille Paglia observed in her controversial book *Sexual Personae*, "There is no female Mozart because there is no female Jack the Ripper." Even if we ignore the sexual context of the remark, it remains true. Jack the Ripper and Mozart do indeed have something in common— to wit, both men were afflicted with a pathological monomania, an obsessiveness that led one to terrible crimes and the other to the highest flights of genius. In the case of Jack-the-Ripper, the psychosis is obvious. No one would question it. In Mozart, it is less obvious; but it is there for anyone willing to look with open eyes. An individual who creates entire symphonies—instrumentation, counterpoint and all—in his head, and then copies them out, like some prophet transcribing visions of God, is not a normal person. Mozart could never have led the life of the average Joe. How could he hold a regular job with all this music constantly, unceasingly blossoming within his mind, demanding to get out and be heard? One is reminded of the difficulties faced by the philosopher Karl Popper during his early apprenticeship as a cabinetmaker. Popper found himself so helplessly distracted by epistemological problems that it compromised the quality of his French polish!

The men most responsible for changing our world, creating our prosperity, and developing our ideas are all, in some respects at least, pathological cases. From the vantage point of the common man, they are lunatics. They are often regarded as dangerous to the welfare of society, and in closed societies, they are put down by force. Galileo represents a paradigmatic case. Catholic apologists have attempted to blame Galileo for the church's persecution of the great Italian scientist. Galileo, through his arrogance and contumacy, brought the church's condemnation down upon himself. No doubt, this is how it happened. But to place the blame on Galileo is an absurdity only a special pleader could take seriously. Geniuses are often very arrogant and contemptuous of authority. It is their nature to be so. Putting up with their inordinate pride is the price we pay for the privilege of having them dwell among us and spreading their unique light on our benighted world. Galileo was the great hope of Catholic science. In condemning him and putting him under house arrest, the Catholic authorities not only silenced their greatest scientific mind, but also suppressed a whole host of other potential geniuses who might have continued Galileo's work. Thanks to these Catholic prelates, Catholic Europe would remain a scientific and cultural wasteland for an additional two hundred years, and the scientific revolution would remain the achievement of Protestant Europe. And all because a handful of church dignitaries were offended by Galileo's intractable arrogance! Imagine that: men of God who, in keeping with the example of Christ, are supposed to practice humility and forbearance, wreaking their vengeance on the greatest mind of their faith, merely because of a few pinpricks stuck in the tender sides of their inflated egos. The Catholic Church has paid a very heavy price for its folly. It can only be hoped that they have learned from their mistakes.

We can all of us learn a very valuable lesson from the story of Galileo's persecution. If we want progress in the arts and sciences, in entrepreneurship and technology, we may have to cut the exceptional individual some slack. It is, in any case, foolish to persecute him merely because he wounds our vanity or incites our envy. We should not be shocked if the exceptional individual breaks the rules and heaps scorn upon traditional ways of doing things. If we desire progress, we will just have to grin and bear it.

It could be argued that this issue of the demonic character of genius applies only to artists and creative people and not to businessmen and entrepreneurs. This, however, is not entirely true. It is, to be sure, a greater problem in artistic fields, but that doesn't mean businessmen and entrepreneurs don't manifest similar antisocial tendencies. As Schumpeter has noted, "the typical entrepreneur is more self-centered than other types, because he relies less than they do on tradition and connection and because his characteristic task—theoretically as well as historically—consists precisely in breaking up old, and creating new, tradition." [*Theory of Economic Development*, 92] Consider, as one example, Cornelius Vanderbilt—by all accounts, an absolutely hideous man, with hardly a charitable bone in his entire carcass. Yet, despite his ruthless greed and wanton lack of human feeling, he was a brilliant administrator, a man who really knew how to get things done, as his business affairs well prove. Or consider, to take a contemporary example, Steve Jobs, the CEO of Apple: a man who, down through the years, is notorious for his arrogance and his lack of consideration for others, yet who, nevertheless, is largely regarded as the greatest entrepreneur and midwife of innovation of the age. The men who make the most difference in the progress of the human race—the most indispensable men—do not always have the most upright character. If we want to benefit from their vision, their leadership, their energy, we do well to put up with their vices.

Of course, there is a limit to such tolerance, as there is to anything. We shouldn't let them commit rape, pillage, murder, mayhem, etc. If they commit felonies, they should go to prison, like anyone else. But they should not be persecuted for making outrageous statements, or for wounding the vanities of the rich and powerful, or for offending prevailing moral uniformities, or for making piles of money, or for being elitist, or for being unpleasant and rude. (All of this, of course, assumes a desire for "progress." For those, however, who detest progress, who would prefer significantly lower average life spans, a higher infant mortality rate and lower living standards, then the persecution of the exceptional human being becomes a veritable duty.)

Having sketched several principles which might prove helpful for the development of a new, more realistic theory of economics, I will conclude this essay with a brief attempt to apply these principles to the current economic situation. The last quarter century has witnessed an extraordinary revolution in capital markets. Nearly any economic asset can easily be turned into a financial instrument that can be traded anywhere in the world. The globalization of financial markets effectively liberates the speculator from government regulation. If the

U.S. government threatens to "over-regulate" the securities markets in America, speculators can simply take their business somewhere else. "We'll eventually be financial organizations headquartered on a ship floating on mid-ocean," one intransigent speculator boasted. (Millman 1995, 231)

While the globalization and regulatory liberation of speculative finance have received at least some attention from business journalists, another innovation in high finance has pretty much remained unnoticed by even the most astute observers of the current financial scene. I have in mind the ability of non-banking institutions to create money. Detailing how this is accomplished goes well beyond the scope of this essay. I will merely note that the nation's shrewdest financial analysts, such as Doug Noland of David Tice and Associates, regard this innovation as critical to grasping the brave new world of speculative finance. Those economists and financial analysts who continue to assume that *only* banks can create money will fail to understand the extent to which the Federal Reserve has lost control of the money supply.

Even under the best of circumstances, the development of a sort of wildcat financing infrastructure would be a cause for concern. Yet that is not only difficulty faced by the governors of the Federal Reserve. They must also come to grips with the increasing immeasurability of money. With the exceedingly rapid development of new and immensely complicated financial instruments, money is becoming harder to define. No one, not even the chairman of the Federal Reserve, knows how much money is really out there. The banking authorities have not merely lost control of the money supply; they are blinded to its size as well.

Under such circumstances, is it any wonder that markets have become prey to illusions of quixotic dimensions? The bursting of the tech and dot-com bubbles apparently left the illusions of most investors intact. For how else can we explain the recovery of the Stock Market in the face of the greatest accumulation of debt in human history? The United States has amassed more than 53 trillion dollars worth of debt. Even more worrisome is the rate at which this debt is growing. In recent years, household debt has grown much faster than the economy—an unsustainable trend fraught with sinister implications and unpleasant consequences. But most critically of all is the debt of the financial sector, which in recent years has accelerated at an alarming rate, with a debt to growth rate 28 times that of general economic growth. (Hodges 2005)

Debt levels of this magnitude have prevented the economy from sustaining a full and healthy recovery following the recession of 2001. They impose burdens on consumers and businesses that hamper investment and spending. Until we begin to clear a good portion of this debt, the U.S. economy will continue to flirt with catastrophe.

Clearing the debt, to be sure, poses some serious problems of its own. During a recession, the economy normally cleanses itself of most of the bad debt accumulated during the preceding boom. But in the 2001 recession, debt levels were so high that it became impossible to clear them without suffering serious ramifications. So the authorities at the Federal Reserve, in league with financial speculators, pumped fresh debt into the economy to keep the whole thing from blowing to pieces. They contrived to use government sponsored institutions like Fannie Mae and Freddie Mac to recycle bad debt and turn it into a fresh source of liquidity via home mortgages. Unfortunately, this source of debt eventually evaporated, so that the wizards of high finance now must scramble to find ever new sources. At some point, a day of reckoning must bring this process to an abrupt and catastrophic conclusion. Either the economy will experience a severe debt crisis leading to the sort of deflation experienced during the Great Depression, or (more likely) it will descend into a long and protracted episode of intense stagflation.

If we examine the U.S. economy impartially, intent upon seeing things as they are, not as we might wish them to be, it becomes very difficult to see how this conclusion can be evaded. In 2004, total debt in U.S. was $53 Trillion, or $175,154 per capita. Another $60 trillion, representing contingent social security and medicare, could easily be added to this figure. Does anyone seriously believe that the economy can grow itself out of *this* debt burden?

There may be a few opportunistic cynics among us who do not regard this debt burden as serious because a good portion of it is owed to foreigners. A trip to any local gas station would, I should hope, shake them from their dogmatic illusions. The fact is, America competes on the world market for oil; and when we run up a huge current account deficit, we inevitably weaken the dollar and force up the price of oil imports. Since our entire economy, from its hell-bent hyper-consumerism to its techno-industrial base, runs primarily on oil, this renders the prognosis for a full-fledged recovery any time soon extremely grim. We may never again see anything to approach the prosperity of nineties. America has reached, and now passed, the zenith of its greatness. It is all downhill from this point on.

What, then, in more specific terms, does the future have in store? While we can never be certain what will happen in the years to come, we can make several educated guesses as to what *might* happen. I believe the following three conjectures are well founded and more than probable:

1. The U.S. economy—and the world economy in general—will experience either chronic stagflation or a severe debt crisis leading to general worldwide depression. I doubt there is any way, short of a major war, that this can be avoided. As this book goes to its publisher, the financial markets are beginning to unravel, as one banking or investment institution falls by the wayside. This is merely the beginning of a major credit debacle that this writer has seen looming on horizon for some time.

2. The end of cheap oil will bring about the greatest period of economic regression since the decline of the Roman Empire. Rome's economic regression came about with the end cheap labor. The Roman economic system depended on a steady supply of inexpensive slaves. When Tiberius decided to abandon the wars of conquest on the Rhine, the supply of fresh slaves ceased. Large landowners became so desperate for laborers that they began seizing people on the roads. Eventually, the increase of slave prices destroyed Rome's inter-regional commerce, forcing more and more estates to supply all their own needs. This in turn led to the decay of the cities and towns, which depended on the exchange of labor and goods with the hinterlands.

The powerful Roman bureaucracy could not be maintained without a considerable supply of taxes. As the economy contracted, it became increasingly difficult to meet the expenses of a continental state, particularly the expenses of maintaining an army. Without a reliable, patriotic army, the Roman Empire could not fend off the barbarian invasions. The Western half of the empire inexorably crumbled into anarchy, poverty, and, ultimately, feudalism. (Weber 1976, 389-411)

America and the West face a similar crisis, only this time high oil prices, rather than high slave prices, will be the triggering cause. Our way of life depends on cheap energy. Imagine how different our lives would be if none of us could afford to drive a car. Yet that is precisely what is at stake here. As gas prices rise, automobiles will become increasingly expensive to drive, until only the rich will be able to use them. As transportation becomes increasingly expensive, people will have to make substantial changes in their lifestyles, especially in where and how they live.

Even more worrisome is the effect these changes will have on the production and distribution of food. Agriculture is no less dependent on cheap oil than industry. Not only farming equipment, but fertilizers and pesticides often use petroleum-based products. The question is whether we can produce and distribute enough food to maintain the high levels of population that have been made possible by the industrialization of agriculture in a post-industrial, post-petroleum era. If we can't manage this transition we will have a very ugly situation on our hands. Unless we take the inevitable depletion of oil reserves seriously and begin taking steps to solve these problems, we may not be able to avoid the horrors of famine, anarchy, and the complete demoralization of society.

It would be foolish to assume that some other cheap energy source must inevitably be discovered and all we have to do is wait to be delivered from our unhappy predicament. We have no reason to believe that this will happen. None of the proposed energy substitutes for oil are in the least promising. Hydrogen, for example, requires energy to bring it into existence. Where is this energy to come from? Some have suggested nuclear power. This would make a good short-term solution. It would certainly buy us time. But nuclear power is a finite source just like oil. Maybe it could keep us going for a century or more. Yet what will happen when we run out of uranium?

In short, unless we discover some other source of energy that is both cheap and inexhaustible, the industrial system is doomed.

3. By the middle of the twenty-first century, the welfare state will have run its course. Even if we ignore the effects of higher energy prices, there is no way that we can maintain a system of increasing entitlements. According to Congressional Research, by 2014 the Social Security trust fund will require other federal receipts to help pay benefits. By 2050, the ratio of workers to Social Security recipients could be as low as one to one. The system will obviously not be sustainable on such a basis. The burden of supporting Social Security and Medicare will impact the entire welfare system, placing an insupportable strain on government finances. (Berman 2000, 30-31) Raising taxes might help a little bit, but raising them too much could prove counter-productive, as the law of diminishing returns would almost certainly, at some point, begin to kick in. The fact that the federal government is currently running up huge deficits only makes the situation more pregnant with disastrous consequences. Serious reform of the welfare system, especially of the Social Security and Medicare systems, will be forced upon us whether we like it or not.

4. Income inequality will worsen, placing great stress on the viability of American democracy. The globalization of commerce is gradually undermining the manufacturing based of the U.S. economy. If the trend continues, the country will become divided between high paid professionals in information related jobs on the one side and mere peons slaving away in low paying service jobs on the other. Computer automation could eventually render a large section of the working population useless. What need for clerks and manufacturing labor when computers can do the work for so much less? In California, the occupations with the highest projected declines are order clerks, sewing machine operators, and typists. What will these people do after they are laid off? The occupations with the most projected openings in California include retail salespersons, cashiers, food service workers, and waiters and waitresses. In other words, degrading service jobs. (EDD 2004, 10) We are heading toward a society which exemplifies the worst sort of elitism imaginable: a cognitive elite of information workers and professionals on the top, with a horde of service people, tending the needs of the elites, on the bottom. It doesn't take much insight into human nature to understand that such an arrangement

would lead to an intensification of social conflict and resentment. It is unlikely that a democratic, consensual system of government can last long in a society split between a small elite of information professionals on the one side and a large mass of service workers on the other.

These are merely projections of current trends. If the trends could somehow be reversed, there might be hope for a different outcome. But before these trends can be reversed, they must be taken seriously. Perhaps the greatest threat comes from ideologues who will try to use these problems to further their partisan agendas. Ideologues regard every social problem as an opportunity to advance the cause. Hence, a libertarian, when confronted with the demise of social security, is eager to suggest privatization. While that might be preferable to doing nothing, to regard privatization of social security as a viable solution requires a predilection for wishful thinking. Let us face facts: Social Security is a welfare program. It redistributes money from the working middle-class to senior citizens, rich or poor. It is unclear how a welfare program can be privatized, since wealth redistribution goes against the principles of a private market.

The solutions provided by socialist ideologues are even worse. They would like to dramatically increase taxes on wealth, grant labor unions new powers, and raise the minimum wage to giddy heights. Such a policy would seriously threaten economic development and growth. By removing monetary incentives for risk-taking, entrepreneurship, and the self-development of human capital, it would lead to a reduction of savings, investment, and innovation and could very well bring about a serious depletion of talent within the professions of medicine and law. Why would anyone risk everything they own in a perilous business ventures if most of the profits will be taxed away should they succeed? Why would anyone spend years studying to become doctor if, at the end of all that toil and trouble, one would earn no more than a common ditch digger? Income redistribution in moderation may not cause much harm; but when taken to extremes, it can destroy an economy.

Answers to the problems confronting American society will never be found in ideology. Only within the framework of a disillusioned realism can we ever hope to find solutions to the difficulties which the womb of time is preparing for us.

7. Notes on Business Cycle Theory

Mainstream economics—by which I mean, the sort of economics that is taught in universities and promulgated in the mainstream press—is clearly in a grievous state and has been so for many decades now. Despite all their theories explaining how business cycles occur and all the statistical evidence they have compiled detailing what happens when an economy goes into an inevitable malaise, economists are still up a creek when it comes to prognostication. Nor is it simply a matter of not being able to say precisely when an economy will rise or fall. Exact predictions in economics are impossible. But economists should have at least a rough idea of where the economy is likely to go. Even concerning this very modest goal, mainstream economists fail more often than not. In a June 1990 poll, 88 percent of economists predicted a continued economic expansion. (Prechter 1995, 19) A month later, the economy promptly nose-dived into the worst recession in a decade. Economists really ought to do better if they expect any intelligent person to take them seriously.

Their grasp of the financial side of economic reality is little better. Mainstream economists were as clueless about the nineties' Stock Market as they were about the economy as a whole. "Economists are as perplexed as anyone by the behavior of the Stock Market," Stanford economics professor Robert Hall confessed. To the question, "Is the Stock Market too high?" Berkeley economics professor J. Bradford De

Long answered, "No one knows." (1996) Another economist, Mike Norman, places the whole scandal in perspective. "Until last year, economists got even less respect than Wall Street analysts; now, we're just a notch above," admits Norman. "Admittedly, this reputation is well-deserved, because it comes from our less-than-stellar ability to get economic forecasts right. With all that data and plenty of powerful computing ability, you'd think we could produce better forecasts. Heck, even the local weatherman puts us to shame" (Thorton 2003)

Is this not incredible? What good are all their graduate and postgraduate degrees, all their mathematical and empirical training, all their models and analysis, if they cannot explain something so simple as the behavior of the Stock Market?

Now as long as the economy is humming along at a good pace and most people are doing well, the fact that the overwhelming majority of professional economists are clueless about business cycles provokes little interest. Why should any of us care, as long as the paychecks keep filling up our bank accounts and our credit card debt is manageable? But as soon as the economy begins to flounder and we find ourselves facing unemployment and crushing debts, we are likely to take a different attitude towards the intellectual malfeasance of mainstream economists. Their ignorance now appears implicated in our misfortune. Perhaps if they knew more about business cycles than do palmists and tarot card readers, we could turn to them for guidance in times of crisis. But given their track record, this would not be a very wise thing to do.

Who, then, should we turn to in a time of economic crisis? Is there anyone out there who understands these mysterious fluctuations in economic activity that lead so inevitably to booms and busts? Or is the science of economics, and especially of business cycle research, one vast and perpetual morass of unintelligibility?

To know nothing is to be in a lamentable state. Even worse is to think one knows when one is actually quite ignorant. Most economists don't regard themselves as ignorant. Many see themselves as great interpreters of economic fact, men whose understanding and wisdom soars well above the common herd. Icarus had his wings, all wax and feathers, and economics its "science," all mathematics and intellectual pretense; yet neither, I fear, can hold fast under the bright sizzling glare of truth. Economists have compiled all sorts of theories to try to explain the business cycle, none of which, alas, can be counted on as a reliable guide to fiscal and monetary policy. Consider, as one example, one of the more influential business cycle theories within the economics profession today, the Keynesian theory, as expounded by the pundit-master of liberal economics himself, Paul Krugman. "As is so often the case in economics (or for that matter in any intellectual endeavor), the explanation of how recessions can happen, though arrived at only after an epic intellectual journey, turns out to be extremely simple," Krugman smugly assures us. "A recession happens when, for whatever reason, a large part of the private sector tries to increase its cash reserves at the same time." (1998)

This explanation, like so many propagated by Lord Keynes and his followers, raises more questions than it answers. Business cycles, we are told, happen when, for some inexplicable reason, a whole lot of people decide to increase their cash holdings. But why should such a thing ever occur in the first place? Why would so many people decide to start stuffing their mattresses with cash? How can we explain so singular an occurrence? Is it mere coincidence? A malignant conjunction of the planets? Or is it perhaps a wave of temporary hoarding insanity that spreads through the population like a vulgar fashion or a bad cold? It is very odd that a man of Krugman's stamp, who is so sure that he alone is right and that everyone who disagrees with him is a complete dunce, should offer so ridiculous a theory. For it should be clear that Krugman's Keynesian theory of recessions suffers from an egregious superficiality. Imagine if some medical researcher had written an editorial in the *New York Times* insisting that the common cold is caused by a sore throat! Yet Krugman's statement is no more credible. Increased cash reserves is merely a symptom of a recession, not its cause. If you cannot provide a coherent explanation of why people increase their cash reserves at the start of an economic crisis, you will never explain why recessions happen.

If mainstream economics cannot provide us with an adequate explanation of the business cycle, who on earth can? Has any progress at all been made in explicating this great mystery? Well, yes, some progress has been made. Not in mainstream economics, but on fringes, a few economists can give you at least a rough idea of the *how* and *why* of recessions. The best theories are those that arose at the beginning of the twentieth century in Austria. Two men in particular deserve mention: Ludwig von Mises and Joseph Schumpeter. In 1911, they each published a book introducing a new theory of the business cycle. Mises' theory, introduced in his classic *The Theory of Money and Credit*, is known as the Austrian theory of the trade cycle, because it relies heavily on the work of the two great founders of the so-called "Austrian school" of economics, Carl Menger and Eugen Böhm-Bawerk. Schumpeter's theory, which, due to its unique and heterodox nature, has no special name of its own and belongs to no particular school (though it dovetails nicely with certain aspects of the Austrian theory), was first introduced to the world in the pathbreaking *The Theory of Economic Development*. While neither of these theories is fully adequate, they both provide the essential groundwork for grasping the inner workings of the business cycle.

Mises theory begins with an examination of the interest rate. Mises' teacher, Böhm-Bawerk, had argued that the phenomenon of interest could only be accounted for on the basis of what he called "time-preference." The interest rate, this theory claims, stems from the fact that individuals prefer present spending to future spending. If a man borrows $100 for one year at ten per cent, this is tantamount to saying that he would rather have a $100 now than $110 a year from now. In the words of Mexican economist Faustino Ballvé: "If the entrepreneur obtains money, he is able to have today what he could otherwise not have until tomorrow. When he obtains a loan, *he buys time*: the interest that he pays is the price of the advantage he obtains from having at his disposal immediately what he would otherwise have to wait for." (Hazlitt 1959, 204, 205)

With this theory of time-preference well in hand, Mises proceeds to analyze what happens when the banks (usually at the behest of the government) seek to stimulate the economy by "artificially" lowering the interest rate. Whenever the interest rate is artificially lowered, it *ipso facto* falls below the level consistent with the time-preference of the public. This means that the new interest rate fails to express what is really going on in the economy. A "genuine" decrease in the interest rate would mean that the public's time-preference had changed: most people would prefer to save now and spend later. This in turn would bring about an increase of savings and more money for the banks to lend to entrepreneurs. But when the interest rate is lowered artificially, there exists no corresponding increase in savings. Instead, the banks merely create money by expanding credit. The bank, for example, lends money to Peter. Peter pays off Paul, his contractor, and Paul deposits the money back in the bank. Then the bank turns around and lends Paul's savings-deposits to someone else. Through this process the bank expands credit well beyond its original reserves. A bank with $100,000 in savings deposits can quickly multiply its credit to well over a million dollars. The only restraint on this process is what is called a reserve requirement. Banks have to keep a certain percentage of a customer's savings-deposits as a reserve, so that they will always have cash on hand to pay depositors who want to withdraw money from their accounts. But these reserves requirements aren't very hefty—sometimes as low as three per cent. The capacity to expand credit is very real.

Now according to Mises' trade cycle theory, when banks lower interest rates by expanding credit, entrepreneurs suddenly find that they can invest in lengthy and time-consuming projects which, on the basis of the original interest rates, would never have been profitable. Mises argues that in assuming this, the entrepreneurs have committed a major error. Herein lies the problem; for it turns out that these new projects are not really profitable, because there exist no real savings to fund them. The time-preference of the public has not really changed. The average Joe still wants to spend as much of his money on consumer goods as he did before. The entrepreneur's investment is based on a mirage. The amount of capital goods, the number of machines and tools, remains the same. The only thing that has changed is the amount of money that can be spent for capital goods. The inevitable result of this state of affairs is a rise in the price of capital goods. Entrepreneurial projects suddenly become more expensive. The entrepreneur, thinking that, with the decrease in the interest rates, he can afford new investments in capital goods, has been fooled. He failed to anticipate that the price of capital goods would rise before he could carry out his entrepreneurial investment all the way through. "Business had been seduced by the governmental tampering and artificial lowering of the rate of interest [into acting] as if more savings were available to invest than were really there," is how Austrian economist Murray Rothbard, in his exposition of Mises' theory, explained the process. "As soon as the new bank money filtered through the system ... it became clear that there were not enough savings to buy all the producers' goods, and that business had *malinvested* the limited savings available. Business had overinvested in capital goods and underinvested in consumer products." (Mises 1978, 84)

Although this theory is certainly preferable to anything found in contemporary mainstream economics, there are still a number of things seriously wrong with it. To begin with, the theory is clearly motivated by an ideological prejudice against any kind of state intervention in the market. The Austrian school has been infiltrated and taken over by partisans of *laissez-faire* who dogmatically believe that all government interference in the economy is bad. The economist, however, must not allow his ideological biases to influence his conclusions. The economist should focus exclusively on elucidating economic reality, irrespective of policy implications. Policy implications are the province of ideologues—that is, of those who have already made up their minds well ahead of time and have no interest in the truth.

If we look at the Austrian theory impartially, without the biases engendered by a political or ideological point of view, we will find that the Austrian vision, although so clear in some directions, is clouded in others by a fog of wishful thinking and ideological presumption. At the very commencement of their theory, we find them lapsing into error. The interest rate, they claim, is a product of "time-preference." But is this really true?

While this view of the matter may have a certain amount of logical plausibility, it fails to account for several important empirical realities, the most critical of which involves the question of motivation. Do lenders really charge interest rates because they would rather spend more money now than later? No, not quite. Their motivation is really a great deal more complicated than that. Very few people stop to consider what money will be worth to them in a year's time. The future is a realm of great uncertainty—so much so that it is very unlikely that time-preference plays an important part in the calculations of more than a handful of lenders. And it probably plays an even smaller role in the calculations of savers and borrowers. People save for a variety of motives that have little if anything to do with time-preference. The most common motive is uncertainty about the future. The proverbial "save for a rainy day" falls under this category. People also save because they don't have enough money to buy what they want right now. While there is an element of time-preference in such saving, to regard it solely as a matter of time-preference is naive, because that is not how people think about it. Most people do not think in terms of time-preference, and so if you want to predict their behavior, you better not overemphasize the time-preference factor.

The economist Frank Knight had a much better grasp of this issue than anyone within the Austrian camp. In his classic work *Risk, Uncertainty, and Profit*, he wrote: "The saving of capital seems to us to be in fact the result mainly of two or three motives of which the desire for increased consumption of goods in the future is only one and probably one of the less important. Like other acts of man in society, it is largely a mere matter of established custom, good form, the thing to do, the *mores*. Then we must emphasize the impulse to create. Probably the greatest single source of saving is the putting of income back into a business, because of sheer interest in the business and the desire to make it grow. That the desire for the increased income is not the dominant motive in much of this is proved by the fact that men invest as desperately in an enterprise never likely to be profitable as they do in the most prosperous concern, and by the further fact that much of the reinvestment in society is made by directors of corporations who will not get the fruits of the work for themselves at all. The truth is, we believe, that the real motives of human life, at least of those people who do big things, are idealistic in character. The business man has the same fundamental psychology as the artist, inventor, or statesman. He has set himself at a certain work and the work absorbs and becomes himself. It is the expression of his personality; he lives in its growth and perfection according to his plans." (1921, 162-163)

Knight's analysis suggests that there is something else wrong with the Austrian theory: namely, that it is too rationalistic. It places too much faith on rationalistic calculation, when, as a matter of fact, a great deal of motivation arises from idealistic and irrational impulses. Even more important is Knight's allusion to "established custom" and "mores." The Austrian theory tends to regard individuals as little more than rationalistic profit-maximizers. Many small business owners seek only to make enough money to get by. From a purely monetary standpoint, they might have been considerably better off as an employee of a massive corporation. But because they prefer working for themselves to making more money, they choose to stick with a business that barely produces enough revenue to keep itself from going under.

The Austrian theory, because of its rationalist naiveté concerning human motivation, runs afoul of the facts in other areas as well. According to the Austrians, as soon as the interest rate falls, entrepreneurs flock to banks looking for loans to fund projects which, at a slightly higher rate, would be judged unfeasible. But is this what really happens? Perhaps in some instances. Does it happen in all instances? I doubt it. Since not all entrepreneurs are profit-maximizers eager to expand their enterprises at the first opportunity, we have no right to conclude that a fall in interest rates will always trigger enough entrepreneurial borrowing to bring about the kind of malinvestments in the capital goods industries predicted by the Austrian theory. In some instances, perhaps it might. But in others, it probably won't. And if it cannot explain all instances, then the Austrian theory cannot be regarded as a complete theory applying to all cyclical phenomena.

Another shortcoming in the Austrian theory involves its underestimation of the profound effect of uncertainty. By uncertainty, I don't mean merely a failure to guess what will happen. The Austrian theory obviously stresses the role that misperceptions about the true state of the economy play in savings and investment. Businessmen, the Austrians contend, are led to misperceive the true state of the capital market by the artificial lowering of interest rates. But this assumes that, without interest rate manipulations, businessmen would not have misperceived the true state of the capital market. Is this a plausible assumption?

No, as a matter of fact, it isn't, because it fails to take into account the radical uncertainty of economic life. There are some things about the future we simply do not know and can't even guess. This is precisely what is meant by uncertainty. In a fluxing economy, where consumers' tastes are often changing and some businesses are emerging while others are lapsing into bankruptcy or finding themselves gobbled up by stronger competitors, no one knows for sure which products consumers will be buying in a year's time. It's all a matter of guesswork, shrewd prophecy and luck.

Businesses, in their effort to come to grips with the uncertainty of economic life, devise various methods of increasing their control over consumer wants, to make them less unpredictable. Companies are eager to create demand for their products. This means manipulating consumers through advertising and aggressive sales tactics.

The Austrian theory, by ignoring this element of consumer demand, falls prey to several errors, the most serious of which is its overestimation of the factor of consumer sovereignty. "On the market of a capitalistic society the common man is the sovereign consumer whose buying or abstention from buying ultimately determines what should be produced and in what quantity and quality," explained Ludwig von Mises in his brief polemical work, *The Anti-Capitalist Mentality*. "Big business always serves—directly or indirectly—the masses." (1956, 1-2)

Mises strongly disapproves of the opposing view which claims that consumers are brainwashed by corporations through sophisticated advertising techniques. "It is a widespread fallacy that skillful advertising can talk the consumers into buying everything that the advertiser wants them to buy," he wrote in his *magnum opus, Human Action*. "The consumer is, according to this legend, simply defenseless against 'high-pressure' advertising. If this were true, success or failure in business would depend on advertising only. However, nobody believes that any kind of advertising would have succeeded in making the candlemakers hold the field against the electric bulb, the horsedrivers against the motorcars, the goose quill against the steel pen and later against the fountain pen. But whoever admits this implies that the quality of the commodity advertised is instrumental in bringing about the success of an advertising campaign. Then there is no reason to maintain that advertising is a method of cheating the gullible public." (1949, 321)

Mises argument, though perfectly sound as far as it goes, nonetheless spreads more confusion than light on the subject. The question in advertising is not whether businesses could ever use propaganda techniques and hypnotic suggestion to sell candles in place of light bulbs or horsedrivers in place of automobiles. What is at stake involves a far more subtle point. Left-wing critics of capitalism who believe consumers are so gullible that they can be manipulated by multi-national corporations into buying anything are clearly guilty of exaggeration. But this does not mean that the opposite view is appreciably more tenable.

That most corporate advertising is suggestive and manipulative, rather than informative and objective, no disinterested observer would ever deny, as even some of Mises' own followers have admitted. Consider the following remark courtesy of the Austrian economist Wilhelm Röpke: "It is undeniable that the 'sovereignty of the consumer' ... is seriously impaired by the suggestions which advertising puts out in an attempt to replace his true needs by imaginary ones. At the same time advertising becomes a dangerous instrument of monopoly ('monopoly of opinion') and of big business." (1942, 143)

The point I am trying to make, however, is not so much a moral as a psychological one. Central to the Austrian theory is the notion that the efficiency of economic processes is largely evaluated by how well it serves the desires of consumers. Any intervention in the market that thwarts consumer sovereignty is regarded by Austrians as a waste of precious resources. From this premise, Austrians conclude that intervention in the credit markets leading to lower interest rates and expansion of credit must always lead to lower economic efficiency. Investments based on expanded credit are always, according to this theory, "malinvestments." But is this really true in *all* cases?

Let us think about this for a moment. Suppose the banking system, under prompting from the Federal Reserve, dramatically increases credit. What will happen? If, as the Austrian theory assumes, the credit expansion is first directed toward production goods, this will mean an increase in capital investment and a corresponding decrease in consumption spending. Is this necessarily a bad thing? Yes, answer the Austrians, because the capital would have been "malinvested." Why malinvested? Isn't an increase in capital investment a good thing? Consider the following point made by Mises himself: "There is only one way that leads to an improvement of the standard of living for the wage-earning masses, viz., the increase in the amount of capital invested." (1952, 152)

If increases in capital investment lead to a higher standard of living for the masses, why should Mises object to the increase of capital brought about by credit expansion? Why is he so certain that all investment created by credit expansion must lead by grim necessity to malinvestment? He explains his position in *Human Action* as follows: "What [economics] has in mind when asserting that impoverishment is an unavoidable outgrowth of credit expansion is impoverishment as compared with the state of affairs which would have developed in the absence of credit expansion and the boom. The characteristic mark of economic history under capitalism is unceasing economic progress, a steady increase in the quantity of capital goods available, and a continuous trend toward an improvement in the general standard of living. The pace of this progress is so rapid that, in the course of a boom period, it may well outstrip the synchronous losses caused by malinvestment and overconsumption. Then the economic system as a whole is more prosperous at the end of the boom than it was at its very beginning; it appears impoverished only when compared with the potentialities which existed for a still better state of satisfaction." (1949, 564-565)

Mises introduces this theory to address what would otherwise appear, from an Austrian point of view, as an anomaly. Historically, business cycles have occurred hand-in-hand with rapid economic progress. The sharpest and most severe cyclical activity in American economic history occurred in the very period that witnessed the most rapid economic growth (i.e., the second half of the nineteenth century). In order to account for this inconvenient fact, Mises assumes that consumers will always be better off without credit expansion.

This argument takes too much for granted. Mises assumes that all market prices, including interest rates, will always register precisely what consumers want. Hence, any market "interference," even if engineered by non-governmental market participants (e.g., the banks), must always lead to a loss of consumer satisfaction. The problem is that Mises tacitly assumes that consumers *know* what will satisfy them. That is a most improbable assumption. Consumers may know what they want in terms of basic necessities, but in an advanced capitalist society, economic activity is only partially directed towards "basic necessities." The greater part is devoted to "quality of life" consumption—that is, to luxuries, VCRs, computers, audio CDs and DVDs, garden tools, cameras, camping gear, etc. Between such items there is no great difference in consumer satisfaction. If, for instance, credit expansion led to over-investment in technological goods at the expense of investment in camping gear and sportswear, would this inevitably lead to a loss of consumer satisfaction amounting to impoverishment? No, not at all.

Technological goods, like TVs, computers, stereos, and VCRs would merely be less expensive, in relative terms, than tents, sleeping bags, and jogging shorts. Consumers, prompted by lower prices and advertising, would merely watch more videos and play more computer games and spend less time in the woods or on jogging trails. Who's to say that they would be any less happy or less satisfied? Maybe a few will be less happy; but since most people are not sure what they want, it probably won't matter much one way or the other. Consumer satisfaction is obviously impaired in extreme cases, as when consumers have to settle for bread and water instead of meat and wine, or bikes and go-carts instead of cars and motorcycles. When the comparison, however, is between boats and campers, or lobster and sushi, or game consoles and DVD players, arguments over consumer satisfaction and the thwarting of consumer sovereignty lose much of their polemical force.

If we then factor the variable of advertising into the equation, it becomes even less clear how consumer sovereignty arguments can be used to support the malinvestment view of credit expansion. Although advertising cannot create consumer demand out of thin air, it can help "educate" the consumer to prefer whatever products are most favored by production. If credit expansion really has seriously distorted the production process, especially within the capital good industries, as Mises insists, then there seems little reason to doubt that advertising can be used to readjust consumers tastes to fit the new structure of production. While such readjustments will never be absolutely perfect, it is unlikely they would have been perfect even if there had been no credit induced "malinvestment" to complain of. For we cannot reasonably assume that all "malinvestment" is caused solely by credit expansion. Investors make unwise decisions all the time, irrespective of the monetary manipulations of the Federal Reserve. Nor is it true, as the Austrian theory implies, that all (or even most) investments are motivated by considerations of economic efficiency (that is, by concern for profits). Many people chose a specific line of business, not because they are looking to get rich, but because they feel specially called. A man may seek to become a contractor, not because market prices indicate to him that there is a high demand for such work, but because he feels a special aptness for directing construction projects.

I fear that, in some respects at least, Austrians misinterpret what is essential to the market process. Their emphasis on consumer sovereignty, rather than entrepreneurial innovation, constitutes one of the greatest weaknesses in their theory. Consider, as an example of this, Mises description of the entrepreneur in *Human Action*: "Like every acting man, the entrepreneur is always a speculator. He deals with the uncertain conditions of the future. His success or failure depends on the correctness of his anticipation of uncertain events. If he fails in his understanding of things to come, he is doomed. The only source from which an entrepreneur's profits stem is his ability to anticipate better than other people the future demand of the consumers." (1949, 290)

The entrepreneur is here regarded as a mere agent or lackey of consumers. His function does not extend beyond administering to the needs of his customers. Is this an accurate description of the entrepreneur? Is the entrepreneur really nothing more than the lickspittle of consumer appetite? If so, how can we explain the dynamic, innovative, progressive quality of the capitalist achievement? If the "titans of industry" are simply the sycophants of consumer taste, how can we account for their roles as leaders of economic development? Could someone who is merely concerned with satisfying the petty needs of his customers possibly be the very same person who, by introducing utterly new and disturbing innovations, completely overturns and renders obsolete all the old, customary and approved ways of doing things? It would seem hardly likely that the timid personage of Mises' description and the bold, innovative entrepreneur of capitalist history could be one and the same person. Serving the needs and whims of consumers is all fine and good as far as it goes. But the entrepreneur can hardly be explained on so slender a basis.

The Austrian account of the business cycle fails precisely because it does not take sufficient account of the role that entrepreneurial innovation plays in the capitalist system. Capitalism is not a static, non-cyclical system. What separates capitalism from all previous systems of political economy is its dynamic, ever-progressing, innovative nature. Before capitalism arrived on the scene, society was static. In the last two hundred years, capitalism has utterly transformed society from a sleepy agrarian order to a highly advanced techno-industrial civilization.

Mises is also misguided in his suggestion that capitalist progress is simply a matter of an "increase in the amount of capital invested." Innovation—by which is meant the introduction into the economy of new, more "efficient" methods of production—does not depend solely on increase in capital. It depends instead on a more felicitous use of available capital. As Joseph Schumpeter explained: "The slow and continuous increase in time of the national supply of productive means and of savings is obviously an important factor in explaining the course of economic history through the centuries, but it is completely overshadowed by the fact that development consists primarily in employing existing resources in a different way, in doing new things with them, irrespective of whether those resources increase or not. In the treatment of shorter epochs, moreover, this is even true in a more tangible sense. Different methods of employment, and not saving and increases in the available quantity of labor, have changed the face of the economic world in the last fifty years. The increase of population especially, but also the sources from which savings can be made, was first made possible in large measure through the different employment of the then existing means." (1934, 68)

Schumpeter's great insight into the nature of capitalist enterprise will help us draw a far more convincing portrait of the business cycle than the one provided to us by Mises and other "orthodox" Austrian theorists. The key to capitalist development and progress, Schumpeter asserted, is entrepreneurial innovation, which involves combining the resources of production in new and economically progressive ways. The entrepreneur is anyone who has the "initiative," "authority," and "foresight" to carry out "new combinations" in production. His central task, as Schumpeter puts it, is to lead "the means of production into new channels." (1934, 92)

Schumpeter places special emphasis on the role that entrepreneurs play in introducing "new combinations" into the economy. Society often resists innovation. Businesses that feel threatened by a new method of production may act to stifle it. Consumers may feel reluctant to try a new product, especially if it violates some rooted moral prejudice of the community. But even in the face of determined and hostile opposition, the entrepreneur perseveres. For this reason, the entrepreneur, according to Schumpeter, is the principle catalyst and leader of economic progress:

"It is ... the producer who as a rule initiates economic change, and consumers are educated by him if necessary; they are, as it were, taught to want new things, or things which differ in some respect or other from those which they have been in the habit of using." (1934, 65)

But perhaps the most significant source of resistance to entrepreneurial innovation comes from the investment community, which may look askance at a proposed innovation because of its unproven economic potential. Under ordinary conditions, investors will prefer lending to established businesses whose products have stood the test of time. Although any investment contains an element of risk, entrepreneurial investments are the most precarious of all, because they have no track record that would enable the creditor to calculate the risk involved in making the loan. No one can tell whether a new method of production involving, in many cases, entirely new products, will ever succeed. The outcome of any economic innovation always contains a large element not merely of risk, but of uncertainty, that is, of incalculable risk. If investors were perfectly rational, they would never lend money to entrepreneurs seeking to introduce new combinations into the economy. It is much safer to stick with established businesses that have demonstrated the worth of their products and their methods of production over time.

How, then, do entrepreneurs find the capital necessary to fund their innovations? Who will lend them the necessary money? Do they have to rely entirely on "irrational" investors? Or is there some other method that will enable them to, in effect, take capital from the established businesses and put it into their own daring schemes?

There is, in fact, one important method which entrepreneurs and the investment community use to redirect capital from proven, established businesses to boldly innovative firms specializing in new techniques of production. This is the method of credit expansion. Credit is created quite literally out of thin air and then lent to entrepreneurs, who use it to buy the production goods necessary to carry out their innovations. Schumpeter even goes so far as to say that credit creation is the only method by which entrepreneurs' demand for credit can be met. (1951, 39) I don't believe this is altogether true, since historically, entrepreneurs have used other methods (often bordering on downright larceny) to raise the purchasing power necessary to fund their projects.

But that credit creation has, historically, been a critical source of capital for entrepreneurial development can hardly be denied by the impartial observer.

Orthodox Austrians would argue that economic progress and entrepreneurial innovation cannot be based solely on credit creation. Savings are required to fund innovation. While this is true to some extent, it nonetheless fails to grasp the main point at issue. It would be naive to suppose that the very segment of the community most eager to save would also be the segment most likely to invest in risky new production schemes. It would appear that, on this issue at least, the Austrians have been led astray by their time-preference theory of savings. Not everybody saves money because they want to be able to spend more at a future date. Many save money as a hedge against uncertainty: that is to say, they save because they are afraid of future contingencies that will imperil their financial position. Still others save because they believe it is the right thing to do.

Now anyone saving for these reasons would probably shrink from being involved in risky schemes such as those proposed by chance-loving entrepreneurs, eager to direct capital into new, untried ventures. Such timid souls will seek to place their savings in financial institutions that promise safe investments, which in this context means: investments backed with collateral and "tested" methods of production and sale. This would rule out investments in entrepreneurial innovation from the very start. In the capitalist system, an impasse is created between the saver and the entrepreneur that can only be bridged through credit expansion (and other forms of economic skullduggery). By expanding credit, banks and other financial institutions can divert savings from "safe" investments involving established methods of production into the hands of innovators eager to try new combinations. This enables economic resources to be transferred into the hands of those most fit to make good use of them. More than anything else, economic progress depends on diverting capital into the hands of those who will put it to best use. Of all economic systems, historical capitalism has enjoyed the most success in achieving this goal.

There is another factor related to the whole problem of savings versus entrepreneurial investment that also needs to be noted. In the early stages of capitalism, limitation of consumption is essential to produce the funds necessary for capital investment. Without frugality and thrift, capitalism could never have taken its first steps. What the sociologist Max Weber called "worldly asceticism" is the necessary moral foundation of early capitalism. As capitalism progresses from one triumph of production to another, it soon finds itself confronted by a serious dilemma. The entrepreneur or the capitalist, before he can turn a profit, must sell his products. At some point along the line, the worldly ascetics have to become consumers. Businesses, in order to turn a profit, will do everything in their power to encourage the transition from worldly asceticism to hedonistic consumerism. Using manipulative advertising techniques, they will attempt to induce consumers to buy their products. These products, they will suggest, can vastly improve the quality of the consumer's life, especially the quality of his (or her) sex life.

In tandem with this shameless psychological manipulation, businesses develop methods that make it easier for consumers to buy their products. Retailers sell on the "installment plan" or issue "credit cards" to facilitate consumption. The end result of this is that the entire capitalist engine, on the retail side, becomes thoroughly consumer-orientated, so much so that a consumerist ethic is born and material acquisition increasingly becomes one of the most important indicators of social status.

The consumerist orientation of modern capitalism can easily be verified by statistics on personal savings. In 1990, Americans saved 7.8 percent of their disposable personal incomes. By 1995, that figure had fallen to 5.6 percent; by 1999, it had fallen to 2.4 percent. With personal savings so low, where on earth is the fledgling entrepreneur ever to find the capital necessary to fund his projects?

Established businesses fund the lion's share of their capital expenditures out of their own profits. An entrepreneur whose only capital is some idea or innovation obviously cannot rely on such a source for his expenditures. Where, then, is he to raise the monetary capital necessary to put his innovations into effect?

Here again we find ourselves confronted with the importance of credit expansion to entrepreneurial innovation and economic progress. While credit expansion does not in itself create any new production goods, if the bulk of it is used for capital expenditures, it will bring about a shift in the economy from consumer goods to capital goods. More production goods will be created than would otherwise have been the case. Mises referred to this sort of increase in capital through credit creation as "forced savings" (*erzwungenes Sparen*).

There are, then, two reasons why credit creation facilitates entrepreneurial innovations: (1) it helps divert capital from established businesses into entrepreneurial ventures; and (2) it creates additional savings that, as a consequence of excessive consumerism, would not otherwise have existed under mature capitalism. If these were the only effects of credit expansion, there would be no reason why banks shouldn't go on inflating credit *ad infinitum*. However, this conclusion, embraced by so many mainstream economists under the influence of Keynes and other palpable economic quacks, constitutes a serious misjudgment. For like so many things in life, credit expansion leads to both "good" and "bad" consequences. The "good" consequences are the aforementioned facilitation of entrepreneurial innovation. The "bad" consequences run along the lines predicated by the Austrian theory.

The Austrians, as will be recalled, argued that credit expansion must inevitably lead to "malinvestment" in production goods. While some of the theoretical constructs upon which this theory is based are flawed, the basic thrust of the theory appears more or less sound. Malinvestment is a necessary consequence of credit inflation, especially when the inflation is prolonged. This is true despite the number of successful innovations introduced into the economy by entrepreneurs because of the credit expansion. The innovations will lead to greater total output in the long run and a more efficient use of resources; but they cannot, in and of themselves, prevent the serious dislocations in the economy brought about by the sustained expansion of credit. Any inflation of credit must be regarded as financially unsound, despite whatever beneficial consequences may result from an increase in economic innovations.

To understand how credit inflation inevitably leads to economic malaise, we need to take a closer look at the phenomenon of entrepreneurial innovation. What happens when an entrepreneur successfully introduces a new, more efficient method of production or a new, more "satisfying" product? Schumpeter notes at least three important consequences. To begin with, entrepreneurial innovation leads to "new methods by which *more* of a product already produced before can be got out of them save quantity of labor and natural agents." (1951, 38) More products at less cost means a deflationary impetus, that is, a tendency towards lower prices, as we see, for example, in the computer industry, where better products are continually being offered for lower prices.

The second important consequence of entrepreneurial innovation is what happens to established businesses producing rival goods. At the start of the boom capital is diverted from old firms to new through credit expansion. This means, in practical terms, that capital costs rise for established firms, which leads to reduced revenues. Later on, the revenues of these older businesses suffer additional curtailment as new, innovative firms seize control of the market. If these older firms fail to adapt to the new circumstances, they will go out of business. Their factories, machines, and production methods may all have to be scrapped or converted to other uses. Schumpeter described the process by which innovation renders obsolete whole industries as "Creative Destruction." "The history of the productive apparatus of a typical farm, from the beginnings of the rationalization of crop rotation, plowing and fattening to the mechanized thing of today—linking up with elevators and railroads—is the history of revolutions," wrote Schumpeter in *Capitalism, Socialism, and Democracy.* "So is the history of the productive apparatus of the iron and steel industry from the charcoal furnace, or the history of the apparatus of power production from the overshot water wheel to the modern power plant, or the history of transportation from the mailcoach to the airplane. The opening up of new markets, foreign or domestic, and the organizational development from the craft shop and factory to such concerns as U.S. Steel illustrate the same process of industrial mutation—if I may use that biological term—that incessantly revolutionizes the economic structure *from within,* incessantly destroying the old one, incessantly creating the new one. This process of Creative Destruction is the essential fact about capitalism. It is what capitalism consists in and what every capitalist concern has got to live in." (1942, 83)

The third consequence of entrepreneurial innovation is that it tends to spawn swarms of imitators or entrepreneurial wannabes. Again, to quote Schumpeter: "Since ... entrepreneurial qualification is something which, like many other qualities, is distributed in an ethnically homogeneous group according to the law of error, the number of individuals who satisfy progressively diminishing standards in this respect continually increases. Hence, neglecting exceptional cases, ... the successful appearance of an entrepreneur is followed by the appearance not simply of some others, but of ever greater numbers, *though progressively less qualified.*" (1934, 228-229, italics added)

The appearance of less qualified entrepreneurs is one of the critical factors in the business cycle. Keep in mind that, initially, the entrepreneur tends to rely very heavily on credit creation to fund the capital necessary to introduce his innovation into the economy. If the innovation succeeds, this, along with the inflationary impetus caused by credit expansion, leads to widespread optimism in business and financial circles. Investors and aspiring entrepreneurs, captivated by the enormous profits earned by the first wave of entrepreneurs, rush into the market in the hope of getting a piece of the action. At the same time, bankers and investors, noticing how profitable entrepreneurial innovation has suddenly become, are also eager to join the feeding frenzy. The consequence is that on the one hand you have investors who are increasingly desirous of lending additional funds to entrepreneurs and on the other hand entrepreneurs who are less and less qualified to use those funds in profitable ways. This will inevitably lead to the accumulation of bad debt. Here we find one of the primary sources of the "malinvestment" which Austrians regard as so conspicuous a feature of the trade cycle.

But it gets worse as the behavioral logic of the situation plays itself out. As noted earlier in this essay, economic action is profoundly affected by the radical uncertainty of life. Now while it may be possible to predict the consequences of some entrepreneurial innovations, others have ramifications that nobody can guess. Who in 1990 could have predicted what the Internet would be like in the year 2000? Only a handful of visionaries had any notion of the Internet's possibilities. Many leaders in the business community, including the estimable Bill Gates, regarded the Internet as a mere plaything with limited commercial possibilities. Then sentiment turned completely around. During the late nineties, investors greatly overestimated the Internet. In the first years of twenty-first century, investors are finally beginning to acquire a more realistic understanding of both the possibilities and limitations e-commerce.

Because entrepreneurial innovations represent, in many instances, entirely new products or methods of production, it is not easy to estimate their long-range effect on the economy. The very fact that an innovation is *new* means that it has no track record. When an entrepreneur introduces some "new combination" into the economy, he and his investors are entering completely uncharted waters. Under such circumstances, there is no guarantee of success. In at least some instances, the investors are likely to lose all their money.

We touched upon this issue earlier in relation to the problem of entrepreneurial investment. Entrepreneurial innovations are inherently risky; they are not safe investment bets. Rational, self-maximizing investors would do well to avoid them, preferring established businesses with "proven" track records. Credit expansion, by giving an illusion of plentiful investment capital, changes the mentality of the investor. Keynes satirically described this aspect of the psychology of investment when he wrote: "Most, probably, of our decisions to do something positive ... can only be taken as a result of animal spirits— of a spontaneous urge to action rather than inaction, and not as the outcome of a weighted average of quantitative probabilities." (1936, 161) "Animal spirits" might be putting it too strongly. But credit expansion obviously encourages risk-taking. If taken to excess, it can lead to reckless speculation across the board, especially in stocks and real estate.

The reckless optimism engendered by credit expansion makes it relatively easy for any entrepreneur, whether qualified or not, to gain access to capital. This has both good and bad effects: good, because even the obscure entrepreneurial genius with little or no track record can acquire business capital; bad, because now even complete entrepreneurial idiots, as well as confidence men and other dubious characters, can find a place at the investment trough. From this we can derive the two major consequences of credit expansion: first, a diversion of capital from old methods of doing business to new methods; and second, a diversion of capital to entrepreneurial schemes that never amount to anything. Good judgment on the part of investors can help mitigate this sort of "malinvestment," but since there is no surefire method to distinguish a successful innovation from a disastrous one, bad investments will be made. The advantage of capitalism over other economic systems is that the market penalizes investors for making bad decisions. If investors put their money behind good innovations, they prosper. If they put their money behind bad innovations, they lose out. Credit expansion intensifies this process by increasing the availability of investment capital. During the expansionary phase of the business cycle, innovations are tested. Because the results will always be mixed, a recession becomes inevitable. Business cycles, in this respect, are necessary evils. In their absence, it is unclear how entrepreneurs would ever be able to test their innovations on the market.

With this insight in hand, the character of the business cycle takes on a whole new significance. Instead of regarding the business cycle as merely the inevitable consequence of reckless credit expansion, it should be seen as a great facilitator of entrepreneurial experimentation. And just as experimentation is the very touchstone of progress in science, it plays the same role in economic innovation. The expansion phase of the business cycle can be seen as the trial period for entrepreneurial innovation. Those innovations that prove their economic worth in the market survive the recession and live to see the subsequent boom. Those innovations that prove infelicitous are "liquidated" by the very recession they help bring about.

This view of the business cycle, which, despite a few changes here and there, comes pretty close to the theory espoused by Schumpeter in his *Theory of Economic Development*, still requires further elaboration. Specifically, we need to examine some of the other effects of credit expansion beyond those attributed to entrepreneurial investment and Creative Destruction. Only a very naive economist could believe that all the credit manufactured through "banking operations" and other financial chicanery winds up in the hands of entrepreneurs. Much of it probably does, either directly or indirectly, but some of it almost certainly winds up in the hands of speculators and other non-entrepreneurial investors, while the remainder is eventually pocketed and spent by consumers. The importance of this can hardly be underestimated. When excess credit flows into the hands of speculators, the consequence is almost inevitably some sort of market bubble, usually in asset prices or real estate. The process goes as follows: the first injection of excess credit drives up the prices in a given investment market, while this, in turn, leads to further investment in the same market, as investors seek to get in while the going is good. The market is thus driven up further and further, until a full-fledged bubble emerges. This is in essence what happened to the Stock Market in both the twenties and the nineties. Credit excesses fueled a speculative bubble market in stocks. That such bubbles cannot be maintained *ad infinitum* hardly needs proof. Sooner or later, they must burst, sending waves of financial devastation through the economy.

The effect of credit expansion on consumer spending is no less fraught with unpleasant consequences. Credit expansion heightens the general level of prosperity, thereby increasing what the Keynesians call "effective demand." Unfortunately, there is no way to maintain this effective demand without repeatedly introducing fresh injections of manufactured credit. This process cannot go on forever. Increasing credit is tantamount to increasing debt, and private individuals can only take on so much debt. Eventually a breaking point is reached and further credit expansion becomes unfeasible. This is often what triggers the recessionary phase of the trade cycle. When the banks reach the point where they can no longer expand credit, consumer spending declines and businesses find themselves unable to sell all their products. In order to cut their losses, they curtail production. Workers lose their jobs. This causes an additional curtailment in consumer demand. A period of retrenchment commences in which the economy cleanses itself of all the untenable debt accumulated during the expansion phase.

There is a widespread belief, even among professional economists, that the expansion phase of the trade cycle could be prolonged indefinitely merely by maintaining a policy of continual credit expansion. Consider once more Paul Krugman's explanation for the trade cycle, quoted earlier: "A recession happens when, for whatever reason, a large part of the private sector tries to increase its cash reserves at the same time. Yet, for all its simplicity, the insight that a slump is about an excess demand for money makes nonsense of the [view that recessions are inevitable]. For if the problem is that collectively people want to hold more money than there is in circulation, why not simply increase the supply of money?" (1998)

Like so many mainstream economists, Krugman is clueless about the nature of credit expansion. In a modern industrial economy, increasing the money supply almost always means expanding credit. But any expansion of credit involves a concomitant expansion of debt, since debt is merely the other side of credit. This, in a nutshell, is the key to understanding why credit expansion must ultimately lead to a recession. When you expand credit, you expand debt; and eventually a point is reached where the debt becomes so onerous, that it becomes impossible to expand it any further.

If, however, credit expansion helps foster entrepreneurial innovation and an economic boom, why can't the economy simply grow beyond its debts? The reason this is not possible stems from the fact that the debt is not distributed evenly throughout the economy, but tends to become concentrated among poorly performing firms. Consider the shrewd analysis of economist Wesley Mitchell: "As prosperity approaches its height," wrote Mitchell, "a sharp contrast develops between the business prospects of different enterprises. Many, probably the majority, are making more money than at any previous stage of the business cycle. But an important minority, at least, face the prospect of declining profits. The more intense prosperity becomes, the larger grows this threatened group. It is only a question of time when these conditions, bred by prosperity, will force some radical adjustment."

Mitchell continues: "Now such a decline of profits threatens worse consequences than the failure to realize expected dividends, for it arouses doubt concerning the security of outstanding credits. Business credit is based primarily upon the capitalized value of present and prospective profits, and the volume of credits outstanding at the zenith of prosperity is adjusted to the great expectations which prevail when the volume of trade is enormous, when prices are high, and when men of affairs are optimistic.... Cautious creditors fear lest the shrinkage in the market rating of the business enterprises which owe them money will leave no adequate security for repayment; hence they begin to refuse renewals of old loans to the enterprises which cannot stave off a decline of profits, and to press for settlement of outstanding accounts."

And Mitchell concludes on this ominous note: "Thus prosperity ultimately brings on conditions which start a liquidation of the huge credits which it has piled up. And in the course of liquidation, prosperity merges into crisis." (1944, 56) Again, I want to emphasize the point that credits are merely debts looked at from the other side of the ledger, so that Mitchell could have just as easily written that prosperity leads to a liquidation of the enormous *debts* which it has accumulated. I suspect that the word *credit*, because of its benign associations, has misled many economists. If instead of using the term "credit expansion," economists were in the habit of calling it "debt expansion," perhaps the ominous implications of this whole process, especially when it is allowed to continue without check for years on end, would be more generally appreciated. But the universal tendency toward euphemism in speech has made *credit* the preferred term in describing the phenomenon.

The accumulation of debt would be unpropitious even in the best of circumstances. When it occurs during the boom phase of the business cycle, it is especially disastrous. The general sense of optimism engendered by the expanding economy causes lenders to lose their sense of caution. Banks begin making loans without regard to sound principles of finance. This, in one sense, is good, because, as pointed out earlier, it enables unproven entrepreneurs to raise capital for their pathbreaking innovations. But in another sense, it is very bad. It inevitably leads to the accumulation of bad debt, backed, if backed at all, by inflated assets or bogus real estate values. The consequences of such unsound lending practices should be obvious. At some point, there must be a day of reckoning, a period of recession where the economy attempts to expel all the bad debt from its system.

Krugman has suggested that, if the financial system is inundated with bad loans, why not "junk the bad investments and write off the bad loans?" As a once in a lifetime solution, this might be a way out of an impossible situation, but if it became a routine policy, it would almost certainly undermine the financial integrity of the economy and cause a serious decline in savings and capital. We cannot simply keep writing off all the bad debts we accumulate and still expect people and businesses to save their money and invest responsibly.

We have but one more aspect of the trade cycle to examine before these notes can achieve a dignified terminus. It involves one of the most salient characteristics of the trade cycle—namely, the fact that production goods industries are usually the first to be hit by a recession and that they invariably find themselves hit harder than anyone else. One of the reasons why Mises and other Austrian economists emphasize malinvestment in producer goods is to explain this aspect of the trade cycle. Credit expansion, they contend, leads businessmen to invest more in capital and producer goods than is warranted by the preferences of consumers. I regard this theory as inadequate because it fails to appreciate the role entrepreneurial innovation plays in economic development and the business cycle. If the Austrian explanation proves inadequate, then how do we explain the intensification of the trade cycle among production good industries? If it is not caused by malinvestment, then what does cause it?

The economist John Maurice Clark in an article written as long ago as 1917 provided the best explanation. Clark pointed out that all producers of industrial equipment must meet two separate demands of their customers: first, they need to maintain the industrial equipment already in use; and second, they must furnish any new equipment needed for expanded production. "Both these demands come ultimately from the consumer," wrote Clark, "but they follow different laws." (1944, 238) Demand for replacement equipment tends to be steady, because equipment wears out at a predictable rate. But demand for new equipment arises out of shifts in consumer demand. If suddenly demand increases for a particular product, businesses have to order more machines so that they can increase output. The industry that constructs the new machines enjoys a period of increased production. Since machines are fairly durable and can be used for years before they need to be replaced, once the new machines are made, there is no need to add additional equipment, except to replace worn-out machines. This means that once the machine industry satisfies the increased demand for new equipment, demand for new machines must fall. The machine industry will suddenly find itself in a recession. Thus any change in consumer demand must always lead to a recession within some sector of the production goods industry. The larger the shift in consumer demand, the greater the fluctuation in production goods.

Clark illustrates this principle by imagining "a town which grows rapidly up to the size at which its industrial advantages are fully utilized and beyond which its normal production can expand but slowly. When the point of transition is reached from rapid to slow expansion, the town may find that it has outgrown itself by the number of people engaged in the extra construction work involved in the process of growing. Houses to take them in, stores to feed and clothe them, trucks to haul the materials they work with, offices, etc., all will be demanded, and thus a boom may be created which is none the less temporary for being based on tangible economic needs. The experience of the boom town has been common enough in the growth of our western country, and the blame need not be laid entirely upon the vagaries of mob psychology." (1944, 242)

Nor need it be blamed entirely on credit expansion, in the manner of the Austrians. Of course, credit expansion will certainly intensify this phenomenon of the trade cycle, and malinvestment will worsen it. Thus the element of truth in the Austrian diagnosis. But it is a mistake to blame the whole phenomenon on entrepreneurial errors caused by easy money policies. For even if every last dollar of the credit expansion were invested in entrepreneurial innovations that ultimately prove their worth in the market, there would still be an intense fluctuation within the producer goods industries. Only in a static economy could the Austrian diagnosis ever hope for complete vindication. In a dynamic, progressive economy, where consumer demand is always being created anew by the introduction of pathbreaking innovations, shifts in demand are endogenous to the system. A progressive economy must for this very reason find itself prey to fluctuations. The business cycle is the price we pay for economic progress. Even if we could have progress without credit expansion (which is unlikely), we would still not be able to rid ourselves of the trade cycle altogether. The distortions introduced by credit expansion undoubtedly intensify the fluctuations of the business cycle, but even without credit expansion, fluctuations would still occur. The trade cycle is rooted within the very nature of the market system. It is a product of capitalism's inherently dynamic, and hence unstable, constitution.

I have titled this essay "Notes Toward a Theory of the Business Cycle" to stress the provisional character of what is offered here. I regard this theory merely as a well-informed conjecture about business cycles. Empirical research will be required to determine whether, and to what extent, this conjecture accords with reality.

Before any research is conducted, certain limitations of the theory must be understood, lest it should be tested upon circumstances where it clearly doesn't apply. This theory, it should be realized, is not valid for all forms of capitalism. It holds good (if it holds good at all) only for the sort of industrial capitalism that flourishes best in Europe and North America. It does not hold for most Third World economies or for Communist or Post-Communist regimes, because these economies lack the requisite entrepreneurial base. Before credit expansion can spur economic innovation, there must exist an entrepreneurial class capable of leading the economy in new and revolutionary directions. In most Third World countries and Post-Communist nations, this entrepreneurial class does not exist in sufficiently large numbers. The attempt, therefore, to create economic progress through credit expansion in such countries is bound to lead to failure. It will, in fact, lead to all the results predicted by the Austrians—malinvestment and spoliation on a grand scale.

Economic action, as conducted in the real world of fact (as opposed to how it works in textbooks) is always characterized by a certain element of spoliation. This is true regardless of the economic system involved, whether predominantly capitalist or socialist in nature. As Vilfredo Pareto noted, "Societies which admit private property ... offer men two essentially different ways of acquiring wealth. One is by producing it directly or indirectly through the work and services of the capital they possess. The other is by acquiring the wealth thus produced by others. These two methods have at all times been employed, and it would be rash to believe that they will cease to be employed in the foreseeable future. But because the second method is generally under moral reproof, people willingly close their eyes to its employment, holding it to be something sporadic and incidental. In fact it is a general and enduring phenomenon." (1966, 139)

Quite so. But not all forms of spoliation are created equal. It depends on who is bagging the plunder and what they are doing with it once they have it in hand. The tremendous wealth of the capitalist West did not arise merely because capitalists are better at spoliation than non-capitalists, but because capitalists have made much better use of whatever loot they have pilfered. Feudal aristocracies squandered the wealth they stole on stupid luxuries. Communists spent their expropriations on military projects. But capitalists devoted the lion's share of their ill-gotten gains to business investment. Thus theft was used to help raise the capital that made nations like America and Great Britain rich and powerful.

With this in mind, we can state the conditions under which credit expansion (which is a form of spoliation) leads to economic progress. Two conditions, in particular, must be met: first, there must exist in society a class of entrepreneurs willing and eager to redirect capital into promising new innovations; and second, this class of entrepreneurs must be among the principle beneficiaries of the credit expansion. If the newly created credits wind up in the hands of timid men or the idle rich or the lazy and thriftless poor, it would be as if all the newly created money had been flushed down a massive toilet. You will simply have runaway inflation and the gradual impoverishment of all decent and hardworking men.

The key to civilization and prosperity is the spontaneous development of methods whereby the vices of human nature are made to work *for* society instead of *against* it. Spoliation works for society when it helps transfers capital into the hands of those most fit and willing to make good use of it. How spoliation is made to work in this way is anyone's guess. One thing is for sure: it is not something that can be legislated or "intended." It arises spontaneously, out of the mores. Either a given society has the mores and institutions that allow spoliation to work for the good of the country, or it doesn't. At the present state of our knowledge, that is about the most that can be said about it.

8. The Economics Profession: An Autopsy

Is orthodox economic theory, as professed within academia, in a state crisis? I would argue that the word *crisis* is too mild to describe the actual state of the economics profession. If it were in crisis, those within the profession would at least have some inkling of the problem. But the majority of economists seem blithely oblivious to the fact that the entire superstructure of orthodox economics is a complete and hopeless sham. While it would be an exaggeration to compare modern economics with, say, alchemy or numerology, the differences aren't as great as the judicious critic might wish.

In the late nineties, the British economist Paul Ormerod published a book entitled *The Death of Economics* which argued that "the orthodoxy of economics, trapped in an idealised, mechanistic view of the world, is powerless to assist ... a world economy in crisis." (1997, 3) Many professional economists greeted the book with scorn. "Paul Ormerod must be a bitter old man who regrets that he chose to specialize in forecasting macroeconomics as a profession," wrote one amazon.com reviewer. "I find it hard to believe that Ormerod is an economist due to the continuous oversight/misrepresentation in his book." Another reviewer complained of "factual inaccuracies and petty point scoring" and concluded: "This obituary is premature. Reports of the death of economics have been greatly exaggerated." (Shortall 1996)

It would be naive to expect economists, who have a vested interest in protecting the methodology upon which their careers are based, to listen with patience and respect to any attack directed against the foundations of their so-called science. Ormerod himself noted a "clear correlation" between the degree of hostility shown his book "and the amount of taxpayers' money which the economist concerned and his or her institution receive to carry out conventional economic research." (1997, vi) But it goes beyond mere pecuniary interest. For many academic economists, it is primarily an ego problem—a question of overweening pride. They shrink from admitting that all those years of drudgery in graduate school were a colossal waste of time. Their self-respect is at stake; and where self-respect is at issue, rational argument becomes futile.

While I do not agree with everything in Ormerod's book, his contention that mainstream economic theory is isolated from reality can hardly be denied. Economists claim that their theories describe "how the world actually operates," but they see "no need to examine this empirically." (1997, 20) This alienation from reality manifests itself most shamelessly in the occult art of economic forecasting. In my essay "Notes Toward a Theory of the Business Cycle," I mentioned the dismal record of economic forecasting. Ormerod provides further evidence of the failure of economic prognostication. "The record of economists in understanding and forecasting the economy at the macro-level is not especially impressive," writes Ormerod. "Indeed, uncharitable writers might be inclined to describe it as appalling." (1997, 93) Ormerod goes on to detail some of the huge failures in forecasting. The Japanese recession, he notes, "by far the deepest since the war, was not predicted. Neither the strength of the recovery in America in the second half of 1992 nor the slow-down in the first half of 1993 was really anticipated. And in Europe, neither the turmoil in the ERM nor the depth of the recession in Germany was foreseen by the models." In fact, according to a survey by the Paris-based Organisation for Economic Co-operation and Development, its own forecasting records and those of the IMF were no better at predicting the future course of inflation and output than was the assumption that these two economic variables would remain unchanged. Economic forecasting, whether done by international economic organizations, governments, or universities generally has a dismal track record. And this remains true regardless of the ideological propensities of the forecasters. "A survey of the accuracy of British economic forecasts, for example, carried out by the London Business School in 1993, concluded that differences over time between the predictions from the various schools of thought are very small," attests Ormerod. "But the most striking fact to emerge from this study is that errors in forecasts are much greater than differences between apparently contending schools of thought. This is by no means a new discovery, but it represents valuable confirmation of previous studies over the years which have come to the same conclusion." (1997, 104-105)

In other words, economic forecasts are close to worthless. If we wish to get an idea of where the economy is likely to go, we might do better consulting an astrologer or a psychic than we would a professional economist. And although the value of economics cannot rest solely on making forecasts and guessing the future, the fact that the prognostications of economists are unlikely to be a jot more accurate than those of soothsayers, spiritual mediums, political cranks, and other such frauds does not speak well for the discipline. Something is terribly wrong with most of what passes for orthodox economics. Many of the basic theories of economics have little if anything to do with reality. They are mere abstract figments of an excessively pedantic imagination. The general theory of equilibrium, for instance, derived from the theoretical cerebrations of the Swiss economist Leon Walras, is, as Ormerod puts it, "a travesty of reality." Yet this theory, despite its glaring absurdities, has become one of the profession's holiest of holies. Anyone who dares to question its importance and validity places himself well beyond the pale and demonstrates, in the eyes of the economic fraternity, that he and his views can be easily dismissed out of hand.

This is not to imply that economists don't have reservations about the general theory of equilibrium. Economists well know that, as a description of reality, the theory leaves a great deal to be desired. But it is not the theory's descriptive content that constitutes the main problem. No, it is the theory's methodological *raison d'être* from which all the trouble stems: its wholehearted embrace of mathematical mechanism.

The philosopher Thomas Kuhn, in his famous book *The Structure of Scientific Revolutions*, argued that every science requires what he called a paradigm, which Kuhn defined as a kind of interpretive framework that guides the scientist in the development of both the methods and the goals of his research. Most so-called "normal science," Kuhn argued, involves little more than "an attempt to force nature into the preformed and relatively inflexible box that the paradigm supplies. No part of the aim of normal science is to call forth new sorts of phenomena; *indeed those that will not fit the box are often not seen at all.*" (1962, 24, italics added)

The general equilibrium theory, with its utterly arrogant and intolerant commitment to quantification, measurement, and a sterile, math-based logic, amounts to little more than a Kuhnian paradigm. Such paradigms, as Kuhn went to great lengths to explain, are of course necessary before anything remotely describable as science can take place at all. The process of knowing cannot begin without an interpretive framework or paradigm. As Kant famously said, "Thoughts without content are empty, perceptions without understanding are blind." Theories are needed to make sense of that vast heap of disparate perceptions known as experience. "Our intellect does not draw its laws from nature," admonished Kant, "but imposes them on nature." Or rather, as Kuhn puts it, "Surveying the rich experimental literature … makes one suspect that something like a paradigm is prerequisite to perception itself. What man sees depends both upon what his previous visual-conceptual experience has taught him to see. In the absence of such training there can only be, in William James' phrase, 'a bloomin' buzzin' confusion.'" (1962, 113)

Kant's assumption that the mind imposes laws on nature involves a bit of philosophical license, a regrettable lapse into idealism. Contrary to what idealists continually assert, the mind does not impose anything onto reality. Only a very conceited philosopher would make so bold an assertion. But the mind does require theories or frameworks or paradigms (call them what you will) before it can interpret and comprehend experience. This poses a bit of a problem for our intrepid methodologist. How can our ideas describing reality possibly be true if such ideas must be based on previous theories which are *not* (and never can be) derived from reality? The philosopher Karl Popper proposed a solution to this paradox as follows: "Our intellect does not draw its laws from nature, but tries—with varying degrees of success—to impose upon nature laws which it freely invents." (1963, 191) In other words, our interpretive frameworks are not the rigid categories proposed by Kant or the arbitrary paradigms of Kuhn, but are fluid and provisional theoretical constructs which can be adjusted and improved over time. To be sure, such adjustments are not easy. Kuhn is correct when he stresses the inflexible nature of these interpretive paradigms. The point I wish to stress in contrast to Kuhn is the indubitable fact that not all paradigms are created equal, that some are clearly more superior as interpretive frameworks than others. Kuhn seems to imply that all paradigms are more or less equal, that truth, or at least the truth of all interpretive frameworks, is altogether relative. This view of the matter is clearly implied by his contention that there exists no cumulative development in the maturity and refinement of scientific paradigms—a very questionable assertion, to say the least. The paradigms that dominate scientific interpretation and research today are clearly more powerful and reliable than the paradigms that dominated what passed for science in the Middle Ages.

If all that Kuhn was really trying to say is that later interpretive schema are not necessarily better than earlier ones and that progress in the development of paradigms can never be taken for granted, then there would be no reason to quibble. Obviously, the progression of knowledge is not guaranteed. For any number of reasons, a specific science or discipline may regress over time. As a matter of historical fact, this has not happened in the hard sciences, which have enjoyed substantial progress since the seventeenth and eighteenth centuries. Progress in the social sciences, on the other hand, has been less propitious. In terms of the accumulation of fact, a great deal of work has been done. But in terms of our understanding of those facts, the social sciences for many decades now have been doing little else than spinning their cognitive wheels. In terms of broad understanding, do we really know that much more about society or politics or the economy than was known fifty years ago? No, I don't think so. Only in psychology has real progress been made. The rest of social science remains largely moribund, with progress existing only within overly specialized (and hence largely trivial) domains. In terms of general theory, no social scientist understands society a jot better than Max Weber, Joseph Schumpeter or Vilfredo Pareto did.

How can this be? Why has progress within the social sciences come to a sudden halt? I would venture to guess that the reason has to do with the paradigms that dominate research and scholarship within the social sciences. Social science is afflicted with bad paradigms, with interpretive frameworks that fail to correspond with reality. The most conspicuous example of a bad paradigm is the so-called Standard Social Science Model, which asserts, in the words of anthropologist Margaret Mead, "that human nature is almost unbelievably malleable, responding accurately and contrastingly to contrasting cultural conditions." (Pinker 2002, 25) Those who interpret social facts on the basis of this utterly untenable and scandalously utopian interpretive paradigm will end up with a very warped view of society.

Although economics has escaped the corruption of the Standard Social Science Model, it has not been so fortunate regarding other questionable paradigms. In particular, the paradigm of the general equilibrium theory, with its sterile mathematical formalism, has held economics in a death grip since at least World War II. An examination of this entirely gratuitous interpretive framework holds the key to understanding why economics has become so irrelevant to the real world.

Interpretive theories or paradigms become dominant within a particular science because of their ability to solve what are considered the main problems of the field. The early pioneers of general equilibrium theory and mathematical economics nearly all had backgrounds in the physical sciences. Walras and Pareto were engineers; Jevons held a position as assayer to the Australian mint; Irving Fisher, before earning the first Ph.D. ever awarded by Yale, published works on astronomy, mechanics, and geometry. These engineers and mathematicians, when they turned to the study economics, were put off by the literary bent of the leading thinkers of the discipline. Men like J.S. Mill, David Ricardo, Jean-Baptiste Say, and Adam Smith were either men of letters or businessmen who wrote for the general public. Smith and Mill were prominent philosophers as well as economists. To men of scientific training the study of economics, as practiced by these literary gentlemen, was sorely lacking the scientific rigor found in the disciplines of physics and chemistry. They believed that economics, before it could become a respectable science in its own right, had to make use of the methods of the hard sciences. Inevitably, this meant applying advanced mathematics to economic research. "It is clear that Economics, if it is to be a science at all, must be a mathematical one," insisted Jevons. (Schumpeter 1951, 103) Mathematics, it was thought, would bring greater precision to the discipline. "Familiarity with the [concepts of mathematical economics]—and with such notions as systems of equations, determinateness, stability, all of which admit of simple explanations—changes one's whole attitude to the problems that arise from theoretical schemata of the quantitative relations between things," averred Joseph Schumpeter, who, although he rarely used mathematics in his own economic work, never missed an opportunity to champion the cause. Mathematics gives to economic problems, argued Schumpeter, "a new definiteness"; "new methods of proof and disproof emerge; the maximum of return may be distilled from the little we know about the form of the relations between our variables; and the logic of infinitesimals disposes automatically of much controversial matter that, without its help, clogs the wheels of analytic advance." (1954, 955-956)

Schumpeter's points can be summarized as the *precision argument for mathematical economics*. There are other arguments that can be advanced in the econometric cause as well. A closely related argument stresses the role that mathematics plays in one of the most critical theories of modern economics, the theory of marginal utility, which states that men value, not an entire good or service, but only the last available or marginal unit of the good or service. (1949, 123) The theory assumes that individuals "carry out rational calculations and consume an amount of any particular product such that the utility derived from the consumption of the final unit of it—the marginal utility—was equal to the cost of obtaining that unit." (Ormerod 1997, 50)

Apologists for mathematical economics have made the claim that the concept of marginal utility is essentially mathematical, and that by subjecting it to methods of higher mathematics the economist is merely following the logic of the concept to its ultimate conclusions.

I will have more to say of this anon. But first let us glance at one other argument made on behalf of mathematical economics, perhaps the most plausible of all. One of the most distinctive features of economic reality is the interdependent nature of economic phenomenon—the fact that so many processes and events exercise a sort of reciprocal causation on one another. The general theory of equilibrium was developed in part to describe the interdependence between economic variables. "It is the mutual dependence of economic phenomena which makes the use of mathematics indispensable for studying these phenomena," wrote Vilfredo Pareto, the most brilliant of the early mathematical economists. "Ordinary logic can serve well enough for studying the relations of cause and effect, but soon becomes impotent when it is a matter of relations of mutual dependence. The latter, in rational mechanics and in pure economics, necessitate the use of mathematics." (1909, 180)

What is wrong with these arguments? Doesn't economics deal with quantities, with such things as prices, marginal propensities, gross national product, the money supply, and other such *numeric* indicators, all of which provide a precise accounting of relevant economic facts? Shouldn't economics make use of all the tools at its command, including the mathematical ones?

It involves an enormous error of judgment to think so—an egregious misunderstanding of the scope and relevance of economic knowledge. While it is true that certain economic values can be represented numerically, only a very shallow intellect would conclude from this fact that economics can be a mathematical science. Economics can never be a mathematical science—not in any meaningful sense of the word. The primary obstacle rests in the fact that human action and human willing are central to economic phenomena—that without such action and willing, no economic phenomenon would ever arise.

This point, which seems obvious to good sense, has been completely ignored and forgotten by the vast majority of economists. Yet it was understood by the classical economists—by those who originally opposed the development of mathematical economics. The arguments advanced by Irish economist John Elliot Cairnes have lost none of their relevance in the fourteen decades since they were first published:

"So far as I can see, economic truths are not discoverable through the instrumentality of Mathematics," Cairnes wrote in the 1870s. "If this view be unsound, there is at hand an easy means of refutation—the production of an economic truth, not before known, which has been thus arrived at; but I am not aware that up to the present any such evidence has been furnished of the efficacy of the mathematical method. In taking this ground I have no desire to deny that it may be possible to employ geometrical diagrams or mathematical formulæ for exhibiting economic doctrines reached *by other paths;* and it may be that there are minds for which this mode of presenting the subject has advantages. What I venture to deny is the doctrine ... that economic knowledge can be extended by such means; that Mathematics can be applied to the development of economic truth, as it has been applied to the development of mechanical and physical truth; and, unless it can be shown, either that mental feelings admit of being expressed in precise quantitative forms, or, on the other hand, that economic phenomena do not depend upon mental feelings, I am unable to see how this conclusion can be avoided." (1888, iv-v)

Nothing more need be said on the subject than this. The inability to quantify mental states—that is, the palpable absurdity of measuring, numerically, acts of willing—provides enough evidence to dismiss mathematical economics out of hand. But since prejudices on behalf of this shallow superstition are so rooted, I will provide additional evidence against it.

The early fabricators of mathematical economics suffered from an intellectual disease which the great Austrian economist, F.A. Hayek, identified as "scientism." Borrowing the term from the French, Hayek defined scientism as "a slavish imitation of the method and language of science." (1952, 24) Behaviorism, which, along with the Freudian imposture, ruled the psychological roost during the first half of the twentieth century, represents a cardinal example of this attitude. The behaviorist banished from his universe everything subjective and immeasurable, including ideas, beliefs, desires, feelings, and even consciousness. As behaviorist E. C. Tolman put it, since "all that can ever actually be observed in fellow human beings ... is behavior, the study of mental states is unnecessary." (Polanyi 1962, 372) This sort of myopic hubris led behaviorists to adopt views that have no meaningful correspondence with reality, such as J.B. Watson's infamous boast: "Give me a dozen healthy infants, well-formed, and my own specified world to bring them up in and I'll guarantee to take any one at random and train him to become any type of specialist I might select—doctor, lawyer, artist, merchant-chief, and yes, even beggar-man and thief, regardless of the talents, penchants, tendencies, abilities, vocations, and race of his ancestors." (Pinker 2002, 19)

Of course, we now know that behaviorism was incapable of doing any such thing. The ruling paradigm of behaviorism was simply wrong. Human nature cannot be understood entirely from the outside. To banish introspection because it is not "scientific" or "objective" is to do away with a tool indispensable to psychological knowledge.

The application of mathematics to economics is analogous to the application of behaviorism to psychology. It evinces, not insight or understanding, but a morbid insensibility to the sources of economic knowledge coupled with an intellectual snobbery that is revolting to good sense. The behavior of human beings simply cannot be described let alone elucidated and understood by mathematical formulas and equations. Inanimate objects can be understood simply by describing them, mathematically or otherwise, because such objects have no souls, no sensibility, no motives, no consciousness, no purpose. They are non-teleological entities. To understand them in their physical aspect is to understand them to the very depths of their being. With human beings it is far different. Without reference to their desires and motives, their thoughts and feelings, human beings cannot be understood at all. Their physical bodies tell us nothing essential about them. Yet it is only their bodies, their superficial external shells, that can be weighed and measured. None of their mental states—not their motives, not their desires, not their thoughts or feelings—can be expressed intelligibly in numerical form.

Any attempt to quantify human nature assumes a mechanical view of human action. Men become, under this view, mere machines. Economists, for their part, view men as little more than utility maximizing machines—as, in other words, a *homo oeconomicus*, the individual who seeks nothing else but to achieve his objectives in the most cost efficient manner possible. This particular figment of the economist's imagination has weathered much criticism of late—so much criticism, in fact, that many professional economists no longer attempt to defend it. Instead, they claim, with some but not complete justification, that they don't believe in any such thing, that the *homo oeconomicus* is little more than an oversimplified abstraction, a useful tool for analysis. But if it is a mere abstraction, what is it abstracting from? That human beings sometimes behave as little more than utility maximizers and rational calculating machines is occasionally true; but to reduce all their relevant economic activity to this one abstraction constitutes a wanton travesty.

The most critical problem with mechanical descriptions of human behavior is that they inevitably ignore everything they cannot explain. The general equilibrium theory, which is a mechanistic theory *par excellence*, is entirely static in scope; it largely ignores the developmental element of economic reality. Machines don't develop; they simply go through their particular motions in a zombie-like fashion. So it should not surprise us that a mechanistic model of the economy should either ignore or misunderstand the developmental side of capitalism. Economic development is a product, ultimately, of applying new ideas to old problems. That, in short, is what innovation is all about; and it is innovation, more than anything else, that fuels economic development. The general theory of equilibrium cannot explain innovation, as Schumpeter himself admits. "Continuous changes, which may in time, by continual adaptation through innumerable small steps, make a great department store out of a small retail business, come under 'static' analysis," wrote Schumpeter. "But 'static' analysis is not only unable to predict the consequences of discontinuous changes in traditional way of doing things; it can neither explain the occurrence of such productive revolutions nor the phenomena which accompanies them. It can only investigate the new equilibrium position after the changes have occurred. It is just this occurrence of the 'revolutionary' change that is our problem, the problem of economic development in a very narrow and formal sense." (1934, 62-63)

I must emphasize how critical this whole issue is. The capitalist system is not a mechanism, it is a process in continuous development, driven by innovation. Anyone who does not understand this is incapable of understanding capitalism. Mechanistic theories, because of their inability to explain capitalist development, constitute a hindrance to understanding economic reality, obstacles thrown in the path of the intellect. As an example, consider the role that human creativity plays in economics. Because creativity cannot be explained mechanically or expressed numerically, economists tend to ignore or downplay its influence. Yet it exists as an economic reality for all that, and economic theory does itself little good by pretending that it doesn't exist or (even worse) that it lacks theoretical significance. The creativity of capitalism has transformed the world beyond the recognition of our ancestors. In the face of this transformation, modern economics gapes like an idiot, utterly oblivious to the meaning of it all.

This brings up another serious problem of mathematical economics. The systems of equations used in economic theory simply cannot convey the deeper realities involved in economic processes. There is a peculiar sort of obtuseness at the core of mathematical economics. Its brilliance is entirely formal and technical; there is no depth or profundity to it. It sees the vague forms and shapes of economic phenomena without, however, understanding them.

This may seem like an intolerably vague way of putting it; but I doubt it can be expressed any more clearly than this. It is one thing to be able to identify or describe a thing; but to say one *understands* it is a different matter altogether. Understanding involves an identification of the deeper relations and causative forces behind the object of inquiry. The business cycle, for instance, cannot be understood without knowledge of the economic and social factors that bring it about. To merely express the business cycle mathematically does little to illuminate the understanding. Mathematical equations, at best, lend but a *semblance* of understanding to the matter at hand. They evoke a kind of aesthetic response, a feeling of intellectual satisfaction that is easily confused with genuine insight.

As an illustration of this psychological illusion, consider the notorious equation of exchange, $MV=PT$, where M equals the quantity of money, V equals "velocity," or the rate at which money circulates through the economy, P equals the average price level of goods and services, and T equals the quantity of goods and services in the economy as a whole, also sometimes regarded as "real income." The equation seems to state an obvious truth: namely, that the amount of money spent equals the amount of goods sold. But if we look at it more closely, we discover that, behind all the pretentious algebraic symbols lurks a serious error.

What, precisely, is this surreptitious error? To put it as simply as possible, the main error is that the equation really doesn't *explain* anything. The main point of MV=PT is to explain the price level. Since V and T are believed to be roughly constant over time, the argument is made that the price level must be determined by the quantity of money. Thus, if the quantity of money is increased, the price level will rise; that is to say, inflation, which measures the rate at which the price level increases, will rise. If, on the other hand, the quantity of money is decreased, then the price level will fall and deflation will ravage the economy.

In very rough terms, this is somewhat true. An increase in the money supply will, all things being equal, tend to bring about more inflation. The problem, however, with the equation of exchange is that it implies that the whole process by which this comes about is entirely mechanical, as if the economy were simply a giant Swiss watch made of countervailing levers and pulleys.

In the real world, the price level is not determined mechanically, as the equation of exchange would have us believe. Money is a good like any other. Its value is determined by the subjective preferences of individuals. If individuals decide to hoard money rather than spend it on goods and services, the demand for money will increase, and the price level will fall even if the money supply remains constant. How, perchance, does the equation of exchange hope to illustrate such a circumstance? The simple truth of the matter is that it cannot. Human desires do not exist in the world described by MV=PT, which can only explain an increase in the demand for money as a decrease in its velocity! And what does it mean to say that velocity has decreased? It means nothing. The really important and fruitful question would be: *why* has velocity decreased? Only when you begin to understand the actual motives of economic agents—of the men and women who decide what happens in the economy—can you make sense of what is *really* going on. Nor can these motives be understood by mechanical models, with their hopelessly quantitative biases. Motives always involve qualitative judgments. People don't think mathematically, in terms of variables and equations. They think qualitatively, in terms of vague estimates and educated guesses. Economists, when considering the motives and judgments of economic agents, must think qualitatively as well. Otherwise, they will understand nothing.

As an example of how the quantity theory of money misleads and confuses its proponents, consider Milton Friedman's analysis of monetary policy during the Great Depression. Friedman argues that the Great Depression was caused by the Federal Reserve's monetary mismanagement. In particular, Friedman sites the fact that the money supply dropped by about a third during the early years of the depression. (Skousen 2001, 401-403) Why did it do so? Here, under the influence of the equation of exchange, Friedman goes astray. He would have us believe that the great contraction in the money supply was caused by the Fed's unwillingness to aggressively pour liquidity into the banking system. This assessment, however, only makes sense if we assume that the relationship between the price level and the monetary supply is as mechanical as the equation of exchange makes it. In reality, the relationship between the money supply, the price level, and the economy as a whole is not a simple mechanism, easily grasped by mathematical symbols, as any forthright attempt to understand economic phenomenon will reveal. Understanding economic reality means getting at the deeper causes of economic events. What, may we be so bold as to inquire, *caused* the money supply to contract during the Great Depression? It would be misleading to blame it merely on monetary contraction caused by mismanagement. If we want to grasp what was really going on during the Great Depression, we have to dig further, we have to ask more questions. The cause of the Great Depression, Friedman argues, was the Fed's tightening of monetary policy. But why did the Fed tighten monetary policy? The Fed tightened because it had no choice. The Fed had been pursuing easy money policies during most of the twenties, leading to an enormous expansion of credit. When credit expands dramatically, the *quality* of credit inevitably declines, leading to an alarming increase in bankruptcies and loan defaults. Mathematical economists, with their emphasis on the mechanical and the quantifiable, often overlook this aspect of the situation. The equation of exchange completely ignores the *quality* of money, assuming, instead, a mechanical relation based on quantity alone. By overemphasizing the quantitative element of the problem, mathematical economists end up believing that every contraction in the monetary supply can be met with a comparable expansion in liquidity. Never mind whether the contraction was initially caused by a previous expansion; nor let us worry our heads about the problem of the *quality* of expanded credit. As long as the numbers add up right in the end, everything should be fine.

For those who may be under the illusion that this issue is merely of academic significance, of little importance in the real world, I must needs point out that Friedman's analysis of the Great Depression has deeply influenced the conduct of the Federal Reserve in recent years. When the economy, after years of speculative excess, began tottering at the edge of a massive collapse in 2000, how did the Fed react to the crisis? It dropped interest rates as far as it could and flooded the banking system with liquidity. This has been the Fed's *modus operandi* ever since Alan Greenspan became its chairman in 1987. Every crisis has been greeted with the obligatory interest rate cuts and open market purchases. The consequence of this facile retreat into easy money policies is an economy awash in debt and speculative excess; an economy, moreover, that has become less and less responsive to the Fed's monetarist nostrums. Despite having lowered the Fed Fund's rate to just 1.25 percent in October of 2002, the economy remained moribund for several years.

Things were not so very different during the Great Depression. I have already mentioned the Fed's easy money policies during the twenties—policies that ultimately led to the catastrophic 1929 Stock Market crash. Consider the testimony of economist Benjamin Anderson, one of the shrewdest historians of the Great Depression, concerning the Fed's policies following the crash. "Late in December, 1929, one found the conviction among [the few responsible men in the Federal Reserve System] that monetary ease would have to wait for substantial liquidation of the volume of bank credit outstanding, secured by stocks and bonds. We were strong enough at the time to have gone through an orderly liquidation. But early in 1930 Federal Reserve policy quickly veered in the other direction, and the purchase of Government securities was resumed. The Federal Reserve System was gambling, using dangerous devices to stave off an unpleasant liquidation, and hoping for a return of the prosperity which was 'just around the corner.' They succeeded in making cheap money.

They succeeded in bringing about a further expansion of bank credits against securities. But the Federal Reserve also succeeded in bringing the banking system of the United States into an extremely vulnerable position, tragically revealed when the foreign run on our gold came in late 1931, and when depositors, fearful of individual banks, were taking cash out of these banks and hoarding it." (1949, 263)

Anderson's testimony on this issue is especially valuable, since he was one of the leading critics of the equation of exchange. In fact, in a book published in 1917, *The Value of Money,* Anderson thoroughly refuted Irving Fisher's version of the quantity theory of money. Stressing that any theory of money and credit "must be a dynamic theory," Anderson went on to point out that "a theory like the 'quantity theory' of money, which rests in the notions of 'static equilibrium' and 'normal adjustment,' abstracting from the 'transitional process of readjustment,' touches the real problems of money and credit not at all." (1913, vii)

If we compare Anderson's understanding of the Great Depression to that of Irving Fisher, the leading exponent of mathematical economics during the first three decades of the twentieth century, we find an excellent illustration of the inadequacy of math-based economic models. Anderson well understood that the Stock Market crash "was overdue, and long overdue." Stock market prices, Anderson recognized, "had reached levels so fantastic that a disastrous break was merely a question of time." (1949, 209-10) Contrast this with Irving Fisher's infamous remark, made just two weeks before the Stock Market crash. "Stock prices have reached what looks like a permanently high plateau," Fisher pontificated. "I expect to see the Stock Market a good deal higher than it is today within a few months."

Fisher's mathematical principles clearly led him astray. For all his surface brilliance, Fisher had no real understanding of money and credit, of speculation and excess. He lacked the one thing that is utterly necessary to an economist: good judgment. But judgment is a qualitative matter. It is an art, not a technique. One reason so many economists are attracted to mathematical methods is that it provides a technique that does not require any special gift or talent. A technique can be mastered through mere diligent imitation; an art can only be obtained through a combination of hard work and innate talent.

There exists a peculiar type of intellect that shows remarkable ability at calculation but is deficient in grasping the deeper significance of things. In extreme cases, such types are called idiot savants. Their inability to analyze and judge factual data renders them incapable of looking after themselves. In less extreme cases, such types are called pedants. Although not completely destitute of the ability to analyze facts, pedants often exhibit poor judgment. Their brilliance and ingenuity as human calculating machines blinds them to the deficiency of their analyzing skills, leading to all matter of pretentious and often idiotic prognostications. Irving Fisher's infamous "permanently high plateau" remark is a classic example of the myopia of insight that plagues the quantification-mongers of this sort.

The problem with economics is that the pedants have taken over the profession and turned it into their own private preserve, which they jealously guard from all trespassers. Unless you are as pedantic and narrow-minded as they are, you will never be granted entry into the ivory towers of their sham wisdom. They defend their status as "experts" and "scholars," not with brains or wisdom or sage prognostications, but with mere dribblings of letters from the alphabet pedantically spattered on sheepskin. Professor Pedant most emphatically *is*—as he never ceases reminding us—a *Ph.D.*, and therefore must never be challenged by someone lacking these magical three letters.

Over a hundred years ago, William James warned against the pernicious affects of what he called "the Ph.D. Octopus." "Human nature is once for all so childish that every reality becomes a sham somewhere, and in the minds of Presidents and Trustees the Ph.D. degree is in point of fact already looked upon as a mere advertising resource, a manner of throwing dust in the Public's eyes," James wrote. "The truth is that the Doctor-Monopoly in teaching, which is becoming so rooted an American custom, can show no serious grounds whatsoever for itself in reason. As it actually prevails and grows in vogue among us, it is due to childish motives exclusively. In reality it is but a sham, a bauble, a dodge, whereby to decorate the catalogues of schools and colleges." James clearly saw what would happen if the prestige associated with this bauble were not nipped in the bud. "We ought to look to the future carefully, for it takes generations for a national custom, once rooted, to be grown away from." American universities "should never

194

cease to regard themselves as the jealous custodians of personal and spiritual spontaneity.... They ought to guard against contributing to the increase of officialism and snobbery and insincerity as against a pestilence; they ought to keep truth and disinterested labor always in the foreground, treat degrees as secondary incidents, and in season and out of season make it plain that what they live for is to help men's souls, and not to decorate their persons with diplomas." (1903)

Not surprisingly, James' strictures were ignored by the academic establishment. The Ph.D. Octopus is now more extensive than ever; its tentacles, dripping with poisonous spittle, reach into every nook and cranny of the American spirit, grasping by the throat any bold and enterprising spirit who threatens the academic status quo. Mainstream economics is unlikely to suffer reform as long as it remains within the university system. Despite the existence of heterodox schools of economic thought on the fringes, the established *pedantcracy* will not be overthrown any time soon. Such disagreement that exists among the orthodox is largely superficial and does not reach down to fundamentals. Most academic economists accept the essential role of mathematics in economic thought and there is no reason to believe that this will change any time soon.

This brings us back to the central question of this essay: *What is wrong with mathematical economics?* Some of the groundwork that will go toward providing an answer to this question has already been laid. We have found that mathematical economics relies on the tacit assumption that economic forces operate on mechanical principles. We have also taken note of the essential superficiality of mathematical thinking—how it inevitably leads the mind astray, replacing thought with mere calculation. At this point, we are far enough along in our critical analysis to take on the three most prominent arguments made on behalf of mathematical economics. The first of these, *the precision argument*, emphasizes the clarity which mathematical methods bring to economic analysis, the "new methods of proof and disproof" that emerge as a consequence of thinking in quantitative terms. There are a number of things wrong with this argument, not the least of which is the palpable fact that mathematical economics is infamously imprecise in its results. According to Paul Ormerod, forecasts based on the immensely complicated models of mathematical economists "are so unreliable that virtually no model operator in the world dares allow his ... model loose on its own." To avoid detection, economic forecasters "interfere" with the model's output before any results are published. "These 'judgmental adjustments' can be, and often are, extensive," notes Ormerod. "Every model operator knows about the process of altering the output of a model, but this remains something of a twilight world, and is not well documented in the literature." One of the few studies ever done on model tinkering found that, in the absence of such adjustments, the forecasting record of models would have been significantly worse. (1997, 103-104)

It is important to grasp what this means vis-à-vis the credibility of mathematical economics. If economic forecasters, using highly complex mathematical models to make prognostications, are forced to tinker with their numbers to prevent them from producing patently absurd results, this demonstrates, beyond any reasonable doubt, the futility of applying math to macroeconomic thought. When faced with making actual prognostications, economists trust their intuition far more than they trust mathematical methods. Why, then, do they continue to insist that economics must be mathematical? Isn't it time that we expose the sham for what it is and move on?

There is another problem with the precision argument, one that is entirely methodological in nature. Mathematics is a purely analytical science; which is to say, all mathematical truths are essentially logical and, *ipso facto*, circular. They are true because of how their terms are defined. The equation *2+2=4* is true because the numbers *two* and *four* and the *plus* and *equals* signs are defined to make the equation true. Had they been defined differently, the equation might not be true.

Mathematics involves working out the logical implications of the concept of number. Every conclusion of mathematics is implicit in the basic axioms of the science. Mathematics is little more than a vast and immensely ingenious tautology.

Mathematical economics, as long as it remains steadfastly within the realm of pure theory, is no less tautological and circular. Take the famous theory of general equilibrium, which, by describing the economy as a system of equations, attempts to show that all prices and quantities are uniquely determined. (Bannock et al 1972, 421) Many economists regard this theory as one of the foremost achievements in economics.

Schumpeter declared that the theory would "stand comparison with the achievements of theoretical physics." (1954, 827) Yet the theory accomplishes nothing beyond demonstrating the implications of its premises. The achievement of the theory is not that it demonstrates the unique determination of prices and quantities, but that it discovered a set of premises out of which the demonstration could be deduced. It is a clever tautology with little if any application to the real world. The assumptions it is based on are either gross over-simplifications or outright falsehoods. The theory assumes that the economy is made up of a large number of small firms, none of which enjoys any degree of control over the markets in which it functions; that human beings are rational utility maximizers; that no barriers exist for entry into every market; and that all market participants have access to "perfect knowledge"—that is, complete information about prices, quantities of available goods, revenues of firms, etc. None of these assumptions correspond to what we find in reality. They are arbitrarily introduced to preserve the circularity of the theory, so that the proof that all prices and quantities are uniquely determined remains valid.

By establishing their proof, the mathematical economists have achieved, at best, a Phyrric victory. Proof is little more than a kind logical consistency between ideas. The truth of any theory about matters of fact cannot be established by logic alone. The most that can be done on behalf of a theory is to corroborate it with tests or other forms of evidence. To demand a logical proof for a theory about matters of fact is to demand the impossible. Mathematical economics, in proving that, under conditions of equilibrium, prices and quantities are uniquely determined, has accomplished nothing of significance. Even if the theory were in some respects valid, it would still fail on the grounds of irrelevance. Who cares whether prices and quantities are *uniquely* determined? Of what significance is it to explaining economics? What does it help us understand? Very little, if anything at all!

What, then, can we conclude about the precision argument? That it fails to deliver what it promises. Precision in economics is impossible, as is demonstrated by the imprecision of its results. But even if it were possible, it would be useless and irrelevant, because of the tautological character of mathematical analysis. Mathematics can only bestow upon economics an illusory or trivial sort of precision. Such a precision, as the economist Henry Hazlitt would be quick to remind us, "is worse than worthless; it is a fraud. It gives our results a merely spurious precision. It gives an illusion of knowledge in place of the candid confession of ignorance, vagueness, or uncertainty which is the beginning of wisdom." (1959, 99)

Having disposed of the precision argument for mathematical economics, we can next turn our attention to the marginal utility argument, which insists that the very concept of marginal utility demands the use of advanced mathematics, particularly calculus, with its emphasis on infinitely small steps and, *ipso facto*, the analysis of marginal quantities. Calculus is a forbidding subject, way above the heads of most people. By bringing calculus to bear on problems of economics, the discipline is turned into an occult science understood only by specially trained experts, who can turn around and claim that anyone who does not understand calculus is not qualified to criticize or even question their recondite pronouncements. There is no reason, however, to allow mere pedants to intimidate lay people with advanced mathematics. The application of calculus to marginal utility constitutes a palpable fraud. No form of utility, whether marginal or otherwise, can ever be quantified or measured. Indeed, the very concept of marginal utility is itself somewhat overrated in economics, even among non-mathematical economists. It was originally devised to explain why a substance such as gold, which doesn't seem to have much practical utility, is more valuable than a substance like water, a commodity essential to life itself. The economist Ballvé explained the concept as follows: "The economists who formulated the theory of marginal utility took account of the fact that economic utility is the power to satisfy any want.... Hence the difference between the utility of iron and that of gold is not determined by comparing the serviceability of *all* gold and *all* the iron in the world, but consists in the difference between the economic services, expressed in terms of supply and demand, that can be rendered by the *last available unit* of the one or the other metal." (1956, 23)

If this is all that the law of marginal utility sought to establish, there would be nothing objectionable in it. But economists have not been content to leave well enough alone. They have been eager to apply it well beyond the bounds of common sense and reality. One such extension of this law is the assertion that consumption is subject to diminishing marginal laws of return, so that each additional unit consumed provides less satisfaction. The first ice cream cone provides greater utility than the fifth. Although this might seem pretty obvious at first blush, if we go a bit deeper into human nature, we find that it isn't always true that the fifth of anything necessarily provides less utility, less satisfaction than the first. Suppose, for instance, you have two siblings. In that case, the fifth cone might provide more satisfaction to one of the siblings, if the other sibling only received four. Since satisfaction is a very subjective matter, there is no guarantee that the theory of marginal utility will always hold true. Many people are more concerned with status than they are with the actual physical satisfaction they may receive from consuming a given unit. Moreover, economic decisions are rarely based on the utility derived from the actual consumption of a specific good. Instead they are based on an estimation of *possible* utility. Consumers, when they buy anything, are simply trying to guess what will *likely* bring them satisfaction. The guess is something different from the actual satisfaction—as frustrated consumers know all too well. To apply advanced mathematical constructs to such vague and immeasurable quantities as utility is to engage in an activity that has more in common with blind man's bluff than with legitimate scholarship.

While the marginal utility argument for mathematical economics is just a ruse, an attempt to intimidate the uninitiated with the mind numbing complexities of calculus, the last argument this essay will examine is somewhat more plausible. Indeed, as I mentioned earlier, it is the most plausible argument of all. I refer to the mutual dependence argument. In economics, hardly anything happens by a single cause. There are often many causes, most of which mutually influence each other. One example is the causative effects of wealth on the economy, the fact that the production of wealth *tends* to undermine the very conditions that brought it into being, so that, in Pareto's words, wealth "is its own grave-digger, it destroys what gives it birth." (1909, 300) Wealth fosters political demagoguery and welfare statism, both of which exact a toll on wealth and wealth making. Wealth also softens men and manners, leading to demoralization in the face of a hostile world eager to plunder or destroy wealth. Another example of interdependency might consist in how various economic variables mutually influence each other, such as inflation, interest rates, the money supply, the employment rate, national income, and the like. An increase in the money supply, especially if accomplished through credit expansion, will lower interest rates, increase employment and investment, stimulate economic growth and raise national income. But it will also increase debt, which will eventually lead to more defaults and (possibly) a contraction in the money supply, which will cause deflation, unemployment, and bring about a lower national income.

The apologists for mathematical economics insist that the only way to take account of the interdependence of economic phenomena is by expressing it in mathematical equations. The problem with this line of reasoning is that it fails to take into account the all too obvious fact that there exist no fixed mathematical relations between economic phenomena. Economists can, of course, gather economic data and stick them into equations. For instance, a mathematical economist could create a set of equations which attempts to describe the relation between the inflation rate, the money supply, the national income, the employment rate, and so on. He could even find numbers for these variables and plug them into the equation. Unfortunately, every economic situation is unique and thus requires its own unique equation. This is one of the reasons why mathematical models perform so poorly. It is impossible to squeeze human behavior into an equation: human beings are just far too ingenious and unpredictable for that.

The most that can be said on behalf of these equations is that they can be used to model, in a very abstract and not very adequate fashion, how mutual dependence works in theory. They cannot, however, explain how mutual dependence works in reality. Indeed, by using mathematics to illuminate economic problems, the real issues are masked. The only way to grasp the relations between various economic phenomena is to study each of the relations as they interact with each other, and by mental construction attempt to grasp the web of mutual dependence that connects them all. This is what the mathematical economists do at the beginning of their constructions, guided, not by mathematical rigor, as they would like us to believe, but only by the light of their feeble intuitions; the mathematical equations are only added afterwards, but artificially and arbitrarily, lending the illusion of precision and logical rigor to what is little more than a piece of algebraic legerdemain.

Yet the problem goes even further than the inapplicability of the equations themselves. The mathematical logic behind the whole thing is itself a fallacy of some note. Strictly speaking, there is no "mutual dependence" between economic factors—not, in any case, in the mathematical sense of the term. The relations between economic factors are always in some sense causative. Certain factors may "depend" on others, as the inflation rate depends on the relationship between total output, the money supply, and the demand for money. But such dependence is purely tautological: it exists in the meanings of the terms. The *real* dependence, the relation between the various factors existing *in the real world*, is always causative and must be understood as such if its nature is ever to be grasped. This is not to say that there exists a direct causal link between all or most economic phenomena. Inflation does not cause an economy to boom, despite what economists say. On the contrary: inflation, or the rise in the price level, is merely a *symptom* of what causes the boom. The real cause is usually an expansion of credit, often brought about by the central bank, working at the behest of the government or the business community.

To avoid confusion, it would probably be preferable to use such phrases as "reciprocal causation" or "multiple causation" to describe the relations of economic phenomenon rather than "mutual dependence," with its suggestions of mathematical logic and mechanism. It would be even more advisable to do away with all the nonsense about equilibrium. This term was originally borrowed from physics. It has little if any bearing on economics. At best, it is a mere metaphor—and not a very apt one at that. As I have stated before, the equilibrium theory assumes a static economy; in Pareto's words, "economic equilibrium is the state which would maintain itself indefinitely if there were no changes in the conditions under which it is observed." (1909, 109) Originally, the idea of a static, changeless economy had value as a kind of thought experiment. The economist imagines a fictitious state where no change occurs and then examines what would happen if one change is introduced, then a second change, a third change, and so on. At some point, economists forgot that it was just a tool and turned it into one of their idols. Although many economists question its validity, it is still taught as orthodoxy in the universities, and "retains a strong grip on the intellectual sympathies of academic economists themselves."

(Ormerod, 1997, 76-77) Wouldn't it be better to rid ourselves of the concept altogether? Economists of the Austrian school have a concept which accomplishes all the legitimate analytical goals of equilibrium without all its dubious mathematical baggage. This concept is called the "evenly rotating economy," which Ludwig von Mises defined as "a fictitious system in which the market prices of all goods and services coincide with the final prices." The purpose of this imaginary construction is to "analyze the problems of change in the data and of unevenly and irregularly varying movement" by confronting them "with a fictitious state in which both are hypothetically eliminated." This method is necessary, argues von Mises, because there exist "no means of studying the complex phenomena of action other than first to abstract from change altogether, then to introduce and isolate the factor provoking change, and ultimately to analyze its effects under the assumption that other things remain equal." (1949, 247-248) In other words, the evenly rotating economy is little more than a thought experiment that helps the economist figure out what might happen under simplified conditions. The conditions are simplified to make them comprehensible. The real economy is far too complex for the human mind to grasp in its entirety. Hence the need for simplifying the vast complexity of reality into something more amenable to the human scale of comprehension.

Simplification will, it must be admitted, always involve a certain amount of cognitive distortion. We must always keep this in mind. The conclusions of economic analysis are little more than educated guesses or approximations. They can never attain a complete or fully adequate comprehension of economic reality. Economists would do well to remember this and adopt a humble attitude not merely toward their theories, but, more critically, toward the prognostications which are derived from these theories. Economists can never know with certainty what the economic future will bring. But a little humility can go along way toward reducing error in their forecasts.

The first order of business for the economics profession must be to rid itself of the incubus of mathematics. While there may be some value in math for accumulating and analyzing economic statistics, there is no place for math in economic theory. Economic theories must rest on an understanding of economic processes; and since these processes ultimately derive from human action, which itself is a product of human motivation, the implicit mechanism of mathematical methods can only lead the intrepid economist astray. If economics is ever to become a useful science again, it must descend from the lofty abstractions of mathematical analysis and return to the real world, where men of flesh and blood buy and sell in a real market and where the notion of economic equilibrium is a remote fantasy.

Part 3: Philosophy

9. In Defense of Intuition

"The more we know, the better our intuitions." —Christina Stead

The last three decades have witnessed an extraordinary revolution in one of the main disciplines of philosophy. For two millennia, epistemology, the study of human knowledge, has largely been confined to the speculations of rationalists and uncritical empiricists. Philosophers spent their time developing theories based, not on research, but on "introspection,"—in other words, on sloppy and uncritical observation. They were primarily interested, not in getting at the empirical truth of the matter, but merely in constructing theories that gave the appearance of an explanation. In doing so, they created a whole host of artificial problems, which they bequeathed to later generations of epistemologists, thus condemning centuries of philosophy to sterile debates about the meaning of words and other such hopeless muddles.

In the last thirty years, all this fruitless pedantry has been swept aside by the discoveries of cognitive science, which seeks to bring the methods of science to the study of epistemology. No more abstruse reasoning; no more verbal constructions based on hunches and introspective delusions; no more rationalistic hubris: now epistemology has finally become a science as reputable as physics or chemistry. At last we are beginning to understand how the mind works.

One of the first great shibboleths of speculative epistemology to fall by the wayside is the conviction, held by many philosophers, that human thinking, especially efficacious human thinking, is essentially logical in nature—that, in other words, thought and logic are intertwined right from the start, so that to think correctly one must think logically. Consider, as one example of this attitude, what J. S. Mill, an empiricist philosopher, wrote in his *System of Logic.* "By far the greatest portion of our knowledge, whether of general truths or of particular facts, being avowedly a matter of inference, nearly the whole, not only of science, but of human conduct, is amenable to the authority of logic. To draw inferences has been said to be the great business of life. Every one has daily, hourly, and momentary need of ascertaining facts which he has not directly observed; not from any general purpose of adding to his stock of knowledge, but because the facts themselves are of such importance to his interests or to his occupations. The business of the magistrate, of the military commander, of the navigator, of the physician, of the agriculturalist, is merely to judge of evidence, and to act accordingly. They all have to ascertain certain facts, in order that they may afterwards apply certain rules, either devised by themselves, or prescribed for their guidance by others; and so they do this well or ill, so they discharge well or ill the duties of their several callings. It is the only occupation which the mind never ceases to be engaged." Mill concludes by describing logical reasoning as "the common judge and arbiter of all particular investigations." (1843, 5)

Mill, despite his status as the leading empirical philosopher of his generation, made no effort to corroborate these claims with empirical evidence. He simply took them for granted as true, as if they were so obvious that they didn't need empirical corroboration. In succumbing to this sort of anti-empirical dogmatism, Mill is hardly alone. In philosophy it is often assumed that rational thinking and logical thinking are one and the same. This is the "classical" view of rationality, the view that has dominated philosophy since Plato and Aristotle.

Through an exhaustive empirical study of human cognition, cognitive science has found that the classical view of rationality is wrong. "For many centuries, philosophers and others who have studied the human mind have believed that reason takes place according to the laws governing logic," writes Morton Hunt. "But the findings of cognitive science run counter to it: logical reasoning is not our usual—or natural—practice, and the technically invalid kinds of reason we generally employ work rather well in most of the everyday situations in which one might suppose rigorous deductive thinking was essential." (1982, 121)

If human beings don't in fact reason logically, how do they go about making inferences and reaching conclusions? According to cognitive science, *real* human thought proceeds largely by analogy and experience. "Naturalistic reasoning doesn't use the rules of inference but tends to be 'content-specific'—it uses rules that work in a particular area of experience." (1982, 138) Hence, the more experience an individual has of a particular subject or field, the better his judgments about it. If Peter has more experience troubleshooting computers than Mary, he will tend to have better judgment about computer problems than she will. To be sure, this is not always true. If Mary is a genius and Peter a dunce, Peter's judgment about computer problems may be worse than Mary's. But if we compare two individuals of equivalent intellectual ability, the one with more experience will tend to demonstrate better judgment.

There shouldn't be anything controversial in this. If anything, by pointing out such a bald commonplace, I come perilously close to belaboring the obvious. Knowledge, I am asserting, comes from experience. Yet there is more to the issue than this old homily. The word *experience* is scandalously vague. What do we mean when we say *knowledge comes from experience*? How do we, in point fact, *learn* from experience?

When people talk about learning from experience, they tacitly assume that such learning is *personal*, that it is unique to each person. Some things every individual must learn for himself. There is something incommunicable at the very core of experience—something that can be alluded to but never adequately described or explained or passed on through mere words. No amount of book learning, television watching, or college bull sessions can ever convey the wisdom gained from a long and exhaustive experience of a thing.

When I use the word *incommunicable* to describe such knowledge, it is important to understand precisely what is meant. What is incommunicable are not the results, the conclusions of such knowledge, but its justification. We often know something without being able to prove to others *how* we know it. In other words, what is incommunicable is the proof, the evidence supporting the knowledge-claim, not the knowledge itself. If the knowledge is in fact valid, others can use it, but they must accept it on faith. Not having the experiential prerequisites for judging the issue, they must defer to someone who does, or take the time to go learn it for themselves.

The non-expert, therefore, finds himself at the mercy of the expert. If the mechanic tells his customer that his transmission is shot and his brakes worn to the bone, the customer has little choice but to accept this diagnosis on faith. Even if the mechanic attempts to show his customer the damaged transmission and the worn brakes, this will hardly suffice to "prove" the mechanic's case, because his customer simply does not have the frame of reference necessary to make an adequate assessment of such evidence. Having no experience diagnosing and fixing automobiles, the customer has no understanding of their inner workings and can therefore make neither heads nor tails of worn brake pads or leaky transmissions. Being shown these items may make him a little more comfortable accepting what the mechanic tells him, but seeing them provides little more than a superficial understanding of the matter at hand. In any case, he could never have made the diagnosis on his own—at least not with any degree of certainty.

Although the mechanic cannot always explain to his clueless customers the reasons for his diagnosis, he can nearly always explain them to other mechanics. The problem of incommunicability, in this instance, exists largely between the expert and the non-expert. In other cases, the incommunicability of personal knowledge is far more radical, extending even to the individual's own mind. The individual thinks he knows something. The only problem is that he has no idea *how* he knows it. Not only is he incapable of explaining to others, even other experts, how he knows what he knows, he can't even explain it to himself.

Let us return to the problem of the mechanic and the clueless customer. From hard earned experience, some customers develop an intuitive sensibility that often helps them distinguish the honest from dishonest mechanics. Yet this knowledge may exist in nothing more definite than a vague hunch. If the customer has no actual evidence to go by, no references from other customers, no rumors of double-dealing and the like, he may have nothing else to go on but his intuitive feeling of the man. Are such intuitive feelings trustworthy? Can they safely be relied on? It all depends on what the intuitive feelings are based on. If they stem largely from the tribulations of experience, they might turn out to be uncannily right. If, however, they are based on little more than prejudice, hubris, paranoia, or other such questionable sources, they will be close to worthless.

The fact that there exists a type of knowledge that resists demonstration of any sort raises several serious epistemological problems. Since this sort of knowledge, if it has any validity at all, must be based on a personal and incommunicable experience, and since everyone's experience is, at least to some extent, unique, the question arises whether this kind of personal, tacit knowledge can ever qualify as objective. What happens when two people, each insisting that their knowledge derives from personal experience, reach different conclusions about some matter of fact?

Such disagreements are far from uncommon. Suppose you have two individuals, Peter and Paul, each of whom arrives at diametrically opposed views regarding a certain auto mechanic. Peter claims that the auto mechanic is a "good sort of fellow" and can be trusted. Paul, on the other hand, has experienced bad vibes about the mechanic and suspects he is a liar and a thief. How do we determine which of these gentlemen, if either, is correct?

In the absence of evidence, there are at least two ways to settle the difference. You could try to compare the track records of Peter and Paul to determine whose intuitive judgment has proven more reliable. Although this would not settle the difference conclusively, it would give us the best estimate of who is most likely to be right. An even more effective way of settling the difference would be to test the claims empirically: that is, let the mechanic work on one's car and see what happens. Of course, this could be a rather expensive way of determining who is right, especially if Paul's intuitions, rather than Peter's, prove closer to the truth and the mechanic is shown to be a swindler.

The difficulties of evaluating claims based largely on intuition gives rise to a number of cognitive abuses. People tend to view their own intuitions with considerable indulgence and hubris, often accepting them uncritically, as if they were infallible. Or, even worse, they will rationalize them, coming up with all kinds of bogus reasons for believing in things that never could have been discovered through rational thinking. It would make more sense to take our intuitions for what they often are: shrewd guesses of the subconscious which, though clearly not infallible, are often uncannily right.

Cognitive science has found that experts (i.e., people with experience) tend to rely far more on intuition and other non-logical forms of thinking than novices. "I'm continually struck by the fact that the experts in our studies very seldom engage in formal logical thinking," testified Paul E. Johnson, a psychologist and researcher who studied how experts in cardiology, brokerage, and other professional fields solved problems. "Most of what they do is plausible-inferential thinking based on the recognition of similarities. That kind of thinking calls for a great deal of experience, or, as we say, a large data base. If anybody's going to be logical in a task, it's the neophyte, who's desperate for some way to generate answers, but the expert finds logical thinking a pain in the neck and far too slow. So the medical specialist, for instance, doesn't do hypothetical-deductive, step-by-step diagnosis, the way he was taught in medical school. Instead, by means of his wealth of experiences he recognizes some symptom or syndrome, he quickly gets an idea [i.e., an intuition], he suspects a probability, and he starts right in looking for data that will confirm or disconfirm his guess." (Hunt, 139-140)

Johnson's description of how the typical medical specialist thinks gives us a near perfect model of how intuition, under the best circumstances, works. Especially take note of the emphasis on the importance of "a great deal of experience." This is the most critical point in any discussion of the cognitive value of intuition. Without the requisite "data base" to draw from, intuitions are close to worthless. That is precisely what distinguishes the expert from the novice: the expert has a "wealth of experience" to draw from, while the novice has little more than the step-by-step, hypothetical-deductive methods he's learned in school.

Also important is the willingness to test and criticize our intuitions. The medical specialist doesn't take his intuitions for granted. He doesn't assume they are infallible or right. No, he uses them as a starting point for experimentation. He tests them to see whether they might be correct. It is only by testing our intuitions empirically that we can be justified in trusting them as a source of reliable knowledge.

In life, we are sometimes faced with situations in which it is not so easy to test our intuitions. Perhaps we are confronted with a decision that must be made immediately. Someone we barely know offers us a chance to work with in Hawaii. We must decide immediately. What are we to do? Can we trust this individual? In such circumstances, all we have to go by is our intuitions. Suppose our intuition suggests the person can't be trusted? Should we go with him to Hawaii to test whether our intuitions are correct? No, probably not.

Knowing what to do when confronted with intuitions that cannot be tested constitutes one of the most difficult cognitive challenges of the human condition. In the remainder of this essay, I wish to explore the whole question of the validity of intuitive knowledge, focusing in particular on the comparison between intuitive or "personal" knowledge on the one side and "scientific" or "objective" knowledge on the other. This will help foster a greater appreciation for the unique predicament of the human mind, which can only know the world through symbols and representations, never as direct objects of cognition.

As Locke pointed out more than three centuries ago, knowledge is never immediate, but is achieved through the medium of ideas. This insight, if valid, suggests an epistemological dualism between the objects of reality on the one side and the thoughts or ideas through which the mind apprehends them on the other. Now if all knowledge is *mediated* by ideas, this would make literal knowledge impossible. This is indeed the first main corollary of epistemological dualism. Knowledge becomes the art of using symbols to interpret existence, of thinking aptly about things rather than experiencing them directly. The real world must be adapted to the scale and perspective of the human mind before any attempt can be made to grasp or understand it.

Epistemological dualism has never fared well in philosophical circles because of the perception (or rather misperception) that it separates ideas from existence, thus making knowledge impossible. This alleged separation, however, is an exaggeration. Actually, all that follows from epistemological dualism is the conviction that knowledge can never be perfectly adequate, that something is always lost in the translation between the real world on the one side and the world of our minds on the other. This is not the same as saying that knowledge is impossible. Knowledge doesn't have to describe its objects with immaculate perfection. Such perfection is otiose. As long as knowledge is good enough for practical purposes, that should more than suffice. I do not require perfect knowledge of a bus to know that I need to get out of its way as it comes barreling down the street.

But though knowledge can never be altogether perfect or literal, there are degrees of literalness, or something akin to literalness. As an example, consider the following two propositions:

(1) Abraham Lincoln, when he died at 56 years of age, weighed 180 pounds, measured six feet four in height, and had a shoe size of 14.

(2) "Lincoln was a case of American exceptionalism because, in his humble, untaught way, he was a kind of moral genius, such as is seldom seen in life and hardly ever at the summit of politics." (Johnson 1997, 435)

The first proposition is quantitative and statistical, listing measurements of the sixteenth President taken at his autopsy. The second is a statement from historian Paul Johnson that expresses a qualitative judgment of Lincoln's moral intelligence. Obviously, the two propositions are very different in both their degree of objectivity and the type of information they convey. The first proposition is far more precise and thus easier to validate objectively. Not so the second statement, which is somewhat vague and immune to objective validation. What, after all, is moral genius? And what evidence can be brought forth to demonstrate that Lincoln was in fact a genius of the moral variety? There are some people—especially Southerners—who take a very dim view of Lincoln's moral intelligence.

Although more controversial and less easy to validate, the second proposition is nonetheless far richer and considerably more profound than the first proposition. Lincoln's bodily measurements are trivial. They tell us little if anything about the inner man, about Lincoln's mind and character. The second proposition, on the other hand, attempts to elucidate a critical aspect of Lincoln's makeup: his moral insight. Which is more important to understanding Lincoln? Obviously, the proposition about moral intelligence. After all, Lincoln did not save the union and abolish slavery because he was six feet four and had a shoe size of fourteen.

By comparing these two propositions, we can reach several generalizations regarding quantitative versus qualitative judgments. Quantitative judgments tend to be precise, explicit, unequivocal, communicable, and objectively verifiable. They give science its unique objectivity and power over the mechanistic side of reality. They are less useful, however, in dealing with moral, social, and religious issues.

Qualitative judgments, on the other hand, tend to be vague, figurative, inexact, and difficult to validate objectively. In their highest form, qualitative judgments constitute some of the most profound utterances on human nature and the human condition. They are the stuff of great literature, philosophy, and religion. They find their justification, not in shallow proofs or tautological axioms, nor in simple facts or vague generalizations, but in experience—often an extensive experience covering many years and many individual instances. More often than not, these judgments reveal themselves in flashes of intuition emerging spontaneously from the depths of the unconscious. How they come about is not entirely known. They appear to arise from the obscure machinations of the inner mind and are based on that vast mental database of unconscious memories built upon the ashes of experience.

One of the most extraordinary characteristics of intuition is its ability to grasp and convey the subtle nuances, the obscure and recondite nooks and crannies of existence in all its multifaceted glory. Reality, in its deeper reaches, is far too rich for mere words. This is especially true of the profoundest realities of the human condition. Consider the following statement by the philosopher Hannah Arendt: "The human condition is such that pain and effort are not just symptoms which can be removed without changing life itself; they are the modes in which life itself, together with the necessity to which it is bound, makes itself felt. For mortals, the 'easy life of the gods' would be a lifeless life."

Most intelligent adults would probably agree with this statement, though no one could explain precisely *why* they agreed with it. Some might attempt to explain it by rephrasing it in simpler terms or offering elaborations upon its basic premise. They might say, "Yes, it's true: life's a struggle"—or: "Right, a life without challenges, without stress would be a sham life"—or: "I agree: without pain and effort, there would be no point, no meaning in life. Life is essentially about striving after goals." Others might explain their acceptance of Arendt's observation by providing some sort of salient anecdote which purports to illustrate its truth. What you will not get is irrefutable evidence proving the validity of the remark, for that would be impossible. A qualitative assertion of this type simply cannot be "proved" or "validated." The individual must judge the statement for himself based on his own experience and intuition.

Matters become even more complicated when we approach a statement that runs counter to widely held ideological assumptions. Consider the following statement, compliments of the playwright Eugene Ionesco. "No society has been able to abolish human sadness, no political system can deliver us from the pain of living, from our fear of death, our thirst for the absolute. It is the human condition that directs the social condition, not vice versa."

The difficulty of this statement arises, not from its premise, but from its conclusion. Nearly everyone will agree that no society has ever managed to abolish human suffering; but not everyone will agree with the notion that the human condition determines man's social condition. Most people on the left will strongly disagree with Ionesco's statement. Most on the right will have no trouble accepting it.

Here we run across one of the principle difficulties of qualitative assertions based on personal experience and intuition. Assertions that cannot be validated objectively will easily fall prey to the abuses of ideological presumption. In making intuitive judgments about man and society, we all rely on certain tacit assumptions, on an elaborate interpretive framework through which we make sense of the world. Precisely because it is a tacit framework, we are unaware of its influence over our thoughts. Its assumptions are taken for granted, as if they were true *a priori*. Since we don't even realize we have these assumptions, since we have never articulated them to ourselves, we never think to challenge them, or test them, or change them. Yet all our beliefs, convictions, core ideas are shaped by this unconscious interpretive framework.

Buried deep in the interpretive framework of nearly every leftist is the assumption that, by changing social conditions, "society" can alleviate (if not cure) the ills of the human condition. When the leftist comes across any statement that runs counter to this tacit conviction, such as Ionesco's assertion about the primacy of the human condition, he rejects it out of hand. That simply cannot be true, he insists. To say that social conditions are caused by the human condition is tantamount to apologizing for the status quo, for the injustices and horrors of the established order.

Such, in any case, is how the left instinctively regards the issue. Who, then, is right? Does the human condition direct the social condition, as Ionesco suggests? Or is it the other way around, as the left would have us believe?

The question, precisely because it is qualitative in nature, can never be settled to everyone's satisfaction. Examining the facts of history won't give you a clear and unequivocal answer, because the question goes beyond the facts of the matter: it involves the interpretation of facts, so facts by themselves don't cut it. There is no escaping from it: qualitative judgments are necessary in making determinations of this sort; but such judgments are largely intuitive and personal.

Does this mean that all non-quantifiable knowledge is subjective? No, not at all. If knowledge were subjective, this would imply that all claims of knowledge were equal. Yet this is not the case at all. There is only one truth. When two people disagree on some issue, either one of them is right or they're both wrong. You will never find that they're both right. The difficulty arises from trying to determine whose qualitative judgment comes closest to reality. How should we go about assessing the cognitive value of qualitative judgments?

Since qualitative judgments are largely personal, our assessment of them must be personal as well; that is, qualitative judgments must be judged by their source. Do they come from an individual who has a large fund of experience to draw from and a good track record of making intuitive judgments? In that case, we are justified in having at least some faith in his pronouncements. If, on the other hand, the individual doesn't have a good track record, or he has no experience in the matter at hand, we should be very skeptical of anything that comes out of his mouth. The cognitive value of any qualitative judgment depends largely on two main factors: (1) relevant experience in the matter at hand; and (2) an innate gift for making insightful intuitions.

The absence of either of these two factors greatly reduces the cognitive value of a given qualitative judgment. Keep in mind that knowledge is fundamentally practical. The whole point of having knowledge is to increase one's practical efficacy in dealing with the problems of life. Valid knowledge leads to successful outcomes, invalid knowledge to failure and despair. If an individual's qualitative judgments on a particular issue prove helpful in making correct prognostications about future events or solving specific problems, he can be judged to have a fairly reliable intuition on the issue at hand.

It is important to keep in mind that the value of a man's qualitative judgments is always content specific. The fact that a man's intuition is reliable concerning political issues does not mean it will be reliable concerning economic or social issues as well. In judging the reliability of any particular person's intuitive ability, we must first ask: *Does he have the right sort of experience? And if so, what kind of track record does he have? Does his qualitative judgments help solve problems? Or do they only make things worse? Do they lead to reliable prognostications of the future? Or are they invariably wrong?* How these questions are answered determines the cognitive worth of an individual's intuition.

Where we go wrong is to become excessively reliant on what passes for "logical" thinking or "sound reasoning." Many issues confronting us in life cannot be solved by logic or "reason." Logic requires certainty and unequivocal premises. But many problems we face in life do not provide us with certain or unequivocal answers. More often than not, the best we can do is make educated guesses. Good guesses require relevant experience and a gift for making qualitative, intuitive judgments. Sometimes, when the issue involves problems that lay outside our area of expertise, we must rely on the judgment of other people. It would do well for us if we took pains to make good judgments about the reliability of other people's intuition, so that if we must depend on the intuition of others, we place our faith in those who can be trusted to give us good advice.

As an example of assessing the reliability of intuition, consider the case of the English statesman and political thinker Edmund Burke, who provides us with one of the most remarkable feats of intuitive prognostication on record. Examining Burke's insights regarding the French Revolution will provide a test case for how intuition and genius work in the real world. In 1789, the great social transformation known as the French Revolution burst upon the world, with the assembling of the States General at Versailles and the subsequent storming of the Bastille on July 14. Even at the very commencement of these great events, Burke regarded the proceedings with suspicion and distrust. While most of Burke's political friends and allies hailed the storming of the Bastille with exaltation, Burke intuitively sensed an impending catastrophe. In August, he wrote to Lord Charlemont, warning that the events in France could easily take a dangerous turn; it all depended on whether wiser heads would prevail against the congenital ferocity of the Parisian mob.

Within the year, Burke would publish one of the most famous political works in the English language, the *Reflections on the Revolution in France*. As Burke's biographer, John Morley, has pointed out, the *Reflections* came out at "precisely the time when the hopes of the best men in France shone most brightly, and seemed more reasonable. There had been disorders, and Paris still had ferocity in her mien. But Robespierre was an obscure figure on the back benches of the Assembly. Nobody had ever heard of Danton... At the very moment when Burke was writing his most somber pages, Paris and the provinces were celebrating with transports of joy and enthusiasm the civic oath, the federation, the restoration of concord in the land, the final establishment of freedom and justice in a regenerated France. This was the happy scene over which Burke suddenly stretched out the right arm of an inspired prophet, pointing to the cloud of thunder and darkness that was gathering on the hills, and proclaiming to them the doom that had been written upon the wall by the fingers of an inexorable hand. It is no wonder that when the cloud burst and the doom was fulfilled, men turned to Burke, as they went of old to Ahithophel, whose counsel was as if a man had inquired of the oracle of God." (1881, 99)

How did Burke *know* that the French Revolution would likely turn ugly and become a great and bloody catastrophe? In the *Reflections*, Burke poses the following rhetorical questions: "When men of rank sacrifice all ideas of dignity to an ambition without a distinct object, and work with low instruments and for low ends, the whole composition becomes low and base. Does not something like this now appear in France? Does it not produce something ignoble and inglorious? a kind of meanness in all the prevalent policy? a tendency in all that is done to lower along with individuals all the dignity and importance of the state?" (1909, 185-186) This, in its broadest essentials, expresses what Burke *intuitively* sensed about the French Revolution. There was something fundamentally ignoble in it, something sinister and degrading. What Burke saw in the French Revolution was the birth of the modern revolutionary left; that is to say, of a secular movement which seeks to transform the human condition through any means possible, including terror and mass murder. Burke's descriptions of these nascent leftists sound eerily familiar. "Among these are found persons," he wrote, "in comparison of whom Catiline would be thought scrupulous, and Cethegus a man of sobriety and moderation. Nor is it in these clubs alone that public measures are deformed into monsters. They undergo a previous distortion in academies, intended as so many seminaries for these clubs… In these meetings of all sorts, every counsel, in proportion as it is daring, and violent, and perfidious, is taken for the mark of superior genius. Humanity and compassion are ridiculed as the fruits of superstition and ignorance. Tenderness to individuals is considered as treason to the public. Liberty is always to be estimated perfect as property is rendered insecure. Amidst assassination, massacre, and confiscation, perpetrated or meditated, they are forming plans for the good order of future society." (1909, 205-206)

These words were penned three years before the Jacobin reign of terror. No one, not even the most adamant apologists of the old order who, due to their hopes and prejudices, expected the Revolution to fail at any moment, could have anticipated the horrors of the terror. What accounts for Burke's superior insight?

It can hardly be ascribed to logical acumen or special knowledge of the facts. Burke's *Reflections on the Revolution in France* is not exactly a masterpiece of logical reasoning. Nor did Burke, surveying the revolution from England, have any special acquaintance with the facts of the event. Indeed, in some places, Burke seems to have either omitted important facts or gotten them wrong—as Thomas Paine bitterly complained in his *Rights of Man*. Burke's biographer Morley insists "that Burke did not know enough of the subject about which he was writing"—that is, about the *facts* of the revolution. Nevertheless, Morley admits that Burke's "prophecy was fulfilled to the letter." (1881,

103, 100) For not only did Burke anticipate, even if only vaguely, the terror, he also foresaw the despotism of the Napoleonic empire. Was it simply blind luck that enabled Burke to be so uncannily right in his prognostications? Or was there something deeper in the man that enabled him to see what others could not?

At one point in the *Reflections*, Burke notes that when confronted by great events, "our passions instruct our reason." (1909, 217) What could he have meant by this? I'm not sure Burke himself fully understood what made him so violently detest the French Revolution. The reasons for his opposition lay deep within him, in that great repository of learning and experience that made him the leading political thinker and statesman of his age. Burke's political judgments did not arise from dubious speculations or obscure logical deductions, but from twenty-five years experience in politics, where he enjoyed the opportunity to work with and learn from some of the brightest minds of his age. Combine this fund of experience with an intuitive genius of the highest order, and you have all the elements required to make qualitative judgments of great insight. Burke knew how the French Revolution would turn out long before anyone else because he had more political knowledge and greater intuitive intelligence than any of his contemporaries. It is as simple as that.

This also explains some of the shortcomings of the *Reflections*. Since much of Burke's knowledge lay at the threshold of consciousness, he could not fully explain why he felt as he did. He knew that at its core there was something monstrous in the French Revolution, but he did not fully understand what it was. How could he? It was something new, something that had never existed before, at least not in so pure a form. In his *Reflections* Burke struggles to explain this horrifying new reality; in many passages, he delineates various aspects of it. He sees very clearly the rationalism of it, the opposition to tradition and religion, and the moral licentiousness and savagery that it would foster. He understands the threat it poses to European civilization. And he knows that the only way to stop it is to put it down by force. But although his vision of the phenomenon is deep and profound, it is not particularly clear and precise. Too much emphasis is placed on trivial factors. Burke complains, for example, that "a very great proportion of the [French] assembly" is "composed of practitioners in the law." From the moment Burke discovered this, he "saw distinctly … all that was to follow."

However much lawyers may get on our nerves, Burke's suggestion that his great insight into the French Revolution stemmed from the fact that the French Assembly was largely made up of such *canaille* seems a bit over the top. Even if most of these lawyers were, as Burke insisted, "obscure provincial advocates," "stewards of petty local jurisdictions, country attornies, notaries, and the whole train of the ministers of municipal litigation, the fomenters and conductors of the petty war of village vexation," (1909, 180) this alone hardly justifies Burke's forebodings of catastrophe. To a large extent, the *Reflections* is little more than a tremendously ingenious set of rationalizations in which Burke seeks to explain why he feels as he does. Some of the rationalizations are brilliant and true; some are not so brilliant and less true. Burke's deeper intuitions, having been formed from his tacit knowledge of society and politics, could never be expressed in mere words. They could be hinted at, adumbrated, expressed in symbols and metaphor, but never stated literally. Language is too poor a vehicle of expression to elucidate the deepest thoughts of mankind's deepest men.

Of course, it is still possible that Burke was simply lucky—although, given the man's astonishing prescience regarding the ultimate fate of the French Revolution, this would appear unlikely. Burke saw something in the Revolution that frightened him beyond all measure, but which he could not fully explain. How else are we to account for his intensely passionate opposition to everything the French Revolution represented, even to the point of breaking with some of his closest friends and political allies. His friend and parliamentary colleague Charles James Fox is said to have wept after Burke told him, "I have done my duty at the price of my friend. Our friendship is at an end." (Morley 1881, 115) Would Burke have gone to such extremes merely because the French had adopted a suspect constitution or mistreated their Queen? Burke's passionate opposition toward the French Revolution is only explicable if we assume that it arose from deeper causes than those given by Burke himself. In the secular-rationalist mindset of the French revolutionaries, Burke sensed something that would menace Western

Civilization: the birth of radical leftism, with its contempt for religious values and its nihilistic utopianism.

Even if this conjecture about Burke's attitude towards the French Revolution turns out to be wrong, it still provides a good illustration of how intuitive qualitative judgments *can* work. The question we next turn to involves the issue of assessment: how do we determine whether a given claim made on the basis of intuition is worth considering? How, for instance, should a rational person have regarded Burke's *Reflections* upon its publication? From our vantage point some two centuries later, we know Burke to have been right about the French Revolution. But in 1790, when the *Reflections* first greeted the public, the ultimate outcome of the Revolution was not so obvious. This being the case, should a rational person simply have dismissed Burke's *Reflections* out of hand? Or should he have assumed that a man of Burke's genius, learning, and experience *must* have special insight and therefore should be followed to the letter?

Obviously, either of these extremes would be inappropriate. You don't simply ignore or dismiss out of hand the intuitive judgments of men of great wisdom and experience; nor do you accept them blindly. What you do is approach them with great humility. The intuitions of even the wisest men do not always turn out to be true; but they might be true; indeed, they are more likely to be true than the intuitions of less wise person (such as ourselves). Therefore, we should take the *possibility* of them being true very seriously. By the light of our weaker intelligences we should seek for evidence that would corroborate or falsify them. And most of all, we should guard against wishful thinking. Reality does not exist for our personal benefit. In examining any claim to knowledge, we should never forget this simple and humbling truth.

10. Realism and the Spiritual Life

Realism, although tacitly accepted by every sane person, has enjoyed little popularity as an explicit philosophy. Among academic intellectuals, it is often dismissed as naive or superficial, as if only a child could believe anything so simple. Among more sophisticated thinkers, realism is regarded with even more suspicion. The conviction that the external world exists on its own plane of reality, whether we acknowledge it or not, is, to many philosophers, disturbing. They find the notion vulgar and even shocking. Realism, above all else, insists upon the existence of an external world. But what if this external world is made up of nothing else besides matter? What if spirit lives trapped in an absurd bag of fetid protoplasm? What hope is there for the human spirit in a world dominated by gross matter?

In the nineteenth century, fear of materialism turned most philosophers in the English-speaking world into idealists. Idealism, as a coherent philosophical movement, sought to deny the existence of matter. That was Berkeley's principle aim in devising his ingenious slanders against common sense. Materialism was seen as a great menace to religion and society. It had to be demolished at all costs, even if it meant embracing palpable absurdities.

In the end, Berkeley's attempt to derail materialism proved a colossal failure. The dominance of idealism in the nineteenth century led to a reaction in the twentieth, so that nowadays quite a few philosophers, especially those of a scientific bent, have succumbed to the horrors of materialism. To be sure, not all of them are very happy about it. They have become materialists, not because they like it, but because they believe the pressure of scientific evidence gives them no choice.

Now realism prides itself on accepting evidence. The fact that we may dislike the sort of world indicated by the relevant evidence is of little significance to the realist. Honesty demands that we face up to the facts like men. Refusing to believe the truth will not make it go away. If materialism happened to be true, then the intrepid realist would have no choice but to accept it as such.

Fear of realism's alleged materialistic implications has caused many intellectuals and philosophers to regard it with a cold eye. Surely there is more to the world than what a realist philosophy, with its astringent epistemology and general skepticism toward "subjective" evidence, would give us! What good can come of a philosophy that looks askance at any speculation that trespasses beyond the narrow bounds of common sense? A poor sort of diet for the spirit, is this realist philosophy, offering so little in the way of genuine spiritual sustenance for the wary human soul, lost in this dark wood, with so little hope of finding a way out!

There are those who, confronting the loneliness and terror of the human condition, would like to temporarily push aside all notions of cognitive integrity and believe whatever comforting illusions happened to float within their ken; in other words, they wish to take an epistemological holiday so that they can believe anything they like, regardless of how childish or absurd. The "Heaven's Gate" cult, to take but one example, embraced their meretricious illusions with a tenacity of faith and a childlike joy that might have been touching had it not been a precursor to mass death. The arrival of Hale-Bopp, they wrote on their website prior to their wayward plunge into self-slaughter, "is joyously very significant to us at 'Heaven's Gate.' The joy is that our Older Member in the Evolutionary Level Above Human has made it clear to us that Hale-Bopp's approach is the 'marker' we've been waiting for—the time for the arrival of the spacecraft from the Level Above Human to take us home to 'Their World'—in the literal Heavens."

The "Heaven's Gate" cult stands as a warning of what can happen when we cut ourselves loose from the moorings of reality. The whole point of realism is to keep us within the bounds of sanity, our two feet doggedly planted on philosophical *terra firma*. It comes down to an issue of cognitive responsibility. Either we accept the way things are, or we don't. If we choose to ignore the truth, then we open ourselves to all manner of absurdities, some of them patently dangerous. Reality, however uninspiring it may turn out to be in its ultimate aspect, is at least something that can be relied upon, a worthy object of faith. Whereas illusions are mere will of the wisps, phantoms of the mind that can lead to nothing solid and true.

The question, then, confronting those who follow the realist standard is the following: Given the cognitive constraints of a realist philosophy, what hope can there be for a genuine spiritual life?

The first difficulty that confronts us at the commencement of our inquiries involves the accusation that realism logically implies materialism. Before we can go any further, this particular materialist bogeyman must be laid to rest.

Central to any conception of realism is the notion that the real world exists *independently* of the mind. Another way of putting this is that the world would exist whether you or I or anyone else recognized the fact. The truth about the world is true despite what we may think or fail to think about it. The world then, and the truth about the world, is an outlying reality that exists beyond the mind.

This view of the matter is forced upon us by a number of basic observances. In the first place, we know that we can be wrong about the world—that we can believe in things that are not true. The possibility of error arises precisely because there exists a separation between the mind and the world. Since the mind is not identical with the external world, but exists on a different plane of reality from the world, it must actively seek out the world if it would know it. Nor can it hope to know the world as the world "really is"—whatever that might mean. The mind must represent the world in forms native to itself. It must represent the truth about the world in a grammar and language that it alone understands.

We also know that our conceptions of things are not identical with the things themselves. My conception of the world is not identical with the world itself. It is a mere representation through which the mind attempts to grasp something not itself. We know things about the world through our mental representations of them, through the perceptions, conceptions, and ideas we have of them. Cognitive science has discovered that one of the foremost principles governing the development of ideas and concepts is the achievement of human scale. The world is all out of scale with the mind. The immense complexity and vastness of the external world make it necessary for the mind to compress and scale-down this immensity into something more manageable. Examples of this compression are all around us. A work of history will compress, within the space of a few hundred pages, vast stretches of time. Edward Gibbon, in his *Decline and Fall of the Roman Empire*, compressed nearly fifteen hundred years of history into three volumes.

I stress these facts about the mind to highlight the difference between mind and reality, between the mental realm and the physical realm. The mind is something very different from the world—so different, in fact, that it suggests a kind of dualism between the constituents of the mind on the one hand and the constituents of the world on the other. This dualism is known as *epistemological dualism*. In its simplest form, epistemological dualism merely asserts that ideas or conceptions of things are not identical with the things themselves. But it says more than that. According to epistemological dualism, the constituents of the mind, the percepts, concepts and ideas through which it thinks, exist *only* in the mind. Ideas don't exist in external reality, in physical systems. They don't even exist in the brain. They only exist in the mind. Likewise, the constituents of physical reality only exist in physical reality. Physical objects do not nor can they exist in the mind. A battleship is a substantive entity existing in the external world. It cannot exist within someone's mind.

This epistemological dualism, which may appear, at first blush, rather trivial and even pretentious, nevertheless has profound implications for the spiritual life. From epistemological dualism, it is only a short step to psycho-physical dualism. And once psycho-physical dualism is established, the materialist threat to the spiritual life can be safely set aside.

Psycho-physical dualism is derived from epistemological dualism as follows. Once it is established that the constituents of the mind cannot exist in physical reality, this fact alone establishes psycho-physical dualism. The inability to find a place in physical systems for mental constituents demonstrates the irreducibility of mind to matter. And it is this irreducibility that psycho-physical dualism asserts.

What grounds do we have for believing in the irreducibility of mind? After all, scientific materialism claims that mental states are caused by physical states. The Darwinian philosopher Thomas Henry Huxley went so far as to suggest that consciousness is merely a byproduct of the body, with no more power or capability of modifying the body than a steam-whistle is capable of modifying a locomotive. (Popper & Eccles 1977, 72) Under the materialist view, consciousness is utterly irrelevant and has no role in the functioning of the organism. As Paul M. Churchland put it: "The important point about the standard evolutionary story is that the human species and all of its features are a wholly physical outcome of a purely physical process.... If this is a correct account of our origins, then there seems neither need, nor room, to fit any nonphysical substances or properties into our theoretical account of ourselves. We are creatures of matter. And we should learn to live with that fact." (1987, 21) But if we are creatures of matter, if everything we do merely reflects material processes in our bodies, then what is the point of having a consciousness or a mind? Since everything that goes on in the mind is merely a consequence of various brain processes, what is the need for mental constituents and mental processes? Ultimately, the case for psycho-physical dualism comes down to whether you believe that consciousness plays a functional role in the human organism. To say that the mind (and not merely the brain) makes a difference in human life is tantamount to embracing psycho-physical dualism.

Does consciousness, does the mind make a difference? If we were not conscious, if no mental constituents existed, would we be different from what we are? Of course we would be different. Our very humanity depends on being conscious and on having a mind and self. To deny psycho-physical dualism is to deny that which makes us human.

If this seems like mere common sense—well, that's precisely what it is. Yet many philosophers (Daniel Dennett 1991, 33) hold psycho-physical dualism in very low repute—a view which, however, constitutes a mere prejudice, a product, not of wisdom and impartial intelligence, but of party spirit and a narrow scientism. If good sense prevailed among the denizens of philosophy, dualism would be seen, not as some hoary superstition or metaphysical incubus, but as, in the words of philosopher Arthur Lovejoy, the "normal and inevitable outcome of men's effort rationally to adjust their native realistic faith to familiar facts of experience and elementary postulates of reflection." (1930, 42) Good sense, alas, has never been very popular among philosophers. If philosophers had been more intent at getting to the bottom of things rather than furthering their own dubious agendas, they might have understood the contradiction between realism, with its dualistic entailments, on the one side, and materialism, with its monistic entailments, on the other. Realism accepts the existence of matter, as do all practical men of affairs. But it doesn't accept *only* matter. It believes in spirit as well, as part of the duality of existence. And it is perfectly open to believing in other modes of existence, as many as can be discovered by the human mind. Realism's commitment to dualism is open-ended. It does not contend that there are but two principle modes of existence. There may be, for all we know, hundreds of such modes. Reality is not one massive homogeneous blob. Philosophers obsessed with reducing all of existence to just one thing are reductionists in the very worst sense of the word.

So materialism is not something realists need to worry about. There is nothing in realism that requires the adoption of materialism. Quite the contrary, realism, if properly understood, entails a dualism that is logically incompatible with the sort of unadulterated materialism preached by those who believe that every component of reality, including the human mind, can be explained on mechanical principles. "It can indeed be upsetting to think of ourselves as glorified gears and springs," admits the evolutionary psychologist Stephen Pinker. (2002, 10) Yes, it can be upsetting—if for no other reason than it isn't true. Oh, sure, some people (e.g., particularly stupid or unimaginative people) can sometimes act like mechanical devices—which is to say, they can become so predictable as to become annoying, such as the inebriate returning to his bottle. But comparing the minds of such individuals to machines is to indulge in literary license. It is a metaphor—and not a particularly apt one at that. To seriously believe that the mind can be explained on materialist principles, that every aspect of the mind, including the highest flights of intuition and creativity, can be reduced to the operation of mechanical laws within the realm of matter, is to demonstrate a complete lack of judgment on the issue. While it is true that the mind has a *basis* in matter and that its ability to function is strongly dependent on the integrity of the physical brain, this does not mean that the activities of the mind, its thinking, willing, and innovative problem-solving, can be explained mechanically, in terms of the laws of matter. To even suggest such a thing demonstrates a complete lack of appreciation for the complexity of human thought and the creative originality of the mind.

If anyone should entertain doubts about the issue, just consider the ultimate outcome of any belief that thinking and knowing are in any sense reducible to the laws of physics or chemistry. If this were true, it would mean that anyone who could attain complete and perfect knowledge of how the mind is determined, mechanistically, within the realm of matter, would *ipso facto* be able to predict, by deductive methods alone, the thoughts and behavior of any human being that came within his ken, including, strangely enough, the thoughts and behavior of his own self. (Popper 1982, 68) The idea, however, of predicting one's own behavior is absurd, because the predictions themselves would undoubtedly influence the individual's decisions. For this reason, if for no other, all such materialist theories of the mind are absurd. Mind is something fundamentally different from matter. The very phrase *materialist theory of mind* is a contradiction in terms. The mind cannot possibly be materialistic, any more than matter can be spiritual. Mind and matter constitute different modes of existence.

This doesn't mean, incidentally, that mind and matter exist in completely separate realms of reality. Dualism does not seek to separate mind and matter; it merely attempts to distinguish them and to delineate more clearly the pathology of their interaction. But the anti-dualists, many of whom are uncompromising materialists, are loath to admit even the possibility of interaction. They want everyone to believe that the causation goes *only* in one direction, from matter to spirit, from the physical to the mental.

Why are they so intransigent on this point? The main reason would appear to be the desire to reduce everything to the mechanism of matter, including the mind. While it is true that mechanical explanations can explain many things about the material world, they are much less convincing when used to explain the activities of the mind. Cognitive science has discovered that even the simplest cognitive acts are so immensely complicated that attempts to explain them on mechanical principles appear doomed from the start. "Phenomena that were once not even perceived as problems at all have come to be regarded as central, extremely difficult questions in cognitive neuroscience," admits the authors of *The Way We Think*, Gilles Fauconnier and Mark Turner. "What could be more simpler than recognizing that a tree is a tree? Yet when we look at works in cognitive neuroscience, we find this recognition problem listed under 'conceptual categorization,' already regarded as a higher-order problem, beyond the already difficult feat of 'perceptual categorization.'" (2002, 7) If something as simple as recognizing a tree should prove so immensely difficult to cognitive science, what is to be said of issues relating to qualitative judgments and the highest flights of artistic creativity? Most human beings can distinguish hallucinations from normal perception, although both can appear very lifelike. How on earth do they do this? We don't know, they just can. Human beings can also identify people by face or voice. Such recognitions involve qualitative judgments that cannot be explained mechanically, because they do not occur mechanically. Even more inexplicable is the creativity of a Da Vinci or a Mozart, a Michelangelo or a Beethoven. Does any materialist really believe that the Sistine Chapel or the *Eroica Symphony* can be explained on materialist grounds?

When pressed, the materialists retreat into a position Karl Popper described as "promissory materialism," which accepts the untenability of materialism at the current level of knowledge, but believes that materialism will, after centuries of scientific progress, eventually prove victorious. Progress in brain research will cause us to talk less and less about mere experiences, and more and more about brain processes, until mental terms go out of fashion and everything will be described solely in the terms of physiology.

Promissory materialism, as Popper noted, is a "historical prophecy about the future results of brain research and their impact." Popper regarded the theory as "baseless," and argued that the thesis of promissory materialism was no more rational than the thesis that one day cats or elephants could be abolished by everyone refusing to talk about them. (1977, 97) But it is worse than that. At bottom, what the materialists are really contending for is the irrelevance of consciousness. For that is the ultimate thrust of their metaphysical program: to do away with the concept of consciousness, so that they can replace it with the thesis that all of existence is explicable on mechanical grounds. But consciousness most clearly and obviously *does* exist! How can any realist, committed to accepting the truth as the human mind discovers it, deny so obvious a truth as the reality of consciousness?

So the charge that realism is somehow incipiently materialistic can safely be laid to rest. *Realism is fundamentally dualistic.* The realist philosophy stands or falls on the premise that an external, material world exists independently of whether anyone perceives it. Yet this premise itself assumes the reality of a mind capable of perceiving that material world. If only the material world existed, there would be no point in saying that it can exist whether a mind perceived it or not, because no mind would exist to perceive it. And if only the mind existed, nothing could ever exist independent of the mind, in its own plane of reality. Realism therefore must be dualistic. On no other basis does it make a lick of sense.

The refutation of materialism does not, by itself, secure the possibility of a genuine spiritual life. Even under a dualistic philosophy, a spiritual life may prove impossible. The body may so entirely dominate and brutalize the spirit as to leave no room within man's soul for anything other than material interests. We know from experience that matter tends to lord it over the mind. Spirit often seems overburdened and distracted by the insatiable desires and petty anxieties of the body. The degraded position of spirit within the human organism has led many thoughtful individuals to question the value and purpose of life. "Everything in life proclaims that earthly happiness is destined to be frustrated, or recognized as an illusion," testified the philosopher Arthur Schopenhauer. "We feel pain, but not painlessness; care, but not freedom from care; fear, but not safety and security. We feel the desire as we feel hunger and thirst; but as soon as it has been satisfied, it is like the mouthful of food which has been taken, and which ceases to exist for our feelings the moment it is swallowed. We painfully feel the loss of pleasures and enjoyments, as soon as they fail to appear; but when pains cease even after being present for a long time, their absence is not directly felt, but at most they are thought of intentionally by means of reflection. For only pain and want can be felt positively; and therefore they proclaim themselves; well-being, on the contrary, is merely negative." (1958, 573, 575) "Vanity of vanities, all is vanity," testified Solomon, the troubled sage-king of the Old Testament. "Therefore I hate life; because the work that is wrought under the sun *is* grievous onto me, for it all *is* vanity and vexation of the spirit." (Ecclesiastes 1:2, 2:17) And finally we have the testimony of the great poet of naturalism, Lucretius:

> Finally, what's this wanton lust for life
> To make us tremble in dangers and in doubt?
> All men must die, and no man can escape.
> We turn and turn in the same atmosphere
> In which no new delight is ever shaped
> To grace our living; what we do not have
> Seems better than everything else in the world.
> But should we get it, we want something else.
> Our gaping thirst for life is never quenched. (1968, 117)

The conception of the world developed by modern science only provides more grist for the pessimist mill. Human life, according to the theory of evolution, can trace its roots all the way back to the great primordial ooze out of which all life originally developed. Once bacteria and other protoplasmic organisms bubbled forth from the evolutionary stew, they began competing against each other for the resources necessary to sustain themselves and their progeny. Those organisms that, because of the quality of their DNA, were best fit to survive the Darwinian death match by which animal life evolves, pass their genes to further generations. Through a process of mutation and natural selection, more complex organisms develop, until at last, at the end of the long evolutionary chain, human beings emerge.

If this account of the origin of human life is correct, then the human being is a product of evolution. Everything he is, from the color of his eyes to the desires of his heart, stems from an adaptation forged in the Darwinian furnace. Human beings are largely the products of natural selection. We are the way we are because it helped our ancestors survive and pass on their genes.

The picture of human existence that emerges from assuming that human nature is a mere adaptation chosen by natural selection entirely justifies the view that life is essentially a vain and hopeless enterprise. For what is the purpose of the great Darwinian farce of evolution? There is no purpose. According to the Darwinian vision, more or less accepted by modern science, life essentially consists of a battle between organisms to see whose genes will be passed on to the next generation. The organism that passes on the most genes "wins," although to speak of winners and losers in such a context is to emit senseless patter. Under such a regimen, happiness becomes little more than the carrot at the end of stick; pain the whip against the back; and Nature the stern slavemaster, dangling the carrot and cracking the whip without so much as a jot of concern about the ultimate welfare of the poor bedeviled organism. "Breed, multiply, pass on your genes!" cries dame Nature, and cracks her whip. Life under such circumstances would constitute little more than an endless striving after vain goals. Any happiness that might visit the sentient creature would be fleeting and, ultimately, illusory.

In such a world, there would be no point to developing a spiritual life. Man's existence would be at the mercy of pointless genetic imperatives. Spirit would be an imprisoned spectator of man's futile effort to pass on his DNA. All of life would be a vain endeavor, without rhyme or reason.

The conviction that realism is incompatible with a spiritual life ultimately stems from the fear that the Darwinian-materialist view of the world, advanced by modern science, might turn out to be true. Yet here we must proceed very cautiously. It would be foolhardy to assume that merely because the scientific establishment *believes* Darwinism to be true, that Darwinism therefore *must* be true. The fact that this or that group of scholars entertains a given conception of the world means little to the realist if that conception does not accord with the facts of reality. If we want to get to the bottom of the matter, we have no choice but to examine all the relevant evidence and make our own decision.

So what does the evidence tell us about the world? Is it a world "red in tooth and claw," where protoplasmic machines governed by senseless strips of genetic code compete in a Hobbesian war of all against all? Or is there more to existence than the pointless gyrations of genetic dice and evolutionary billiard balls?

The most important question of philosophy involves the relation of man and his spirit to the universe. In other words, it involves the question of whether God exists. Not everyone, of course, will agree that the question of man's relation to the universe is one and the same with the question of God's existence; yet a little reflection on the matter will demonstrate that it is so. The assertion of God's existence is tantamount to declaring that the universe has some overriding purpose to it, that it is not merely a senseless conglomeration of sub-atomic particles. If the universe does have a purpose, this fact will obviously have immense ramifications for man's relation with the universe. If, on the other hand, the universe has no overriding purpose; if the only teleological realities that exist in the world are those that have arisen in conscious beings; then man's relation to the universe takes on another aspect altogether.

I have introduced this subject at a very high level of abstraction. To get a better grasp at what precisely is at stake, it would help to reduce the vast subject to something more in keeping with the limitations of the human mind. Cognitive science, as I have previously noted, has discovered that one of the most important principles governing human knowledge is the necessity to *achieve human scale*; which is to say, to reduce the subject at hand to something more familiar, more easily apprehended by a human brain. (Fauconnier and Turner, 312) To achieve human scale, the mind conceives its objects through a veil of poetry, in thoughts thickly draped in the furnishings of metaphor and analogy. How else could spirit grasp the attributes of matter? Just as I rely on translations to read Dostoevsky, so the mind relies on cognitive translations to understand the external world.

Let's assume for the nonce that God does in fact exist. How would the mind go about symbolizing a reality as complex as the deity? Few things can be imagined so far out of scale with the human mind than God. Is it any wonder, then, that man's theological conceptions appear so fantastic? Attempts to describe God nearly always lead to strange paradoxes and befuddling obscurities. Perhaps if we had a greater appreciation of the poetical element that all such descriptions must perforce contain, then we could avoid some of the worst absurdities. The recognition that our ideas can never be identical with their object and that the mind is not a mirror counsels us to avoid the fallacy of misplaced literalism. Our ideas of God can never be identical with God himself.

In conceiving of God, we naturally draw heavily on anthropocentric concepts. In order to understand God, we make Him like ourselves. We ascribe to Him thoughts and feelings that we imagine we would have if we were in His place. While such humanizing of the deity, given the limitations of the human mind, is inevitable, we would do well not to take such anthropocentric descriptions too literally.

As realists in search of evidence of God's existence, we start with the idea of purpose. According to the best cosmological evidence available from modern science, the universe initially lacked protoplasmic life. Following the big bang some 15,000 million years ago, only hydrogen and helium existed. Other elements were created by the first stars, but they were trapped at the center of stars burning at temperatures in excess of 10 million degrees. Only after the first supernovas were these other elements—many of them, such as carbon, essential for the development of living, purposive creatures—spewed out into the universe, where, by some sort of inexplicable, miraculous commingling, they fortuitously evolved into life forms. The early millennia of the universe were, according to an atheistical cosmology, utterly destitute of life; in other words, if we assume that God does not exist, the early universe becomes a place entirely devoid of teleological significance: a lifeless, meaningless chaos of swirling stars. Billions and billions of stars—*and nothing else*! A universe utterly destitute of purpose.

What does it mean to describe the universe as destitute of purpose? A universe without purpose is a universe where nothing can happen as result of anyone's desire or intention. How then does anything happen at all? How could such a universe breed galaxies, solar systems, planets and, ultimately, life? One possible answer would be through natural law: a purposeless universe comes into existence by following the laws of nature. Is this possible? Perhaps; but even if it did happen this way, it still leaves open the question of how these laws of nature came about in the first place. Some cosmologists contend that the laws of nature as we know them did not exist before the big bang. Indeed, as far as we can tell, neither time nor space existed before the big bang, so that, in a certain sense, the very phrase *before the big bang*, is a contradiction in terms. There can be no *before the big bang* because time ceases to exist when you go back that far. And if time and space did not exist before the big bang, then surely the laws of nature did not exist either.

So then, if we take purpose and intention out of the equation, how do we account for the universe? We have found that the universe could not have originated through the laws of nature, because the laws of nature only come to play after the universe has commenced. Apparently, there is only one way to account for the universe if we exclude purpose: it must have come about by chance. The universe as we know it is a mere accident.

Is this a plausible view? Let us examine some of the evidence compiled by modern science and see whether we can determine how plausible this atheist view really is.

The development of life depends on the values of certain fundamental constants, such as gravitational and electromagnetic force. If any of these constants had been just a little different, the universe would have remained inhospitable to life for the duration of its existence. To give but one example, consider the physical nature of water. Unlike other molecules, water, when in its solid form, floats. Had it been otherwise, the oceans would have frozen from the bottom up and the earth would be covered with ice. There are hundreds of fortuitous coincidences like this, starting from the big bang all the way to the development of intelligent life. To create life out of a universe which, at the beginning, consisted only of hydrogen and helium, requires an enormous amount of grossly improbable accidents. In fact, no less an authority than the astronomer and mathematician Fred Hoyle considers the universe immensely improbable. "The current scenario of the origin of life," Hoyle wrote, "is about as likely as a tornado passing through a junkyard beside Boeing Airplane Company accidentally producing a 747 airplane." Scientists have estimated that there is much less than one chance in a hundred thousand trillion trillion trillion trillion trillion trillion that there exists even one planet capable of producing life anywhere in the universe. (Ankerberg and Weldon 2005)

Faced with such immense improbabilities, the belief in a random universe, destitute of God and purpose, would appear to be unwarranted. Yet we must consider some of the additional arguments made for the atheist position. The most plausible case for an utterly senseless, random universe assumes the existence of alternating universes. What if the universe, at a certain point, stops expanding and collapses back upon itself? This notion, known as the "big crunch," if possible, could help explain how a random universe produces life. Let us imagine that every big crunch is followed by a big bang. If this were to go on forever, there would be no reason why, out of an infinite number of chances, a universe capable of producing life would not at some point spring into existence. In fact, given an infinite number of chances, an infinite number of life-supporting universes would be spewed into existence. Yet, strange to say, the infinity of life-creating universes would be very much smaller than the infinity of life-destitute universes. How one infinity could be larger than another appears, on the face of it, absurd. But this is not the only absurdity the atheist position must reckon with when assuming a string of infinite random universes. Although we imagine them, in terms of human thought, as a string of universes, one happening after another, in reality it wouldn't be that way. Since neither time nor space exists either "after" the big crunch or "prior" to the big bang, none of these universes could be described as existing in a temporal or spatial relationship to any other universe. What sort of relations would in fact exist between these universes would be difficult to say. We are trying to think of something that is well beyond the scope of human thought. To be sure, this does not mean that an infinite "string" of universes is impossible. Just because we cannot conceive of such a thing does not mean that it cannot be true.

Even if it were possible, the notion of an infinite number of random universes does not appear as plausible as a universe created out of some sort of intention or purpose. The current scientific evidence suggests that this intention or purpose existed "prior" to the emergence of protoplasmic life here on earth.

What this teleological phenomenon might be is hard to say. To assume it must be God—whether the God of the Bible or any other sort of divine entity—would be utterly gratuitous without further evidence. David Hume, in his *Dialogues Concerning Natural Religion*, penned one of the most blistering critiques of the argument from design. Hume begins by accepting the argument's basic premise. Fine, he says; let us suppose the universe is the product of intention or design. What else can we deduce from that? His answer: nothing. Knowing that the universe was designed tells us nothing about the designer. It could have been created by an infant god; or a god in his dotage; or a whole boardroom of gods. It could have been created by a good god or an evil god. (1779, 76-79) How are we to tell, one way or the other, without specific evidence?

Suppose we seek to deduce the nature of God from the nature of the universe? Well then, in that case, we run right smack into the problem of evil. If God mirrors the nature of the universe, then this would mean that God would have to mirror the evil in the universe as well. A god that is even partly evil can hardly be equated with the God of the New Testament—or with the God of any other religion, for that matter. Nor is it clear what role such a god could possibly have in the development of a spiritual life.

Evidence of some sort of vague and inexplicable purpose behind the universe would not necessarily warrant theism. More evidence is required before we can make any kind of rational determination on the question of God's existence. But what sort of evidence should we be looking for?

Let us remove one common misconception from the start. This question cannot be settled ostensively. You cannot prove the existence of God by pointing at Him and saying, "There He is." Demanding such proof would be unreasonable. God is not a material object that can be pointed and gaped at. If we mean to search for evidence of God, we must look for evidence relevant to the type of entity or phenomenon that God is alleged to be.

Although there exists no general agreement on the finer points of God's nature, nearly all theists agree that God is a bodiless entity of some sort. Hence the futility of trying to establish the existence of God by pointing at Him. Less agreement exists on God's role in the universe. In broad terms, we can distinguish three basic views: (1) the view that, following the creation, God has withdrawn from the world and plays no role at all in our lives; (2) the view that, while much of the universe proceeds without the direct meddling of God, nevertheless traces of his influence can be spotted in our lives; and (3) the view that God is directly responsible for everything. If we expect to find evidence for the existence of God, we must assume that the first and third views are wrong. If God has withdrawn from the world, he cannot have any influence on our lives and his existence becomes utterly irrelevant. If God is directly responsible for everything that happens, then it doesn't make any sense to look for evidence for God, because everything constitutes evidence of God's existence. Yet paradoxically, if everything is evidence for God's existence, then nothing is evidence for God. For if God is directly responsible for everything and if everything that happens is a direct cause of God's will, how could we ever attain rational knowledge of this fact? Keep in mind that any evidence for God must always be indirect, because God cannot be pointed at and proven ostensively. Indirect evidence requires counterfactuals: that is, we must be able to imagine what the facts would be like if the object of our inquiry did not exist, so that we can compare our counterfactual supposition with what we actually find in the real world. Evidence for God can only exist if we can distinguish between those things in the world that might have been caused by the direct influence of God from those things caused by the mechanism of nature.

If you believe that everything is directly caused by God, in a sense you have assumed the very point at issue. It is comparable to an atheist assuming that anything that happens, no matter how strange or contrary to the conception of modern science, must be the result of natural processes. Once the individual decides that everything must be caused either by God or Nature, he has shut up his mind to the evidence. He is operating on little more than blind faith.

A rational person tries to establish his beliefs on the basis of all the relevant evidence at his disposal. This is not to suggest that evidence will always provide clear and unambiguous answers to our questions. It would be presumptuous of us to expect that the world exists solely to be intelligible to our minds. One of the great difficulties in dealing with the whole issue of God's existence involves the unrealistic expectations that the partisans of each position bring to the debate. There is a tendency to demand utterly convincing evidence, as if the question can be settled conclusively. The theist insists that the atheist make a slam-dunk case for atheism and the random universe hypothesis; if the atheist cannot make such a case, the theist assumes that he has won the debate. And likewise, the atheist demands indubitable evidence from the theist. When no such evidence is produced, each side regards his case as proven beyond all doubt. As a matter of fact, the evidence, as we shall see, is not so clear-cut. To make any kind of determination on the issue involves choosing the least implausible view.

Many people experience a sort of aversion or resentment to admitting that we can never know for certain whether God exists. Yet many of the most important questions we face in life must be settled in a similar fashion. In the modern world, everyone, as they enter adulthood, is faced with choosing a vocation in life. Does anyone know for certain what choice will bring him the most happiness and success? No, that is not a question that yields certainty. Some people may *think* they know it for certain; but that's an illusion. There are too many unknown variables involved in the question to justify certain knowledge. A person may know with certainty what they want to do with their lives; but they can never know if they will succeed at it.

Deciding whether God exists is in some respects very similar to choosing a vocation in life, except instead of choosing a career, you are making a decision as to the ultimate destiny of your life. If God exists, then the universe is more than just an accident. If so, existence may have some ulterior purpose that very much has to do with how we conduct our lives. It suddenly becomes very important that we acquire at least a rough idea of what this ulterior purpose might be and what it portends, not only for our lives here on earth, but also for whatever may confront us after we have shuffled off this mortal coil. If, on the other hand, God doesn't exist and the universe is nothing more than a cosmological fluke, then all we have is our measly little lives and what we make of them. A very different course of action is suggested on such a supposition. Instead of living to please or obey God, we live to please ourselves. Why should we do anything else? The blind forces that rule the universe will one day very soon snuff us out. Therefore we have no choice but to make the best of it while we can.

For many people, the whole question of God's existence ultimately reduces itself to the opposing moral visions outlined above. How many people have become atheists for no other reason than that they wish to do as they please? And how many people oppose atheism largely because of their fear of atheistical antinomianism? The question of God's existence, however, must ultimately be settled on factual rather than moral grounds. If God exists, then it is up to us to acknowledge

His existence and act accordingly. Likewise, if God does not exist, that, too, must be acknowledged and acted upon.

But what if the evidence is too weak on both sides, so that at the end of the day we must conclude that we can never know whether God exists? Shouldn't we then simply admit our ignorance and move on? Unfortunately, this is not a viable option. The question is just far too important, far too momentous for us to retreat into a facile agnosticism. You can no more evade making a decision on God's existence than you can evade making a decision about your life's vocation. Since the question of God's existence is so inextricably bound with the question *What shall we do with our lives?* it cannot be evaded. If that seems unfair, well, that's just too bad. The world does not exist for our personal convenience. There is no such thing as cognitive entitlement. We cannot assume that the great questions of life must be easy. We find, as a matter of fact, that some of them are extremely difficult. Our only choice is to make the best of it: to examine the evidence, weigh the probabilities, and make a decision. Any attempt to evade the question of God's existence is merely to accept the default choice—which in this case happens to be atheism.

A decision, then, has to be made, one way or the other. Can we find any credible evidence of God's hand in the world we live in? If we can find such evidence, then we can at least assume that God *might* exist. If we can't find any such evidence, than the God hypothesis becomes much less credible.

What exactly would constitute evidence of God's hand in the world? The best way to tackle this problem is to use counterfactual reasoning. First we develop a rigorous model or conception of a world without God. Then we compare this model or conception to the factual world of our experience. If our model of a godless world turns out to be a good match for the factual world, then this would clearly strengthen the atheist case. But if it is not a good match, if it falls short in several critical areas, then this opens the way for alternative views, including theism.

Any view of the universe that denies the existence of God *ipso facto* denies the existence of any sort of cosmic purpose or intent. Once you remove purpose from the equation, you are left with only two alternatives for explaining how the universe came about: chance and mechanism. The most plausible atheist cosmologies ascribe the universe to a kind of cosmic interplay between chance and mechanism. The theory of evolution attempts to explain the emergence of life and the development of individual species as an outgrowth of random mutations weeded out through the utterly mechanical process of natural selection.

The goal of atheistic science is to show how everything in the universe can be explained on the basis of chance and/or mechanism. Regardless of where our sympathies ultimately lie, the remarkable success of the bold and fruitful line of research inspired by mechanistic materialism can hardly be denied. Many things in the universe do seem to act according to mechanical laws. The entire inanimate universe can be seen as a massively complex mechanism.

Richard Dawkins, one of the most rigorous and uncompromising defenders of the mechanistic view of the universe, extends this view, as any logically consistent atheist must, to the human race. "We are survival machines," he states in his book *The Selfish Gene*. Our evolutionary "purpose" is to serve as hosts for our DNA. All living things are survival machines of some sort. "A monkey is a machine that preserves genes up trees, a fish is a machine that preserves genes in water; there is even a small worm that preserves genes in German beer mats." (1976, 21) Dawkins' elaboration of the basic premises of Darwin's theories is immensely ingenious. Many Darwinists, it has to be admitted, shrink from embracing the less palatable implications of their creed. Not Dawkins. He makes a specialty of developing the darkest recesses of the Darwinian world view. According to the theory of evolution, organisms evolve through a natural selection of the "fittest." Thus, the giraffe with a longer neck will have a better chance of surviving than the giraffe with a short neck. Over time, all giraffes will have long necks.

Dawkins amends and enriches the Darwinian theory by combining it with genetics. He notes that when Darwinists talk of survival of the fittest, they cannot mean survival of the fittest creature, because all creatures ultimately die. What, then, survives? Only the genes survive. In the case of the giraffe, it's the gene for longer necks. It gets passed on because longer necks bestow a reproductive advantage on those giraffes lucky enough to carry the long-neck gene. What is selected by

243

evolution is not the creatures themselves, but their genes, their DNA. Those genes that bestow upon their carriers the physical and behavioral characteristics that increase the likelihood that they will pass on their DNA to the next generation are precisely the genes that are selected by the evolutionary mechanism. As Dawkins put it, the gene is "the basic unit of natural selection." (1976, 36)

Dawkins has created quite a furor, even within the scientific community, for describing genes as selfish. The philosopher David Stove went so far as to describe Dawkins' theory as "not only nonsense, but very obviously nonsense." (1999, 256) Such objections are unwarranted. If you accept the basic premises of Darwinism, you really have no ground to quibble with Professor Dawkins. He has merely clarified these premises and developed their deeper implications. If genes are the primary focus of natural selection, then the selfish gene theory follows as a matter of course. Survival and reproduction become the most needful thing. If a gene cannot pass itself to the next generation, it ceases to exist. Altruistic genes—that is, genes that encourage self-sacrificing behavior in the host organism—clearly find themselves at a disadvantage when competing against selfish genes. Genes that are particularly adept, either through fair means or foul, of passing themselves to the next generation will be selected. Over time, those physical and behavioral characteristics that increase the likelihood of reproduction will become dominant in the gene pool.

Evolutionary psychologists have attempted to apply Dawkins' insights to the study of human nature. The vision of humanity that emerges is not a particularly edifying one. "Some people think that evolutionary psychology claims to have discovered that human nature is selfish and wicked," writes Stephen Pinker. "But they are flattering the researchers and anyone who would claim to have discovered the opposite. No one needs a scientist to measure whether humans are prone to knavery." (1997, 517) Central to both the selfish gene theory and evolutionary psychology is the concept of "reciprocal altruism," which is little more than self-interested cooperation. In other words, it is sometimes in our advantage to be nice. But note: all such seemingly altruistic behavior is merely selfish behavior in disguise.

The reason for introducing this theory is not to ridicule or condemn it. What we are trying to do is develop a conception of what a truly godless world governed by chance and mechanism would look like. The selfish gene theory constitutes the most coherent and plausible conception of an entirely natural, atheistical, mechanical world to date. If God did not exist, we would expect the biological world to correspond very closely to Dawkins' theories. If Dawkins is right and the world is uncompromisingly atheistic, then it is difficult to imagine what objection can be made to the notion that human beings are little more than survival machines designed to be host organisms for their DNA.

Most religious people would probably regard Dawkins' theory as palpably absurd. It would be unjust to think so. The theory's ingenuity and explanatory power are little short of breathtaking. There exist a great many facts that back it up and strengthen its plausibility. As theories go, it is darn good one. A very good case could be made that theory is *largely* true. The question we will be addressing is whether the theory is *entirely* true. In other words, can it explain *everything* about human life? Or are there some facts that are not so easily reconciled with it? If there are such facts, then the theory cannot be regarded as the whole truth. In that case, other theories will have to be brought in to explain the anomalous data.

Do all the facts fit comfortably within the conception of human life put forth by Dawkins and other mechanistic Darwinians? No, they do not. There are at least a few facts, and rather important facts at that, which do not fit so comfortably within Dawkins' conceptual framework. We will examine six of these facts, categorized as follows:

1. *The fundamental non-mechanical character of mind and will.* Mechanistic theories of the material world have failed to provide an adequate explanation of the mind or the will. I have already indicated why I regard any belief in the mechanistic character of the mind as extremely dubious. Human creativity cannot be explained on mechanical grounds. Nor, to be entirely frank about it, can plain ordinary thought. There is no mechanical method of thought. Human beings do not think logically. They make plausible inferences, interpreting the world in light of intuitive judgments based on past experiences. The complexities involved in even the simplest thought processes strongly suggest that the human mind does not operate on mechanistic principles.

Darwinism can respond to this challenge in one of two ways. It can either claim that science will one day develop the sophistication and expertise necessary to prove that human cognition can be explained mechanistically, or it can acknowledge that thought is just too complicated to be explained scientifically. Neither alternative speaks well for the Darwinian theory. The first alternative is clearly an appeal to faith. While it is possible that the mind might someday be explained on purely mechanical principles, from what we know right now, this would appear grossly implausible. The second alternative is the more honest one, but it fails to close the door to non-mechanistic theories, including religious theories, that might provide a more satisfactory explanation for the mind.

Attempts to explain human decision-making on the basis of mechanistic principles are fraught with even more difficulties. If the ability to make choices could be explained as a mechanical process, this would be tantamount to establishing determinism. In the final analysis, determinism is little more than mechanism applied to human decision-making. If the choices of human beings could be explained mechanically, that would be the death knell of human freedom. Human beings would, in reality, be little more than "survival machines" fashioned by evolution to temporarily house bits of DNA, just as Dawkins has asserted all along.

I must hasten to add that all attempts to explain human decision-making mechanically have failed. Human beings are not machines, as the least observation of human affairs will readily demonstrate. Why, even Dawkins himself acknowledges human freedom. "We are built as gene machines," he writes, "but we have the power to turn against our creators. We, alone on earth, can rebel against the tyranny of the selfish replicators." (1976, 201) Although Dawkins insists that he is not a genetic determinist, that he only believes genes exert a "statistical influence on human behavior," (1976, 331) in taking this position, he is giving up ground on the mechanistic front. Whether Dawkins realizes it or not, he has conceded that not everything in the world is a result of mechanism or chance. There exists at least one other reality, the human will, that operates on principles other than those which Dawkins puts forth to explain the evolution of life. In a sense, he is tacitly acknowledging that there exists more in the universe than his philosophy logically allows.

Does the failure of mechanistic materialism to explain thought and decision-making provide grounds for belief in God? No, it does not. It does, however, demonstrate that, since not everything in the universe can be explained mechanically, alternative explanations, including explanations involving the existence of a God, cannot be dismissed out of hand.

2. *Abiogenesis.* Materialism faces no greater challenge than to explain how chance-driven mechanisms spawn living, sentient beings brimming with values and capable of self-reproduction. How does life emerge from inanimate matter? "The origin of life was the chemical event, or series of events, whereby the vital conditions for natural selection came about," offers Dawkins. "The beauty of the anthropic principle is that it tells us, against all intuition [i.e., against common sense], that a chemical model need only predict that life will arise on one planet in a billion billion to give us a good and entirely satisfying explanation for the presence of life here." (2007, 137-138) Dawkins is here arguing that, given enough chances, it is possible that life will spontaneously emerge from matter. If we got together a "billion billion" kettles and poured several thousand gallons of carbon molecules in them and warmed them up for millions of years, life would bubble forth from at least one of the kettles. This, Dawkins would have us believe, is an "entirely satisfying" explanation for the emergence of life. But *that* depends on how easily we are satisfied. No scientific evidence exists that life can actually emerge in this fashion. And even if it could, another problem exists that proves an even greater challenge for the true-believing materialist.

The life that bubbles forth from one of our billion billion kettles can't be just any ordinary run-of-the-mill type of life. It has to be a very special kind of life: it has to contain DNA, along with the ability to read and follow that DNA. And this DNA itself must be a specific type; that is, it must be fashioned in such a way that it will support free mutations over time. Otherwise, the whole evolution-through-natural-selection paradigm, so central to Darwinian materialism, would be impossible. As Dr. Frances Collins, head of the Human Genome Program, has explained: "Within the genome, Darwin's theory predicts that mutations that do no affect function (namely, those located in 'junk DNA') will accumulate steadily over time. Mutations in the coding region of the genes, however, are expected to be observed less frequently, since most of these will be deleterious, and only a rare such event will' provide selective advantage and be retained during the evolutionary process. That is exactly what is observed." (2006, 129-130) In short, the human genome is "designed" to support evolution through natural selection. How materialistic nature pulled off this tremendous feat has yet to be explained on materialistic grounds. The notion that carbon molecules, warmed in a primordial soup, spontaneously generate unicellular creatures is, in itself, difficult for the human mind to believe: but to imagine that this same primordial soup can generate organisms with a genome so complex in its structure and coding that it allows for the complexities of evolution through natural selection is to embrace an improbability so immense that it verges into palpable absurdity.

Does the inability to explain, on purely naturalistic grounds, the emergence of life prove the existence of God? Not necessarily. Ignorance is not evidence. Abiogenesis may turn out to be an unfathomable mystery which provides evidence for no position. Nonetheless, it does, on its own strength alone, significantly enhance the plausibility of theism.

3. *The utility of religion.* Few militant atheists could ever bring themselves to accept the idea that religion might be beneficial. Yet their reluctance to regard religion in a positive light may not entirely square with some of the most important premises of Darwinian evolution. For if the Darwinians are right and evolution by natural selection is the biological law of the land, then how do we explain the ubiquity of religious belief throughout most of human history? On Darwinian grounds there can be only one explanation: the survival value of religious belief. If believing in God had no survival value, theism would have long ago been weeded out by natural selection. Clearly, this hasn't been the case. The vast majority of human beings have always been religious. Indeed, it is only in recent history that secular belief systems have taken hold. Even today, after three hundred years of scientific progress and

"enlightenment," pure and unsullied irreligion remains confined to a tiny minority.

Sophisticated Darwinians know better than to quibble against the utility of religion. Although recognizing it as a fact, they are quick to point out that the utility of a doctrine does not establish its truth. "If the religious mythos did not exist in culture, it would be quickly invented," acknowledges Darwinism's most persuasive advocate, Edward O. Wilson, "and in fact it has been everywhere, thousands of times through history. Such inevitably is the mark of instinctual behavior in any species. That is, even when learned, it is guided toward certain state by emotion-driven rules of mental development. To call religion instinctive is not to suppose any particular part of its mythos is untrue, only that its sources run deeper than ordinary habit and are in fact hereditary, urged into birth through biases in mental development encoded in the genes."

Religion, Wilson would have us believe, is the product of our instincts. But where did these curious instincts come from? If Wilson and Dawkins are correct, they must have been produced through evolution by natural selection. That is how Wilson explains it. Religious biases, Wilson observes, "are to be expected as a usual consequence of the brain's genetic evolution.... There is a hereditary selection advantage to membership in a powerful group united by devout belief and purpose." Religious instincts, Wilson points out, are closely allied with tribal instincts. The two instincts reinforce each other. Religious instincts are useful because they help reinforce tribal strength and determination. (1998, 257-258) Historically, groups whose tribal bonds were strengthened by religious convictions enjoyed a competitive advantage against groups that lacked religious convictions. The religious tribes succeeded in exterminating the non-religious tribes.

While this is a fairly plausible view of primitive religions, it is less plausible when applied to the Christian religion, which is clearly not a tribal religion. In Christianity we find a religion that insists upon the equality of all human beings before God—hardly an ideal compatible with primitive tribalism. Now if, as is indeed likely, an instinct for religion developed side by side with the instinct for tribalism, so that the two are joined, as it were, at the waist, like a pair of Siamese twins, how then do we explain the emergence and subsequent dominance, within Western Civilization, of the Christian religion?

If the Darwinian argues that Christianity is only anti-tribal in theory, but not in practice, I would say he misses the point. It is true that Christian practice doesn't always follow Christian theory. According to Christian doctrine, this is to be expected. But *that* is not the point at issue. What is at issue is the fact that, on the one side, we find a theory that explains the utility of religion on the basis of its ability to strengthen tribal bonds, and on the other, a very successful religion that exhibits a strong theoretical bias against tribalism. How is this contradiction to be reconciled within the Darwinian framework?

I have conceded that Christianity has not always been successful in subduing tribalism. But in conceding that, I have perhaps conceded too much. While tribalism (or its psycho-pathological equivalent) remains a problem even in countries strongly influenced by centuries of Christianity, it is no less true that individuals born and raised in predominantly Christian nations tend to be less tribalistic than those born and raised in non-Christian nations. For confirmation of this fact, merely compare the civilizations of the West, where Christianity has enjoyed the most influence, with the Civilizations of the Orient. For all its ethnocentrism, the West has demonstrated far more curiosity and openness to the rest of the world than has the Orient. For two centuries Japan excluded itself from the rest of the world. Tribalistic xenophobia cannot be extended any further than that.

Japan's xenophobia provides additional evidence for proving that Christianity has succeeded in attenuating the tribalistic instincts of human beings. Within a half century after its introduction into Japan in the sixteenth century, Christianity had gained as many as 150,000 converts. The Japanese rulers became alarmed. Their Christian subjects, they found, were more devoted to their religion than to the state. In other words, the anti-tribalism at the core of Christianity was working. Japanese Christians were less tribalistic than non-Christian Japanese. The leaders of Japan, fearing that any weakening of the societal bonds could make Japan vulnerable to the West, decided to close their country to the rest of the world and prohibit Christianity.

Wilson's theory has another problem. Religion, he claims, arose because it strengthens tribal bonds, thus granting survival advantage to those tribes that are religious. No doubt this is true in many instances. Religions reinforce altruistic sentiments, inspiring their adherents with a willingness to make the ultimate sacrifice for the tribe. One can readily see the advantage a tribe would derive from instilling warriors with an eagerness to sacrifice themselves in battle. But why should these tribalistic sentiments require religious enthusiasm to bring them to fruition? Why could not some other belief system do just as well, if not better?

If it should be argued that only religious belief can stimulate the sort of mystical ecstasy necessary to inspire self sacrifice on behalf of the tribe, it would be odd that this should be so. If, as the Darwinian contends, religion is all stuff and nonsense, why should it have this bewildering power? Wouldn't it have been more economical, and hence more plausible from a Darwinian perspective, for nature to have selected some other belief system, one that focused more exclusively on the tribal aspect? Keep in mind that religions normally impose many burdens, some of them rather onerous, on their adherents, especially in the form of elaborate rituals involving propitiation and sacrifice. They also contain what Darwinians would regard as dangerous excesses: beliefs in imaginary entities, in various forms of magic, and other "spurious" arcane. Richard Dawkins has gone so far as to compare religious faith to "a kind of mental illness." (1976, 330) If we are talking merely about enhancing a tribe's competitive advantage in the context of Darwinian natural selection, wouldn't a belief system that took out all these burdensome rituals and dubious superstitions have an advantage over those that did not? In other words, wouldn't a far more secular belief system, one which continued to give people hope in immortality but otherwise got rid of all the "troublesome" God stuff—wouldn't such a system enjoy a Darwinian competitive advantage against the more religious, God-centric systems?

It is possible to come up with all sorts of clever rationalizations to explain why religious dogma triumphed over secular practicality; rationalizations, moreover, which, in reference to primitive religions, have a tolerable degree of plausibility. When confronted with more advanced religions, such as Christianity, this Darwinian contention that religiosity can be explained solely as "brain circuitry and deep, genetic history" suddenly becomes far less plausible. There is no getting around it: from a strictly Darwinian point of view, the utility of religious belief is decidedly odd.

Christianity poses an even greater problem to the Darwinian thesis than most religions. Having arrived on the scene only very recently in terms of evolutionary time, it cannot be regarded as a product of natural selection. Its appeal is not to the biological self, but to some other aspect of human nature that does not fit so easily within the Darwinian *weltanschauung*. I will have more to say of this element of Christianity when we discuss the moral effect of religion. For now I merely wish to insist upon the fact that the utility of Christianity poses a serious problem to the mechanistic vision of Darwinism—so much so that a consistent Darwinian would be best advised to deny Christianity's utility altogether.

Of course, not everyone agrees that Christianity has played a beneficial role in mankind's history. Nietzsche, for example, saw in Christianity "the greatest misfortune of mankind so far." (1968B, 634) Others have been quick to note all the crimes and atrocities that have been committed by people acting in the name of the Christian church, or on behalf of some creed or sect claiming to draw its spiritual sustenance from Christ. But amassing a catalogue of so-called "Christian" iniquities proves little. The worst aspect of Christianity has been its intolerance, its dogmatism, and its cruelty. Yet each of these faults goes against the grain of basic Christian doctrine as presented in the life and words of Christ. Christianity cannot cure the ills and horrors the human nature. It can at best mitigate and soften them. And so any attempt to reach an estimate of Christianity's moral worth must avoid using false ideals about human nature as the basis of judgment. Simply because individuals do evil in the name of Christianity does not constitute an objection to Christian doctrine. For these individuals, these vile priests and blood-drenched inquisitors, may have committed greater evils had they been entirely free of Christian doctrine and precept. "The record of mankind *with* Christianity is daunting enough," admitted historian Paul Johnson. "The dynamism it has unleashed has brought massacre and torture, intolerance and destructive pride on a huge scale, for there is a cruel and pitiless nature in man which is sometimes impervious to Christian restraints and encouragements. But without these restraints, bereft of these encouragements, how much more horrific the history of these last 2,000 years must have been!" (1976, 517)

Against the horrors committed by Christian priests and inquisitors must be balanced the solace it has provided for the sick and destitute and the moral enthusiasm with which it has animated the better part of Western Civilization. Those who see only the negative side of Christianity are obviously blinded by party spirit. They wish to dismiss all the good that Christianity has accomplished in this world because it goes against the grain of their anti-religion prejudices. Here we find yet another example of ideas being placed *before* facts, rather than *after* them. Realism, let me repeat, is all about making our ideas conform to reality, not reality to our ideas.

While the inadequacy of the Darwinian explanation for the utility of religion hardly constitutes evidence *for* the existence of God, it does alter the balance of plausibility between atheism on the one side and theism on the other. The theistic vision has no difficulty explaining the utility of religion. If God existed you would expect religion to have utility. The atheist vision has a more difficult time of it, despite the obvious ingenuity of many of its rationalizations.

3. *The moral effect of religion.* Does religion improve morals? Many think so. The conviction that without God, morality would be impossible, runs deep among defenders of theism. "If there is no God, that means everything is permitted," proclaimed Dostoevsky. Many reasons can be given why this might be so. It could be argued that religious belief gives people the incentive to do well. Or that fear of divine retribution discourages people from evil-doing. Or that human beings could never have figured out how to behave without God's help.

The problem with such arguments is that they are not sufficiently empirical. They take too much for granted. They naively assume that morality is a matter of belief when, as the least reflection will show, it depends far more on the will. Belief is one thing; willing is something else altogether.

Sociobiologists and evolutionary psychologists have advanced the idea that genetic determination is statistical. That is to say, genetic determination is only partial. It influences human conduct, but does not control it. I suspect this theory pretty much accords with the truth of the matter. Personal experience testifies to the fact that all human decisions are made under the duress of passion. We can, if we so choose, act against our passions, but doing so exacts a price. The farther we stray from the natural bent of our biological psyches, the greater the strain on the organism. The general tendency is for human beings to give in to their biological cravings whenever they can get away with it. Hence the statistical result of genetic determination. People are capable of acting against their natural drives, especially the weaker ones. But often they give in to them. Or they compromise. Hence the futility of acting against human nature.

Earlier in this essay, I quoted Richard Dawkins extraordinary assertion (extraordinary given its source) that "we alone can rebel against our genes." In a sense, this is true. We can choose to act against our biological cravings. But Dawkins goes even further than this. Noting that "every time we use contraception," we rebel against our genes "in a small way," he finds "no reason why we should not rebel in a large way, too." (1976, 332) Here Dawkins has bitten off far more than he can chew. If genetic determination really is statistical, as Dawkins himself professes, then it is difficult to conceive how rebellion in a "large way" could *ever* be possible. Human beings may be free in the sense that they *can* decide to go against their biological strivings, but as a matter of fact they hardly ever go against them in a big way, and when they do, they usually pay a very large price. Human beings can *choose* to tilt at windmills, but they cannot very well choose to like the results. Human nature does exist. It is not a figment of anyone's imagination; it is a reality that cannot be pushed aside because someone doesn't like it.

Now let us suppose, for argument's sake, that we discover a certain group of people acting contrary to human nature—that is, contrary to their biological proclivities. And not merely acting against these proclivities in a little way, but in the "large way" suggested by Dawkins. Would this prove Dawkins right? No, not necessarily. It all depends on why or how the anomalous behavior came about. Let me give an example.

The novelist Evelyn Waugh once wrote to a friend, "I know I am awful. But how much more awful I should be without the Faith." By *awful* Waugh simply meant that he knew himself to be selfish, vain, inconsiderate, hypocritical, and uncharitable. That is, he was a fair specimen of human nature as it has been described by the humanities on the one side and the behavioral sciences on the other. According to everything we know about human nature, whether from common experience, literature, or scientific investigation, most people tend to be selfish, vain, inconsiderate, and uncharitable, especially toward strangers. All this makes perfect sense according to the Darwinian hypothesis, with its emphasis on "survival of the fittest" and its "Nature, red in tooth and claw" vision of the world. Dawkins, in his book *The Selfish Gene*, notes how many psychological characteristics of man "have been shaped by natural selection for improved ability to cheat, to detect cheaters, and to avoid being thought ... a cheat." (1976, 187-188) Evolution, as Dawkins brilliantly demonstrates, is thoroughly and even ruthlessly amoral. Human beings, biologically considered, behave ethically only when it is in their self-interest to do so. They are never good for the sake of goodness, but only when they can get something out of it. In the evolutionary scheme of things, people can be nice, because niceness pays; but they can never be noble, since nobility would put them at a disadvantage in the evolutionary farce.

If this vision of the world is correct—and nearly all evolutionary science stands unwaveringly in its favor—then we would expect to find virtually no evidence of individuals rising above their biological selves. Oh, to be sure, now and again we might stumble upon an occasional exception; but these anomalies could easily be explained away as mere genetic freaks—moral mutants whose DNA will quickly be selected out of the gene pool by evolution. For the most part, the common run of human nature, with all its weaknesses and limitations, would prevail; genetic statistical determinism *über alles* would be the order of the day.

Do the facts square with this vision of human nature? In many respects they do, as any keen observer of the human comedy will testify. But here and there, a few stray facts can be found that don't fit so easily within the Darwinian ken. For example, social scientists have found that religious behavior is associated with lower rates of criminal behavior. Prison ministries are known to reduce recidivism by more than ten percentage points. (Cornell 1990) This may not seem like much, but given the statistical dominance of human nature and how difficult it is for people to change their fundamental character, it would be foolish to dismiss it out of hand. Religion also has been shown to make people more charitable. Even if two people are statistically identical in every other way, a secular person is 23 percentage points less likely to give than a religious person. (Brooks 2003)

It could be argued, of course, that statistical evidence supporting the moral effect of religion only proves the existence of a correlation between religiosity on the one side and improved morals on the other. It does not, as any statistician will tell you, prove a causal link. Perhaps the causality runs entirely in the other direction. Perhaps people are not good because they are religious, but are religious because they are good. Since it is not so obvious what is the cause and what is the effect, how are we to discover the truth of the matter? A good place to start would be to ask religious individuals what they think of the issue. After all, who has a better vantage point than the individual actor? The causation that stems from human behavior can only be seen, if it can be seen at all, from the inside, that is, from the vantage point of the individual. So what do religious people think about the role of religion in their lives?

This brings us back to Evelyn Waugh's statement quoted earlier. Without faith, Waugh believed he would clearly be a worse person. He once went so far as to declare that, without faith, he wouldn't be a civilized person. Waugh is not alone in believing this. Many people, especially Christians, believe that acting decently requires help from God. "The Christian thinks any good he does comes from the Christ-life inside him," wrote C. S. Lewis. (1942, 54) Matthew Arnold went so far as to define God as a force "*not ourselves* which makes for righteousness." (1968, 189) The conviction that God constitutes the only possible source of goodness has deep roots in the Christian tradition.

It is important to note that this conviction does not arise solely from Christian theology or even from the Bible. Many Christians claim that they have experienced the effect of the "Christ-life" in their own lives. Now nothing is easier than to dismiss such claims out of hand. Evidence based solely on subjective experience obviously raises enormous epistemological difficulties for the rational investigator. There are, however, two errors that must be avoided right from the start. The first error would be to accept all claims based on subjective evidence, regardless of how sincere they might appear. The second error is to reject all such claims, simply *because* they are personal and "subjective."

It is the difficulty of corroborating subjective knowledge, not subjective knowledge per se, that raises the problems. If a dozen people step forward and claim to have been touched by God, this would hardly constitute evidence for theism. Twelve people could easily be deluded or mendacious. But what if millions claim to be touched by God? (Beauregard and O'Leary 2007, 192) What should we make of such claims? Can millions of people be mistaken? Perhaps. Human beings are naturally somewhat credulous. Yet to assume that millions *must* be mistaken because their beliefs violate this or that theory of scientific metaphysics demonstrates credulity in the other direction. While it doesn't prove that it is so, it does suggest that the claim should be taken seriously. This means that some effort should be made to estimate the plausibility of the claim. How plausible is it to say that God can make it easier for people to be good? Here we must be careful not to let our conclusions be influenced by tacit assumptions. Atheists tend to dismiss any explanation that involves God because they assume that all such explanations must be wrong. Theists commit the opposite error. If we want to find out what is really happening, we must look at this with as few presuppositions as possible.

Several facts can be brought forth to corroborate the view that God helps people rise above the common standard of human nature as defined by evolutionary psychology. In the first place, there is the aforementioned correlation between morals and religion. God—or at least belief in God—generally does exercise a positive moral effect on human behavior. Along with this, we find evidence of a transforming effect. People who were once morally troubled have, under the influence of religion, reformed their ways and become better people. Alcoholics Anonymous constitutes a famous example of this transformation effect. At the core of one of the most successful treatments for alcoholism is the acknowledgment of a "Higher Power." Among the Christian community one can find thousands of examples of people who have undergone various moral transformations. Psychologists are discovering that many problems are best treated through religion. "Among all my patients in the second half of my life … there has not been one whose problem in the last resort was not that of finding a religious outlook on life," testified Carl Jung in 1932. "It is safe to say that every one of them fell ill because he had lost that which the living religions of every age have given their followers and none of them has really healed who did not regain his religious outlook." (1997, 69)

The most convincing evidence for the theist case on this issue involves the contrast between religious morality, especially Christian morality, on the one side, and Darwinian human nature on the other. This can easily be illustrated by comparing Christian ideals of sexual morality with the sexual proclivities of human nature as developed through evolution. As Richard Dawkins notes, "human males in general have a tendency towards promiscuity, and females a tendency towards monogamy, *as we would predict on evolutionary grounds.*" (1976, 164, emphasis added) Yet this is not the worst of it. According to the inner logic of natural selection, any gene that encourages a male to impregnate as many females as possible, or a female to bear the offspring of the strongest and wealthiest male, will quickly dominate the gene pool. This explains the behavior of men and women in a secular society, where men turn women into sex objects and women turn men into success objects. "In our society," notes Stephen Pinker, "the best predictor of a man's wealth is his wife's looks, and the best predictor of a woman's looks is her husband's wealth." (1997, 467, 482)

In Christianity, we find an attenuation of this natural tendency toward the objectification of human beings into sex machines on the one side and money machines on the other. Christianity has been particularly successful at reigning in male promiscuity. If we allowed the inner logic of evolution to have its way, society would eventually begin to resemble those oriental communities where the rich and powerful monopolize all the comely women in society through the institution of the harem. From the standpoint of evolutionary psychology, the harem is the most "natural" sexual arrangement. In Islamic societies, where Christianity is persecuted, we continue to find exploitive polygamy on a grand scale. In the Christian West, the institution of monogamy developed in the very teeth, as it were, of genetic selection.

What reason do we have for believing that God might have had a role in this? Why can't we simply explain it as an outgrowth of Christian doctrine? The reason is simple: Mere belief has a limited efficacy on human behavior. To ascribe something to mere belief goes against everything we know of human psychology. Keep in mind what was said earlier about the statistical effect of genetic determinism. Merely because genetic determinism is not absolute doesn't mean that we can easily evade its force. Going against the built-in tendencies of our genetic endowment imposes huge psychic costs. It leads to neuroses and unhappiness. If the dominance of monogamy in the West arose largely from Christian belief, we would expect it to be accompanied by a tremendous rise in mental illness and unhappiness, especially among religious believers. The evidence does not support this. As Patrick Glynn has noted, "It is difficult to find a more consistent correlative of mental health, or a better insurance against self-destructive behaviors, than a strong religious faith." People who attend church regularly are four times less likely to commit suicide, and are more likely to avoid divorce and refrain from drug and alcohol abuse. (1997, 63-64) On the other side of the coin, psychologists have noted for many years that the sexual liberation experienced by non-religious adolescents "has often led to empty relationships, feelings of self-contempt and worthlessness, … and haunting concerns that they were using others and being used as 'sexual objects.'" (Glynn 1997, 65)

Again we find ourselves confronting evidence that goes against the grain of mechanistic Darwinism. Since we know that Darwinism is at least in some respects a highly plausible theory, evidence that goes against it suggests that some other principle is at work other than natural selection. Could it be, as Christians believe, that evidence of individuals finding happiness while acting contrary to the biological imperatives of human nature demonstrates God's effect in the lives of those who put their faith in Him? To act contrary to natural drives and yet still find happiness would involve something akin to a miracle. Perhaps the disdain which the secular person regards the possibility of miracles is entirely unwarranted. According to the inner logic of Darwinian evolution, true goodness, that nobility of spirit that transcends petty concerns with the biological self, is for all intents grossly improbable, because any genes that favor such behavior would long ago have been selected out of the gene pool by evolution. So doesn't this mean that the existence of genuine goodness, of genuine nobility of character, constitutes a real living miracle, and as such, evidence of God's hand in our lives?

4. *The divine source of creative inspiration.* Creativity has always posed difficulties for mechanistic materialism—difficulties which the mechanists usually ignore. No attempt to explain creativity on the basis of mechanical laws has ever been successful. Creativity is so contrary to mechanism that it seems doubtful that it is compatible with a purely mechanical universe. As the philosopher Eliseo Vivas put it: "The product of the creative mind is not a mere combination, but a *creation* in a sense that no behaviorist or mechanist can admit and remain true to his theories. Creative activity takes place very rarely; but when it takes place it adds something new to the content of experience." (1955, 239)

How is it possible that something new can be added to experience? How does this novelty happen? What, if anything, can be known about it? Perhaps the best place to find answers to this question is by consulting actual artists as to the sources of their creativity. After all, the artist is the only person with firsthand experience of the creative act. The rest of us are just clueless bystanders.

In 1896, an obscure American violinist, Arthur Abell, had a three-hour conversation with the composer Johannes Brahms in which the sources of inspiration and creativity were discussed. Although Brahms was very reluctant to talk about the subject, the death of his close friend Clara Schumann along with forebodings of his own death (which would occur in the next year) and the entreaties of his friend, the violinist Joseph Joachim, persuaded him to discuss the matter. Brahms got right to the point: "All truly inspired ideas come from God," he insisted. "Beethoven, who was my ideal, was well aware of this."

Brahms' remarks on the actual process through which he contacted God are worth quoting in full. "To realize that we are one with the Creator, as Beethoven did, is a wonderful and awe-inspiring experience. Very few human beings ever come into that realization and that is why there are so few great composers or creative geniuses in any line of human endeavor. I always contemplate all this before commencing to compose. This is the first step. When I feel the urge I begin by appealing directly to my Maker and I first ask Him the three most important questions pertaining to our life here in this world—whence, wherefore, whither? I immediately feel vibrations that thrill my whole being.... Those vibrations assume the forms of distinct mental images,

after I have formulated my desire and resolve in regard to what I want—
namely, to be inspired so that I can compose something that will uplift
and benefit humanity—something of permanent value. Straightaway
the ideas flow in upon me, directly from God, and not only do I see
distinct themes in my mind's eye, but they are clothed in the right
forms, harmonies and orchestration." (1955, 5-6)

Several years before Abell's conversation with Brahms, he had
discussed the question of creative inspiration with the composer
Richard Strauss. Although Strauss was not a religious man, his remarks
to some extent echo those of Brahms. "When the inspiration comes,"
he told Abell, "it is something of so subtle, tenuous, will-o-the-wisp-
like nature that it almost defies definition. When in my most inspired
moods, I have definite compelling visions, involving a higher selfhood.
I feel at such moments that I am tapping the source of Infinite and
Eternal energy from which you and I and all things proceed. Religion
calls it God." (1955, 86)

Abell talked to several other composers about the same subject.
They all more or less agreed that creative inspiration comes from
God. Puccini described the "great secret of all creative geniuses" as
the "power to appropriate the beauty, the wealth, the grandeur, and
the sublimity contained within their own souls, which are parts of
Omnipotence, and to communicate those riches to others." Richard
Wagner described inspiration as "a universal current of divine thought."
Max Bruch believed that the composer has to "sit in silence and wait
for the direction from a force that is superior to the intellect." (1955,
116, 137, 146)

It could be argued that these composers, all of whom grew up in
the nineteenth century, when Christian sentiment and terminology
still dominated European culture, are merely using religious words as
symbols for the inexpressible. But this criticism misses the mark. All
words are symbols, including scientific words. When people describe
something as inexpressible, all that they are saying is that words fail
to communicate the experience in question. Thus the artist finds it
difficult to express creative inspiration to non-artists who have no
experience of artistic inspiration. Matters are little improved when
"scientific" people assume from the start that creative inspiration
must, ultimately, be a mechanical process, explicable only through the

symbols of scientific investigation. But what if this is not true? What if the symbols of scientific investigation are inadequate to the task of explaining creativity? Would this mean that the use of other symbols must also be deemed inadequate as well?

But why must we use religious symbols? Why not use symbols that are neither scientific nor religious, but merely descriptive? Well of course it would be possible to use non-religious symbols, although it is unclear that such a procedure would remove the central problem facing the atheist view. No matter what set of symbols we use, we still find ourselves confronted with an external power that is claimed as the source of creative inspiration. Consider Tchiakovsky's description of the creative process, which, although it doesn't use specifically religious symbols, nevertheless refers to inspiration as a "magic process." "Generally speaking, the germ of a future composition comes suddenly and unexpectedly," Tchaikovsky wrote. "It takes root with extraordinary force and rapidity, shoots up through the earth, puts forth branches and leaves, and finally blossoms. I cannot define the creative process in any other way than by this simile… It would be vain to try to put into words the immeasurable sense of bliss which comes over me directly a new idea awakens in me and begins to assume a definite form. I forget everything and behave like a madman; everything within me starts pulsing and quivering; hardly have I begun the sketch, ere one thought follows another."

For Tchaikovsky, as with so many other composers and artists, creative inspiration is not something that is willed. It comes of its own initiative and proceeds under its own power. The composer is completely at its mercy. He forgets everything and behaves "like a madman." One thought follows another of its own accord, irrespective of the self or the will. Would it be mere poetic fancy to describe this creative force as God, as Brahms did? What if, following Matthew Arnold's phraseology, we were to describe it as *that power not ourselves which makes for creativity*? But once we have admitted that a *power not ourselves* exists, what possible epistemological scruple would prevent us from calling it a God? What else should we call it? Would atheists feel better if we were to call it the Great Creative Gremlin?

One of the first principles of any realist philosophy is not to argue about words. The word is not important; it is the reality that the word points to and symbolizes that is important. If creative inspiration comes from outside ourselves, as many artists seem to believe, then there must exist an external power. Where does this external power come from? Well, one thing appears certain: it would be grossly implausible to regard this external power as the mechanical byproduct of evolution. Creativity cannot arise from mechanism or chance. It must therefore emerge from some type of mode or entity or substance or being that is not amenable to scientific description; something, in other words, similar to what religious people know as God. If so, then why not just call it God? By any other name, It would still amount to the same thing.

5. *Near Death Experiences.* An estimated seven million people have gone through what are now called "near-death experiences"—experiences are now fairly well known. The individual sees himself gliding through a tunnel toward a point of light, whom many identify with Christ or other religious entities. Some people experience a sort of celestial judgment; their life flashes before them and they begin to regret their mistakes. Others report meeting relatives and loved ones. A few disturbed souls relate hellish encounters. Regardless of the precise character of each near-death episode, none of these experiences can easily be explained on the mechanistic grounds of Darwinian materialism. Although many in the scientific community remain skeptical or even hostile to the notion that such experiences constitute evidence of God or an afterlife, others have not been so quick to reject them out of hand. Rigorous studies have been made. Witnesses have been interviewed, data collected and analyzed, conclusions drawn. The most notable study was authored by Dr. Pim van Lommel and published in the medical journal *The Lancet*. (Lommel et al 2001) "Our results show that medical factors cannot account for occurrence of near-death experiences," the article states. *The Lancet* is one of the world's most respected medical journals, so such pronouncements are not to be taken lightly.

Can near-death experiences be regarded as evidence for God? While it would be rash to regard them as irrefragable evidence for theism, at the very least they can be seen as providing plausible grounds for a rational belief in God. Alternative theories based on conventional scientific assumptions clearly seem less plausible. There exists no strong evidence that NDEs are caused by oxygen deprivation, excessive levels of endorphins, or excessive levels of carbon dioxide in the brain, as has been suggested by various militant atheists. Pam Reynolds, for example, experiences an NDE during a special surgical procedure in which her body temperature was reduced to the point that her heart stopped and her EEG brains waves flattened to zero. (Beauregard and O'Leary 2007, 153-154)

*   *   *

Having examined some of the evidence for theism, we now turn to some of the evidentiary claims made on behalf of atheism.

1. *God's "hiddenness."* Since God cannot be identified and pointed at for all to see, this is regarded as evidence that God does not exist. I alluded to this issue earlier when I pointed out that the existence of God cannot be proven ostensively. Whether this constitutes evidence for atheism is debatable. Scientists tell us that black holes exist, yet no one can prove the existence of black holes by pointing at one and saying, "There it is." The evidence for black holes must be established on a subtler basis than point-and-look. The same is true of God's existence.

2. *Existence of evil.* "God's only excuse is that he does not exist." Stendhal's witticism, which Friedrich Nietzsche regarded as "the best atheistical joke," (1968A, 700) encapsulates the view that the world is so bad and evil that it would be best if God did not exit. If God exists, how do we explain all the pain and suffering, the senseless brutality and genocide, the terrible crimes committed against children, and all the other horrors that fill newspapers and history books? How could an all-powerful, loving God allow such horrors to take place? If God does in fact exist, wouldn't we have to conclude, from the nature of the world he created, that he is not altogether good, as His propagandists continue to insist, but is, in at least some respects, evil? And if God is in some respects evil, wouldn't it be better if he did not exist at all?

Although the problem of evil has always been a thorn in the side of theism, it would be a mistake to assume that naturalistic theories don't have problems of their own explaining evil. Earlier in this essay,

I suggested that Darwinian naturalism cannot adequately explain any sort of goodness that rises above mere self-interested niceness. A similar argument could be advanced regarding the problem of evil. After all, what competitive advantage, in the Darwinian sense of the term, could possibly be attained from murdering everyone who can read, as the Khymer Rouge did in Cambodia? Or flying airplanes into buildings, as Islamic terrorists did on September 11? Or by indiscriminately murdering and eating people, in the manner of Jeffrey Dahmer?

Would it really be so great a stretch to suggest that perhaps the great evil in the world, far from suggesting that God does not exist, provides instead evidence for the existence of some sort of demonic force at work in the world, symbolized in popular religions as the devil? This symbolism may at times verge toward the palpably fanciful; but that does not necessarily mean that there is no reality at the bottom of it. Ultimately, all knowledge is symbolic. People for generations have sensed that certain forms of evil cannot be explained on a purely mechanistic basis; that some kind of mysterious power had to be at work at the bottom of the world's greatest horrors. Thus the symbolism of demonology, Satanism, and the devil. Although much of this symbolism is crude and vulgar, the general notion of mysterious power or influence that helps bring about great evil in the world can hardly be dismissed out of hand. In any case, it explains extreme evil better than scientific naturalism.

Does the existence of a power or influence that makes for evil solve the theistic problem of evil? Perhaps not. The solution to the problem of evil, whether for naturalism or theism, rests in the idea of freedom. As long as human beings are "free" in the sense that they are capable of creativity and moral choice, evil becomes possible. If a deity wanted to create a world destitute of evil, he would have to populate his world with automatons. Grant an animal freedom, and no one can be sure exactly what will happen.

Now if we assume, as I believe any realist must, that human beings are not mere automatons, but creatures of mind and will capable of moral choice and artistic creativity, then which view is more plausible: mechanistic Darwinism or theism? I will address this question at a later point in this essay.

3. *The success and coherence of scientific naturalism.* In the last three hundred years, the triumphs of science have revolutionized the world. Medical advances have significantly reduced human suffering. Technology has greatly reduced the burden of manual labor. Radio, television, and the internet have facilitated the spread of information, leading to greater individual freedom. The automobile has liberated us from the tyranny of distance. Advances in medicine have extended our lives by decades. This revolution of the modern era owes its existence almost exclusively to the development of the scientific method. The methodology of science, with its emphasis on empirical testability and objective validation, has proven its value again and again. No other method of knowledge can compare with it. Theology, on the other hand, has been a colossal failure. Whereas in science, you find agreement not only on the big questions, but also on many of the details, in theology there is no general agreement on questions big or small, but only a mere anarchy of blind guesses, ultimately defended by belligerently dogmatic faiths. In comparing the methodologies of science and theology, which should a rational person trust? Should he trust a methodology that has no proven track record, that has failed to attain consensus on any of the important questions it seeks to explicate, and that has nothing to show for itself beyond centuries of senseless debates and futile speculations? Or should he trust the methodology that brings within its train all the marks of success: a proven track record, a high-degree of consensus, and a widening of the scope of human knowledge that is little short of breathtaking?

It would be foolish to deny the persuasiveness of this argument. The scientific method is the most powerful tool of cognition ever developed by the mind of man. Its excellence, however, does not mean that it is the only method of knowledge at our disposal, nor that it is capable of elucidating every facet of reality. As realists, we should be careful not to fall into the trap of equating scientific knowledge with all of reality. That would be tantamount to assuming that reality must conform to the strengths of the human mind: an assumption that would constitute a lapse into idealism. We must disabuse ourselves of the notion, so flattering to human vanity, that reality exists for the convenience of scientific understanding.

If we are serious about grasping the world around us, we had better ask some hard questions concerning the scope and character of science. To what, precisely, does science owe its tremendous success? I would answer: science owes most of its success to the intelligibility of its data—by the fact that scientific concepts and measurements can be unambiguously communicated to other scientists. When a scientific theory is passed from one scientist to another, very little is lost in the translation. This allows scientists to repeat the experiments of other scientists, thereby bringing a high degree of accountability to scientific research.

Why is science so intelligible? There are primarily two reasons that account for this: (1) the emphasis in science on quantifiable data, on measurement and quantitative analysis; and (2) the emphasis on observation and empirical testability. Science confines itself to those phenomena in reality that are, by their very nature, amenable to unequivocal symbolization. But what about those things in reality that cannot be described or communicated unambiguously? Those who regard the scientific method as the only legitimate method of inquiry are guilty of tacitly assuming that anything that cannot be unequivocally symbolized does not exist. Here, again, we find ourselves confronting epistemological hubris. While it is true that science has been enormously successful—so much so, that it has fair claim to constituting the best method of discovering and ascertaining truth—this does not mean that we can accept the notion that reality must conform to scientific methodology.

According to certain extreme forms of scientific positivism, we can only know that which can be grasped and elucidated by the methods of science. "Whereof one cannot speak, thereof one must be silent," the philosopher Ludwig Wittgenstein famously said. In other words, what cannot be communicated unambiguously cannot be known. Even a slight bit of ambiguity would make a thing unknowable.

Could this view of reality possibly be true? If something cannot be symbolized unequivocally, does this automatically place it beyond the epistemological pale? Must human knowledge attain unequivocal precision before it can be taken seriously? Must we reject all claims tainted with ambiguity?

Those who take such an extreme view would rule out of hand most of what passes for everyday, practical knowledge. So much of our knowledge consists of little more than educated guesses based on incomplete information. Consider, as one example, our knowledge of other people. Can we really say that knowledge of our friends and acquaintances is clear, precise, and quantifiable? No, of course not. It is not even logical. We observe other people from the outside. We know nothing of their inner life beyond what we infer from vague clues and second-hand information. Yet how critical is this species of knowledge, forming, as it surely does, the very basis of all our judgments of the people we live and work with. Woe to us if our judgment goes awry, if our educated guesses about other people miss the mark!

If God does in fact exist, knowledge of him would be somewhat like our knowledge of other people, only more tenuous and probabilistic. We are dealing with data that, because it is not unequivocally intelligible, will never be entirely amenable to scientific methodology. It would be a mistake to dismiss such knowledge out of hand for that reason alone. Reality, as the least reflection on ultimate questions will demonstrate, is unintelligible at its core. Existence is a surd. We can understand how things work within reality; but why they work one way rather than another we can never know. They simply are the way they are and that's as much as we can say.

To sum up: Merely because something is difficult to understand or put into words does not constitute proof of its non-existence. The success of the scientific method does not constitute a valid argument against theism.

4. *Mind-brain dependence.* Critical to the mechanistic-materialist view of the universe is the hypothesis that all mental events are ultimately reducible to brain events. Mind is utterly and irrevocably dependent on matter, so that for every mental event, there must be, as its cause and basis, a corresponding brain event. If this hypothesis turns out to be true, it would pretty much put to rest the religious conception of a soul and the plausibility of an afterlife. If human beings are little more than materialistic survival machines, doomed to eventual extinction, then the question of God's existence becomes utterly superfluous—a matter of idle curiosity, and nothing more.

It must be admitted right from the start that the evidence for mind-brain dependence is fairly compelling. To give but a sample of the evidence, consider the following six facts:

(1) When an individual's brain is directly stimulated and put into a specified physical state, this results in a corresponding specific mental experience.
(2) Injuries to the brain can affect not only the mental capacity of the individual, but his personality as well.
(3) Injuries to specific parts of the brain are directly related to specific types of mental incapacities and personality disorders.
(4) The mental capacities of animals become more complex as their brains become more complex.
(5) The development of mental capacities is strongly correlated with the development of neurons in the brain.

These facts are indisputable; what can be disputed is how they are interpreted, the meaning that is ascribed to them. This is the crux of the issue. All of us, whether we realize it or not, interpret the facts we observe. When a person observes a cat, an image of the cat appears in his consciousness. Does the image, however, signify or prove that the cat exists? Of course not. The image exists only within consciousness. If the observer shuts his eyes, the image disappears. But does the actual cat existing in time and space disappear when the observer closes his eyes? Obviously not. Yet how does the observer know this? Through his intelligence, which interprets the image of the cat as evidence of a real cat.

Interpretation does not stop at the observation of facts. To know that a cat has entered my field of vision is of little importance. What I wish to know is the significance of the fact. What sort of cat is it? Is it my cat, or someone else's? Is it friendly or hostile? Healthy or diseased? My conclusions will depend on how I interpret my observations of the cat; and my interpretations will be influenced by various tacit presuppositions that I may entertain about cats in general.

What if my presuppositions about feline critters are in some way false or defective? Doesn't this mean that my interpretations will also be false and defective? What if I believe that cats are diabolical creatures who pretend to be ill to incite sympathy from credulous humans. Under such an interpretive framework, I will be incapable of noticing whether the cat is in fact deathly ill. "Oh, he's just faking it—cats are notorious for that." Thus would I dismiss any evidence of illness in the animal. The cat could be at death's very door; but if my tacit presuppositions dismiss the very possibility of feline sickness, no evidence will persuade me of the fact. Tacit presuppositions, though necessary for determining the significance of facts, can, if erroneous, blind us to facts.

In discussing the issue of mind-brain dependence and its relation to the question of God's existence, we cannot ignore the role that presuppositions play in assessing evidence. Since the atheist tacitly assumes that God cannot exist, is it any wonder that he automatically regards mind-dependence as positive proof for his atheistic presuppositions? But what is the ultimate basis for this proof? Is it in the evidence, or in the presupposition?

The whole issue of near-death experiences illustrates the difficulties of settling the question of God's existence on empirical grounds. The atheist, when examining the phenomenon of NDEs, can only make sense of such experiences by interpreting them through the filter of his mechanistic-materialist world view, which rules out of hand any explanation that involves the supposition of an afterlife or the existence of a deity. Hence, near-death experiences must be the result of physiological factors directly affecting the brain, such as cardiac arrest, anesthesia, oxygen deprivation, endorphins, and hypercarbia. The problems with this approach can be illustrated by examining one of the evidentiary claims made against NDEs. If the Sylvian fissure in the right temporal lobe is electrically stimulated, this will produce experiences very similar to NDEs. Mechanistic naturalists contend that the ability to reproduce NDEs through brain manipulation refutes the notion that NDEs provide a glimpse into the afterlife. However, the same argument could be made regarding any experience that can be reproduced through electrical stimulation. Suppose the experience of observing an elephant could be reproduced by electrical stimulation. Would we then be justified in assuming that all experiences of elephants must be dismissed as imaginary, as a mere hallucination of the brain and not a reflection of an external reality? Every experience of consciousness involves brain activity, which could theoretically be stimulated through artificial means. Yet this does not mean that all experience is imaginary. Some experiences are real: they are experiences *of* something. That is what realism postulates. When an individual perceives an elephant, there is more to this experience than mere brain stimulation. There is an interpretive intelligence at work which interprets the perception of the elephant as evidence of the existence of a real elephant, existing within the world of matter and time and space.

Earlier in this essay, I advanced several reasons for dismissing the view that mind is ultimately reducible to matter. A psycho-physical dualism is necessitated by the obvious differences between consciousness, thought, and will on the one side and matter on the other. The conviction that everything that happens in the psychical realm is merely the echo or shadow of what happens in the material realm is little more than a baseless superstition. It is reminiscent of the sarcastic claim of Razumihin in Dostoevsky's novel *Crime and Punishment.* "Oh, if you like, I'll prove to you that your white eyelashes may very well be ascribed to the Church of Ivan the Great's being two hundred and fifty feet high," sneers Razumihin in the heat of a debate over the causes of crime, "and I will prove it clearly, exactly, progressively, and even with a Liberal tendency!" This may sound like a joke, but it is a joke in dead earnest. According to the logic of the mechanistic view, there would be nothing absurd in linking the height of a church with the color of someone's eyebrows. If everything is ultimately reducible to matter, if no dualism exists between mind and matter, then everything that exists arises out of the great cauldron of matter. Since the world of matter is characterized by causal links that make everything at least potentially interrelated, the notion of eyebrows being related to the height of a building makes perfect sense on materialist premises. Once you replace freedom and personal autonomy with mechanism, you are left with a deterministic world where everything that happens can be traced through endless causal links to everything else—terminating, ultimately, in the raving absurdity of an infinite regress.

Only within the framework of psycho-physical dualism is the freedom of the human will explicable. That consideration alone should settle the debate. For if monistic materialism were correct, then the experience of human freedom would have to be regarded as little more than an illusion. But if human willing is an illusion, then human thought and human experience becomes utterly illusory as well: mere epiphenomenal blips signifying nothing.

Once we have driven the materialist out of his reductionist stronghold, what is left of the theory of mind-brain dependence as it relates to the question of God and an afterlife? Only this: *that, as far as we know, every functioning mind requires a functioning brain to exist; and that we have no evidence of a mind or a consciousness existing without a corresponding, living brain to back it up and provide a material ground and sustenance.* This is a strong point in favor of the atheist view, but, unless we are willing to embrace the absurdities of an uncompromising mechanistic materialism, it is hardly conclusive.

Having examined the evidence on both sides of the question, now comes the tough part: making a decision. Does God *really* exist, or is the universe little more than a vast, inexplicable, mechanistic megacosm? Does human life have a transcendent significance, or is it an utterly pointless exercise in suffering and humiliation? Is there life after death, or mere pitiless extinction?

The evidence being so equivocal and incomplete, it might seem that the rational course would be simply to admit our ignorance and take shelter under a humble agnosticism. Yet, as I have already explained, this is not a viable option. Too much rides upon the decision. We have no choice but to weigh the evidence and make an educated guess as to which alternative is more likely to be true.

One alternative we can dismiss right from the start. The view that everything that happens, including everything going on within the realm of human consciousness, can be traced to an event in the realm of matter simply does not hold up under critical scrutiny. It leads to a form of determinism that brings in its wake a flood of absurd paradoxes. It assumes, without a shred of evidence, that, at some point in the future, we will be able to explain all mental and psychological phenomena in purely physical terms. How, may we ask, does it know this? It doesn't know it. The eliminative materialism of so many scientists and atheists is little more than an exercise in blind faith, a sort of wishful thinking prompted by a desperate need to believe that the universe is simpler and less problematic than it really is.

Although monistic materialism may be untenable, this, alone, would not establish or prove the verity of theism. There exist alternative systems of naturalism which, it must be admitted, provide a considerably more plausible account of the universe than does the doltish materialism of extreme reductionists. The "biological naturalism" of the philosopher John Searle is an example of one such tenable form of atheistic naturalism. Searle avoids the worst excesses of monistic materialism by admitting right from the start that consciousness cannot be reduced to the subject matter of physics. The complex structures existing in nature that produce consciousness are far too complicated, argues Searle, to be reduced to anything simpler.

Arguing for the complexity and irreducibility of consciousness does nothing toward explaining it. Searle's theory may be more plausible than materialism, but it gains this plausibility by a corresponding reduction in its explanatory power. Loss of explanatory power does not, of course, mean the theory can't be true. The truth of a theory cannot be measured merely by how well it explains things. Reality does not exist to be explained. It exists to be known, which is something different. A theory may be merely descriptive, telling us the way things are. The fact that it fails to explain the deeper mysteries of existence is no objection to it. A theory may serve no other purpose than to demonstrate that a particular thing exists. We can know that a particular thing exists without knowing *why* it exists.

Although Searle's biological naturalism, by eschewing reductivism and monism, avoids the absurdities of mechanistic materialism, it also, for that very reason, abandons the strong atheistic position of materialism for a much weaker one. If mechanistic materialism were true, then theism would be impossible. Searle's naturalism, by eschewing the deterministic and reductivist premises of materialism, also eschews the support these premises provide for atheism. Searle's atheism is adventitious: it is not something that he can derive from the basic principles of his philosophy. He must decide the question on empirical grounds, like any other question of fact.

This means the question of theism versus atheism reduces itself to comparing the evidence for each view. Since the evidence does not unequivocally support either position, we must make an estimate as to which vision of the universe is most likely true. Of course, it is not always clear which alternative is more plausible. Ultimately, it comes down to a judgment call.

Having examined the evidence on both sides as impartially as humanly possible, I find theism to be more plausible than naturalistic atheism. I cannot bring myself to dismiss out of hand the testimony of millions people who claim that God works in their lives merely because such evidence does not square with the mechanistic theories of monistic materialism. I do not regard any sort of monism, whether materialist or spiritualist in content, to be credible. For this reason, I cannot countenance the attitude that scorns certain types of evidence solely on a priori grounds. For the realist, facts always come first. The purpose of a theory is not to prescribe what the facts must be, but to elucidate and explain those facts that an attentive mind discovers.

One particularly important collection of facts that testify very persuasively on behalf of theism involves reports of near death experiences. Naturalist theories, even of the more sophisticated type, are incapable of providing any sort of credible explanation for these phenomena. The best they can offer is the utterly gratuitous assumption that a credible explanation will be forthcoming at an unspecified future date. Until then, however, we have every right to remain skeptical that NDEs can be adequately accounted for on atheistical principles.

Equally important in the debate over God's existence is the evidence of the efficacy of religious belief. I realize that most atheists would deny that such evidence exists. But is that a reasonable position? If we find that holding certain moral and spiritual ideals enhances and enriches human existence, why should we automatically assume that such benefits are based on utterly illusory premises? The efficacy of a belief speaks for, not against, its possible verity.

The issue of efficacy and truth is touched upon by Christ in the gospel of Matthew. "Beware," Christ warns, "of false prophets, which come to you in sheep's clothing, but inwardly they are ravening wolves." A sensible enough warning, to be sure. But how on earth are we to determine whether a given prophet is false? "Ye shall know them by their fruits," we are told. "Do men gather grapes of thorns, or figs of thistles? Even so every good tree bringeth forth good fruit; but a corrupt tree bringeth forth evil fruit. A good tree cannot bring forth evil fruit, neither *can* a corrupt tree bring forth good fruit. Every tree that bringeth not forth good fruit is hewn down, and cast into the fire. Wherefore by their fruits ye shall know them." (Matthew 7:16-20)

Christ's advice about distinguishing false from true prophets can be given a more general application. It applies to *all* estimations of truth. We know something is true (or probably true) because it bears good fruit. What are the fruits of theism? Whether we look to the testimony of believers or the evidence accumulated by scientific researchers, the fact remains that theism, or belief in God, appears to have positive effects on health and well-being. As one researcher, Dr. Herbert Benson, put it: "The data I have presented is that affirmative beliefs and hopes are very therapeutic, and that faith in God, in particular, has many positive effects on health." And not only on health, but on happiness as well. Individuals with a committed faith in God report higher levels of personal happiness and psychological well-being than do nonbelievers. (Glynn 1997, 88, 61-62) The tree of theism provides better fruit than the trees of atheism and agnosticism.

When all the evidence is added up, I believe a fairly persuasive case can be made for a minimal sort of theism. At the very least, a rational person must admit that the case for God's existence is a plausible one. We can go even further than that. We can say, without stretching or exaggerating the facts, that the case for God's existence is more plausible than the case for His non-existence.

For many people, plausibility is not enough. They want to be certain whether God exists. If we cannot know for certain, how can we avoid feeling paralyzed by doubt? This is where faith becomes necessary. In a certain sense, all knowledge is faith—faith that the images of sense and the ideas of the intellect correspond to something in external reality. This does not mean that knowledge is based on "blind" faith. Knowledge is not a wild shot in the dark, but a series of shrewd insights that find their ultimate justification in experience. These insights are never certain: they are mere guesses—acts of faith. If we must act without knowing for certain whether our guesses have the stuff of truth in them, isn't it preferable that we proceed with faith and confidence rather than vacillation and doubt?

Once we have embarked on our adventure of faith, we will find that some faiths are worthier of our trust than others. "By their fruits ye shall know them." It is through trial and error, conjecture and refutation, faith and practice that we navigate through the problems of life. A "true" faith, we would do well to remember, is fundamentally practical. Faith must continually prove its cognitive worth through action. Those mystics or rationalists whose overweening pride leads them to put all their faith in contemplative or speculative knowledge have built their cognitive houses on sand. Ideas prove their worth by being put to the test. If you would know whether an idea is true, you must *serve* the idea, put it into practice, put its cognitive and moral value to the test. In this sense, there is much to be said for Michael Polanyi's conviction that God can only be apprehended by serving Him. (1962, 279)

I began this essay by taking note of a common misperception which regards realism as a threat to the spiritual life. But why should realism be regarded as a threat? The objective of realism is to see reality without illusions. To regard realism as a threat to the spiritual life is tantamount to believing that reality itself is a threat to the spiritual life. In this essay I have given plausible evidence supporting the view that reality is not so constituted as to make a spiritual life unattainable. Indeed, I would go further. For a spiritual life to have any real value, it must be based on truth and fact. A spiritual life based on wishful thinking and fancy would be little more than a life based on a lie—and what, may we ask, would be so spiritual about that? There are some people who believe that there is something inherently spiritual in believing in patent nonsense. To dabble in astrology, divination, channeling, magic, séances, and other dubious superstitions is equated with developing a rich and blessed spiritual life. But how can any life based on error, credulity, and wishful thinking be rich and blessed? And why is such a life "spiritual"? Unless one equates *spiritual* with *fanciful,* there is no reason to identify a fascination with oracular gibberish with a spiritual life. As Santayana warned us, the "obscene supernatural has nothing to do with rational religion"—nor, for that matter, with the development of a spiritual life. Whatever type of life we seek to develop, if we desire it to have any sort of lasting value, it must be based on truth and reality. Hence the necessity of realism. It is incumbent upon us all to figure out what sort of world we live in, and then act accordingly. That is the task that life has set before us.

11. Freedom and the Spontaneous Universe

The presumption that, in every great controversy, one side is right and the other wrong is not well founded. In many cases, both sides are wrong. An illustration of this is provided by the controversy between evolution and creationism. The evolutionists contend that the universe is little more than a cosmic accident. No conscious will or purpose guided its development. The universe simply emerged out of a vast chaos by a series of fortuitous occurrences, none of them planned or intended. Human life ultimately derives from a purposeless void. Creationists counter this vision by insisting that the entire universe, right down to the most trivial detail, owes its existence to a divine being. God is envisioned as a sort of totalitarian dictator who causes everything to happen, including such terrible disasters as the Indian Ocean tsunami, which killed hundreds of thousands of people. Logical consistency leads this view headlong into the absurdities of Calvinism and predestination. If God is little more than an omnipotent micromanager, constantly fussing over every aspect of the universe, then freedom becomes utterly illusional.

The great irony, of course, is that Darwinian materialism, by the logic of its deepest implications, also denies freedom, so that these two doctrines, which have been diametrically opposed for so long, can at least agree on one thing. They both regard freedom as illusory, as a mere phantasm of consciousness. They merely disagree on the force that controls us in our stead. Creationism contends (at least by logical implication) that we are little more than God's puppets, going through the motions of some great eschatological farce. Darwinian evolution contends that we are the mere puppets of mechanism, forced to go through the senseless gyrations imposed on us by matter. In either vision, puppetry becomes the distinctive characteristic of the human condition.

Fortunately, many creationists and even some Darwinists have enough sense to turn a blind eye to the logical implications of their doctrines and accept the reality of human freedom. They simply ignore the contradiction between their belief in freedom on the one side and their cosmological doctrines on the other. But a contradiction is not something that should be ignored: it is a red flag indicating that something is amiss. When a doctrine contradicts the deeper intuitions of experience, this suggests that the doctrine does not accord with reality.

Samuel Johnson once remarked that "All theory is against the freedom of the will; all experience for it." (Boswell 1931, 807) But why should theory deny freedom, even when experience demonstrates its reality? I suspect this paradox stems from the human tendency to over-generalize. Our knowledge of matters of fact largely derives, as David Hume pointed out, "from the relation of cause and effect." (1910, 439) The brain, however, tends to view causal relations as inflexible and necessary. Thus the billiard ball, if struck by a cue or another ball, *must* move with the force of the collision. It has no choice in the matter. There is a kind of necessity to it that can be demonstrated through experimentation.

Science, taking up this theme and using it as the key with which to open the door to the secrets of nature, has revolutionized the world. Interpreting experience as a vast web of necessary causal relations has become *de rigueur* for anyone eager to be seen as scientific, modern, and rational. We make sense of the world by imposing causal relations on it. But in doing so, we also impose implications of necessity and mechanism on everything that happens. Thus our theories have become saturated with a bias toward determinism. When we theorize about anything, including human action, we find our thoughts contaminated by assumptions of causation and necessity. Hence the difficulties we have conceptualizing and understanding freedom. Grasping how one billiard ball affects the motion of another is easy. Grasping how human freedom occurs is not so easy. If we wish to understand freedom, how should we conceive it?

One misconception needs to be debunked from the start. Freedom is not, as some would have it, "the condition of being free of restraints." (Pickett 2000) Absence of restraint is impossible. Restraints hem us in from all sides. We are restrained from doing as we like by the laws of nature, by societal laws and obligations, and even by our own sentiments and passions. How, then, can we ever be free?

Is it possible that the very restraints that limit our freedom also make our freedom possible? Such a notion is not an easy one to explicate; yet I suspect it is true nonetheless. If human beings felt no inner restraints of passion, sentiment, and desire, whatever freedom they enjoyed would be entirely empty, because they could never make use of it. Imagine, if you will, a creature entirely free of emotions and desires. Would he be free? Would he capable of doing as he pleases? No, he would be capable of no such thing. A creature destitute of emotions and desires, passions and sentiments would have no will to exercise. Before the individual can will something, he must have a desire or passion for it. If you drain the emotions from the psyche, all you have is a thoroughly listless and indifferent organism who would have no need for freedom. Freedom of will requires a definiteness of character, with all its emotional and psychological restraints and impediments. Without these restraints, these predetermined traits of character, freedom of the will would be impossible.

Social and political freedom also requires restraint. If you allow everyone to do as they please, what is to prevent the unrestricted action of one individual from impinging on the unrestricted action of others? Removal of all social and political restraints would not make people free; it would only lead to chaos and anarchy, neither of which is compatible with freedom. In order for a society to be free, a framework of social and political laws must exist defining the scope of action for each individual. In a free society, people are free to do as they like provided they do not interfere with the freedom of others.

Determining what this means in a social context is not easy. Almost everything we do potentially affects others. How are we to distinguish between behavior that impinges on the freedom of others from behavior that doesn't? In many countries, it is illegal to fire an employee without cause. Doesn't this, however, impinge on the freedom of an employer? On the other hand, if an employer can fire anyone for no reason at all, doesn't that impinge on the freedom of the employee? Figuring out how to regulate the employer-employee relation so that the freedom of each is maximized is not an easy task. There are no quick and easy solutions, despite what political ideologues may claim to the contrary. Political and social freedom are best served under a social framework of custom and law which maximizes the individual's scope for responsible action. What this means in terms of specific laws and custom can only be determined by experience.

Once we understand that freedom can only exist within a framework of restraint, we can turn our attention to the larger question of developing a cosmology that is consistent with the type freedom we actually experience in the world. We can begin our inquiry by dismissing the extreme versions of theism on the one side and scientific materialism on the other. Neither view is consistent with freedom. We can also dismiss any notions that the universe, at its core, is a mere chaos governed by chance. Freedom can no more be equated with chaos and chance than it can with complete predetermination. Freedom requires order, but the order must leave room for spontaneous, purposive action.

During the eighteenth century, several important social philosophers of the Scottish Enlightenment discovered that complex orderly patterns can arise spontaneously, without the benefit of conscious design. An important social institution, such as a money-based market, does not arise from human design. It is a spontaneous development that often proves superior to anything that might have been consciously planned and intended.

This idea of spontaneous order, of social formations that arise fortuitously, is of great importance. It explains why freedom is superior to bondage. Under freedom, spontaneous social formations have scope to develop. Under bondage, spontaneity is abandoned in favor of consciously planned social formations, based on the intentions and designs of the rulers. Because of the limitations of the human mind and the narrow views of autocratic rulers, these deliberately designed formations generally prove costly and inefficient, especially when compared with the spontaneous formations that would have arisen under conditions of freedom.

What if this notion of spontaneous order, which is so critical to the development of free institutions, is also applicable to the universe as a whole? What if the universe is not, as so many theists believe, a product of conscious intention or design? Would this mean that the Darwinians have been right all along? After all, Darwinian evolution has championed the notion of spontaneous order right from the start. Richard Dawkins has argued, for example, that living creatures are so intricately and efficiently structured that they could not possibly have been designed by a conscious mind. (Steele 1992, 230) If the universe developed spontaneously, without the benefit of a definite plan or intention, doesn't this rule out the existence of God?

Not necessarily. Those who assume that spontaneous order is incompatible with theism are guilty of overlooking some important facts. In the first place, any system capable of spontaneously generating complex orderly patterns could not exist without a sort of meta-order—a substructure of predetermined laws or uniformities that would mark the parameters within which spontaneous development can occur. Recall what I noted earlier about social and political freedom—namely, that freedom requires a framework of restraint defining the scope and limits of responsible action. This insight into the requisites of political freedom is applicable to spontaneity of development within nature. A world cannot emerge out of chaos. There must exist, from the start, a framework of law defining the general direction in which the spontaneous order can evolve. There must also exist objects with specific propensities. It is impossible for characterless objects existing within a vast, bewildering chaos to spontaneously develop into a full blown universe. Even dice have structure and obey laws. The universe, which is far more determinate than a pair of dice, must have structure and laws as well.

Where do these structures and laws come from? You cannot assume that all laws, even those that form the very framework of spontaneous development, developed spontaneously, because that leads to an infinite regress. At some point, there must exist predetermined laws that form the foundation of existence. How do we account for these predetermined laws? We could, of course, simply shrug our shoulders and confess that we have no idea how to account for the basic structural laws of the universe, that they constitute an impenetrable mystery which can only be gaped at in wonder. But such an approach does not rule out trying to make educated guesses as to how the universe came about. In this spirit, I offer the following humble conjecture.

Suppose that God from the very start wanted men to be free. How would He go about giving men such freedom? Well, to begin with, any notion of a fully planned universe would have to be abandoned. Freedom means giving people the chance to make plans of their own. How is this accomplished? Was freedom merely a characteristic which God added to man's nature, like he added a pair of lungs and a stomach? I don't see how this could be possible. How can a creature whose every trait and character are the direct product of God's design be considered free in any meaningful sense of the word? If God is responsible for every last attribute of a man's character, then how are we to account for evil traits and weakness of will? Why would God, who, according to all orthodox theologians, is good, give men traits that lead him to do evil? If God is directly responsible for what a man is, then He must bear at least some of the responsibility for what a man does.

The theological difficulties of a micromanaging God who is directly involved in every aspect of existence can hardly be denied. At the very least, such a view is incompatible with man's freedom; and, even worse, it is logically irreconcilable with God's goodness. We must therefore assume that man is not the direct creation of God. If God intended man to be free, He would have no choice but to allow human beings to develop spontaneously, through the drawn-out mechanism of evolution. This would not necessarily mean that men were allowed to develop randomly, through blind chance. As explained earlier, spontaneous development requires a framework of law defining the parameters within which the evolutionary process can occur. Moreover, the development would also require a general direction. God, we must assume, intended to populate his world with intelligent beings. So the structure of evolution, the laws and conditions governing its general direction, had to be devised with this in mind. And if, as is not implausible, the mechanism veered off course, God would have to intervene in the process to set things right. Indeed, there is evidence suggesting that something along these lines actually occurred. As anyone acquainted with the facts of evolution knows, the development of species proceeds, not slowly and uniformly, as a thoroughly mechanistic model of evolution would suggest, but by unaccountable leaps characterized by rapid evolutionary change. Perhaps from time to time God had to give evolution a bit of a nudge to keep it from veering off track. God's intervention in the course of evolution would not impinge upon the freedom of God's creatures, provided it did not involve micromanaging every last detail.

Unless we are willing to accept the notion that the freedom we experience every time we make a decision or think a new thought is a complete illusion, we have no choice but to reject both the deterministic theories of evolutionary science on the one hand and the neo-Calvinist implications of Creationism on the other. This leaves the field open for the conjecture advanced in this essay—a conjecture which has the additional merit of harmonizing the evidence in favor evolution (particular the evidence for the spontaneous development of species) with the evidence in favor of theism (particular the evidence of purposeful development found in the very structure and meta-order of the universe).

Theists who have not been mislead by crude notions of God as an omnipotent yet benevolent despot need to recognize that the only satisfactory solution to the problem of evil is to assume that God made men free. If men were not free, then the evil they did and the sufferings they endured would be entirely God's responsibility. But if God is good, why would He create organisms predestined for evil and suffering? A loving God would do no such thing. Man's freedom is entirely consistent with a good, loving God. Indeed, one could easily argue that it is mandatory, that a loving God would wish His universe to be populated, not by helpless puppets, but by free and autonomous beings.

Granting men freedom is not without its difficulties. It means that God must give room for spontaneous development in both good and evil directions. This opens the door for all kinds of problems, including what is, for the theologian, the most serious problem of all, the separation of man from God—a separation almost guaranteed by the fact that man, according to this hypothesis, is not the direct creation of God. If at least some of the traits of man developed without

283

God's direct involvement or say-so, then of course men will become estranged from God. The only question is: what will be done about this separation? How will God bring man back to Himself? And how can this union of God and man be accomplished without violating man's autonomy?

These questions go well beyond the scope of this essay. I merely suggest them to give a hint of the fruitfulness of examining this problem from the point of view of the conjecture advanced above. Conjectures prove their value not only empirically, in terms of the number of facts that they explain, but also in the number of interesting questions they raise. I would contend that theists have never fully appreciated the implications of freedom within a divine order. I would further contend that by taking these implications seriously and using them as the starting point for fresh lines of inquiry, we can shed new light on old problems.

Bibliography

Abell, A. (1955) *Talks With the Great Composers.* New York: Carol Publishing Group, 1994.

Alan Guttmacher Institute. (1999) "Teen Sex and Pregnancy"; online at http://www.agi-usa.org/pubs/fb_teen_sex.html [accessed April 11, 2005].

Alterman, E. "Freedom is History (and Vice Versa)," *The Nation,* Dec. 10, 2001; online at http://www.thenation.com/doc.mhtml?i=20011210&s=alterman [accessed April 11, 2005].

Anderson, B. (1913) *The Value of Money.* New York: Richard R. Smith, 1936.

Anderson, B. (1949) *Economics and the Public Welfare: Financial and Economic History of the United States, 1914-1946.* New York: D. Van Nostrand Company, Inc., 1949.

Ankerberg, J. and Weldon, J. (2005) "False Assumptions About Evolution False Assumption 5: Part 2"; online PDF at www.johnankerberg.com/Articles/ _PDFArchives/science/SC3W0300.pdf [accessed April 21, 2005].

Aristotle. *Politics.* Translated by B. Jowett; online PDF at http:// onlinebooks.library.upenn.edu/webbin/book/search?author=Arist otle&amode=words&title=Politics&tmode=words [accessed April 11, 2005].

Arnold, M. (1968) *Dissent and Dogma.* University of Michigan Press, 1968.

Balvé, F. (1956) *Essentials of Economics: A Brief Survey of Principles and Policies.* Translated and edited by A. Goddard. Irvington-on-the-Hudson, NY: The Foundation for Economic Education, 1994.

Bannock, G., Baxter, E., and Rees, R. (1972) *A Dictionary of Economics.* Baltimore: Penguin Books, 1972.

Bastiat, F. (1964a) *Selected Essays on Political Economy.* Translated by S. Cain. Edited by G. Huszar. Irvington-on-the-Hudson, NY: The Foundation for Economic Education, 1964.

Bastiat, F. (1964b) *Economic Sophisms.* Translated and edited by A. Goddard. Irvington-on-the-Hudson, NY: The Foundation for Economic Education, 1964.

Barzun, J. (2000) *From Dawn to Decadence: 500 Years of Western Cultural Life.* New York: Harpers Collins Publishers, 2000.

Bennett, W. (1994) *The Index of Leading Cultural Indicators.* New York: Simon & Schuster, 1994.

Berkeley, G. (1965) *Berkeley's Philosophical Writings.* Edited by D. Armstrong. New York: Collier Books, 1965.

Berman, M. (2000) *The Twilight of American Culture.* New York: W. W. Norton & Company, 2000.

Beauregard, M. and O'Leary, D. (2007) *The Spiritual Brain: A Neuroscientists Case for the Existence of the Soul.* New York: HarperCollins, 2007.

Birnbaum, J. (1993) *The Lobbyists: How Influence Peddlers Work Their Way in Washington.* New York: Three Rivers Press, 1993.

Blanshard, B. (1962) *Reason and Analysis.* La Salle, IL: Open Court Publishing Company, 1962.

Bloom, A. (1987) *The Closing of the American Mind.* New York: Simon and Schuster, 1987.

Bradley, F. (1893) *Appearance and Reality.* Oxford: Clarendon Press, 1893.

Brooks, A. (2003) "Religious Faith and Charitable Giving." *Policy Review* Oct-Nov 2003; available online at http://www.policyreview. org/oct03/brooks.html [accessed April 22, 2005].

Boswell, J. (1931) *Life of Johnson.* New York: The Modern Library, 1931.

Buchanan, P. (1998) *The Great Betrayal.* New York: Little, Brown and Company 1998.

Burke, E. (1909) *The Harvard Classics: Edmund Burke.* Edited by C. Eliot. New York: Collier & Son Corporation, 1968.

Burke, E. (1796) *Select Works of Edmund Burke.* Vol. 3, *Letters on a Regicide Peace.* Indianapolis, ID: Liberty Press, 1999.

Burckhardt, J. (1979) *Reflections on History.* Translated by M. Hotinger. Indianapolis: Liberty Fund, 1979.

Burnham, J. (1964) *Suicide of the West: An Essay on the Meaning and Destiny of Liberalism.* New York: John Day Company, 1964.

Burnham, J. (1943) *The Machiavellians: Defenders of Freedom.* Chicago, IL: Henry Regnery Company, 1963.

Cairnes, J. (1888) *The Character and Logical Method of Political Economy.* Second Edition. London: MacMillan & Co., 1888.

Chomsky, N. (2007) "Noam Chomsky – Wikiquote"; available online at http://en.wikiquote.org/wiki/Noam_Chomsky [accessed January 4, 2007].

Churchland, P. (1987) *Matter and Consciousness.* Oxford: Blackwell, 1987.

Clark, J. (1944) "Business Acceleration and the Law of Demand: A Technical Factor in Economic Cycles." In *Readings in Business Cycle Theory.* Philadelphia: The Blakiston Company, 1944.

Collier, P. (1993) "Incorrect English: The Case of Alan Gribben." In *Surviving the PC University*. Studio City, CA: Second Thought Books, 1993.

Collins, F. (2006) *The Language of God*. New York, Free Press, 2006.

Cornell, G. (1990) "Study of the Effectiveness of Prison Ministries"; online at http://www.prisonministry.org/stats.htm [accessed April 22, 2005].

Damasio, A. (1995) *Emotion, Reason, and the Human Brain*. Harper Collins Publishers, 2000.

Dawkins, R. (1976) *The Selfish Gene*. New York: Oxford University Press, 1976.

Dawkins, R. (2006) *The God Delusion*. Boston: Houghton Mifflin Co., 2006.

DeLong, B. (1996) "Is the Stock Market Overvalued?" *Slate* Dec 21, 1996; online at http://www.slate.com/gist/96-12-21/gist.asp [accessed January 10, 2002].

Dennett, D. (1991) *Consciousness Explained*. Boston: Little, Brown and Company, 1991.

Diggs, J. (2002) "The Health Risks of Gay Sex"; available online at http://www.inoohr.org/homosexualstatistics2.htm [accessed April 21, 2005].

D'Souza, D. (1991) *Illiberal Education: The Politics of Race and Sex on Campus*. New York: Vintage Books, 1992.

Durant, W. and Durant, A. (1997) *Lessons of History*. New York: Simon & Schuster, 1968.

Gandal, M. and Finn, C. (1998) "Teaching Democracy," *Freedom Papers*; online at http://usinfo.state.gov/products/pubs/archive/freedom/freedom2.htm [accessed April 11, 2005].

Glynn, P. (1997) *God: The Evidence*. New York: Prima Publishing, 1999.

Grazia, S. (1989) *Machiavelli in Hell*. New York: Vintage Books, 1994.

Guinier, L. "Making Every Vote Count," *The Nation*, Dec. 4, 2000; online at http://www.thenation.com/doc.mhtml?i=20001204&s=guinier [accessed April 11, 2005].

EDD, State of California (2004) "A Labor Day Briefing for California," online at http://www.calmis.ca.gov/SpecialReports/Labor-Day-Briefing-2004.pdf.

Fauconnier, G. and Turner, M. (2002) *The Way We Think: Conceptual Blending and the Mind's Hidden Complexities.* New York: Basic Books, 2002.

Hayek, F. (1944) "Price Expectations, Monetary Disturbances, and Malinvestments." In *Readings in Business Cycle Theory.* Philadelphia: The Blakiston Company, 1944.

Hayek, F. (1948) *Individualism and Economic Order.* University of Chicago Press, 1948.

Hayek, F. (1952) *The Counter-Revolution of Science: Studies in the Abuse of Reason.* Indianapolis, ID: Liberty Press, 1979.

Hazlitt, H. (1959) *The Failure of the New Economics.* New York: D. Van Nostrand Company, Inc, 1959.

Hazlitt, H. (1964) *The Foundations of Morality.* Irvington-on-the-Hudson, NY: The Foundation for Economic Education, 1964.

Hodges, M. (2005) *Grandfather Economic Report*; online at mwhodges. home.att.net [accessed April 13, 2005].

Honderich, T. ed. (1995) *The Oxford Companion to Philosophy.* New York: Oxford University Press, 1995.

Honderich, T. (2005) "Equality: What it is"; online at http://www.ucl.ac.uk/~uctytho/whatequalityis.htm [accessed May 17, 2005].

Horowitz, D. (1998) *The Politics of Bad Faith.* New York: The Free Press, 1998.

Horowitz, D. (1999) *Killing Whitey.* Dallas: Spence Publishing Company, 1999.

Hume, D. (1739-40) *A Treatise of Human Nature.* London: Penguin Books, 1969.

Hume, D. (1779) *Dialogues Concerning Natural Religion.* New York: Penguin Books, 1990.

Hume, D. (1910) *Harvard Classics: English Philosophers of the Seventeenth and Eighteenth Centuries.* Edited by C. Eliot. New York: Collier & Son Corporation, 1910.

Hunt, M. (1982) *The Universe Within: A New Science Explores the Human Mind.* New York: Simon & Schuster, 1982.

James, W. (1903) "The Ph.D. Octopus"; available online at http://www.emory.edu/EDUCATION/mfp/octopus.html [accessed April 16, 2005].

Johnson, P. (1976) *A History of Christianity.* New York: Simon & Schuster.

Johnson, P. (1991) *Modern Times: The World from the Twenties to the Nineties.* New York: Harper Collins Publishers, 1994.

Johnson, P. (1997) *A History of the American People.* New York: Harper Collins Publishers, 1997.

Josephson Institute of Ethics (2000) "2000 Report Card: The Ethics of American Youth"; online at http://www.josephsoninstitute.org/Survey2000/survey2000-pressrelease.htm [accessed April 11, 2005].

Kant, I. (1902) *Prolegomena To Any Future Metaphysics That Can Qualify as a Science.* Translated by P. Carus. Chicago, IL: Open Court Publishing Company, 1994.

Keynes, J. (1936) *The General Theory of Employment, Interest, and Money.* New York: Prometheus Books, 1997.

Knight, F. (1921) *Risk, Uncertainty, and Profit.* New York: Kelley & Millman, 1957.

Kleiner, C. and Lord, M. (1999) "'Everyone's doing it,' from grade school to graduate school." *U.S. News and World Report*, November 22, 1999, 54-57, 61-64.

Koestler, A. (1964) *The Act of Creation: A study of the conscious and unconscious in art.* Laurel Edition. New York: Dell Publishing Co., 1964.

Kolko, G. (1963) *The Triumph of Conservatism: A Reinterpretation of American History.* New York: Free Press, 1977.

Krugman, P. (1998) "The Hangover Theory: Are recessions the inevitable payback for good times?" *Slate*, Dec 3, 1998; online at http://web.mit.edu/krugman/www/hangover.html [accessed April 14, 2005].

Kuhn, T. (1962) *The Structure of Scientific Revolutions.* Third Edition. University of Chicago Press, 1996.

Lakoff, G. (2004) *Don't Think of an Elephant!* White River Junction, Vermont: Chelsea Green Publishing, 2004.

Lakoff, G. and Johnson, M. (1999) *Philosophy in the Flesh: The Embodied Mind and Its Challenge to Western Thought.* New York: Basic Books, 1999.

Landes, D. (1999) *The Wealth and Poverty of Nations: Why Some Nations are so Poor and Some are so Rich.* New York: W. W. Norton & Company, 1999.

Lewis, C. (1942) *The Case for Christianity.* New York: MacMillan Co., 1960.

Locke, J. (1964) *An Essay Concerning Human Understanding.* Abridged and edited by A. Woozley. New York: New American Library, 1974.

Lommel, P. et al (2001) "Near-death experience in survivors of cardiac arrest: a prospective study in the Netherlands." *Lancet* Dec 15, 2001.

Lovejoy, A (1930) *The Revolt Against Dualism: An Inquiry Concerning the Existence of Ideas.* New Brunswick, NJ: Transaction Publishers, 1996.

Lucretius (1968) *The Way Things Are.* Translated by R. Humphries. Indiana University Press, 1968.

Lustig, J. (1982) *Corporate Liberalism: The Origins of Modern American Political Theory, 1890-1920.* University of California Press, 1982.

Mack, D. (1994) "Are Parents Bad for Children?" *Commentary*, March, 1994.

Mannheim, K. (1936) *Ideology and Utopia: An Introduction to the Sociology of Knowledge.* Translated by L. Wirth and E. Shils. New York:: Harcourt Brace Jovanovich, Publishers, 1936.

Mencken, H. (1958) *Prejudices: A Selection.* Selected by J. Farrell. New York: Vintage Books, 1958.

Mencken, H. (1956) *Minority Report: H. L. Mencken's Notebooks.* New York: Alfred A. Knopf, 1956.

Mencken, H. (1991) *The Impossible H. L. Mencken: A Selection of His Best Newspaper Stories.* Edited by M. Rodgers. New York: Doubleday, 1991.

Michels, R. (1915) *Political Parties: A Sociological Study of the Oligarchical Tendencies of Modern Democracy.* Translated by E. Paul and C. Paul. Gloucester, MS: Peter Smith, 1978.

Mill, J. (1843) *A System of Logic.* New York: Longman's, Green and Co., 1941.

Miller, A. (2006) "Alice Miller — Child Abuse and Mistreatment"; online at http://www.alice-miller.com/index_en.php [accessed January 4, 2007].

Millman, G. (1995) *The Vandals Crown: How the Rebel Currency Traders Overthrew the World's Central Banks.* New York: The Free Press, 1995.

Mises, L. (1934) *The Theory of Money and Credit.* Translated by H. Batson. Irvington-on-the-Hudson, NY: The Foundation for Economic Education, 1971.

Mises, L. (1949) *Human Action: A Treatise on Economics.* Third Revised Edition. Chicago, IL: Contemporary Books, Inc, 1966.

Mises, L. (1952) *Planning For Freedom.* South Holland, IL: Libertarian Press, 1980.

Mises, L. (1956) *The Anti-Capitalist Mentality.* New York: D. Van Nostrand Company, Inc., 1956.

Mises, L. et al. (1978) *The Austrian Theory of the Trade Cycle.* Auburn, AL: Ludwig von Mises Institute, 1996.

Mitchell, W. (1944) "Business Cycles." In *Readings in Business Cycle Theory*. Philadelphia: The Blakiston Company, 1944.

Morley, J. (1881) *Burke*. New York: John Wurtele Lovell, 1881.

Mosca, G. (1939) *The Ruling Class*. Translated by A Livingston. New York: McGraw-Hill Book Company, Inc., 1939.

Murray, C. (1984) *Losing Ground: American Social Policy, 1950-1980*. New York: BasicBooks, 1994.

Myers, G. (1909) Gustavus Myers, *The History of the Great American Fortunes*. New York: Random House, 1936.

National Center for Juvenile Justice. (1999) *Juvenile Offenders and Victims: 1999 National Report*; online PDF at http://www.ncjrs.org/html/ojjdp/nationalreport99 [accessed April 11, 2005].

National Institute on Drug Abuse (2004) "NIDA InfoFacts: High School and Youth Trends"; online at http://www.nida.nih.gov/Infofax/HSYouthtrends.html [accessed April 11, 2005].

Neuman, R. (2001) "The Empire Strikes Back." *Village Voice*, October 3, 2001, 53.

Nietzsche, F. (1968a) *Basic Writings of Nietzsche*. Translated by W. Kaufmann. New York: Modern Library, 1968.

Nietzsche, F. (1968b) *The Portable Nietzsche*. Edited and translated by W. Kaufmann. New York: Penguin Books, 1982.

Nigro, N. and Scott, R. (1983) *Principles of Economics*. Macmillan Publishing Co., Inc. New York, 1983.

Nock, A. (1991) *The State of the Union: Essays in Social Criticism*. Indianapolis, ID: Liberty Press, 1991.

Noland, D. (2000) "Joseph Schumpeter on Credit" *Credit Bubble Bulletin*; Online at http://www.prudentbear.com/archive_comm_article.asp?category=Credit+Bubble+Bulletin&content_idx=9155 [accessed April 17, 2005].

Oakeshott, M. (1933) *Experience and Its Modes*. Cambridge University Press, 1933.

Ormerod, P. (1997) *The Death of Economics*. New York: John Wiley & Sons, Inc., 1997.

O'Toole, K. (1997) "Rock and Roll: Does it influence teens' behavior?" *Stanford Online Reporter*; online at http://www.nida.nih.gov/Infofax/HSYouthtrends.html [accessed April 11, 2005].

Pareto, V. (1909) *Manual of Political Economy*. Translated by Schweir, A. New York: Augustus M. Kelley, 1971.

Pareto, V. (1916) *The Mind and Society*. Translated by A. Livingston and A. Bongiorno. New York: Harcourt, Brace and Company, 1935.

Pareto, V. (1966) *Vilfredo Pareto: Sociological Writings*. Selected by S. Finer. Translated by D. Mirfin. New York: Frederick A Praeger, 1966.

Peikoff, L. (1985) Philosophy and Psychology in History. *Objectivist Forum*. October 1985.

Peikoff, L. (1991) *Objectivism: The Philosophy of Ayn Rand*. New York: Dutton.

Peikoff, L. (1995) *Objectivist Forum*. October, 1995.

Pirenne, H. (1925) *Medieval Cities: Their Origins and the Revival of Trade*. Translated by Frank D. Halsey. Princeton, NJ: Princeton University Press.

Pickett, Joseph P. et al. eds. (2000) *American Heritage Dictionary of the English Language: Fourth Edition, 2000*. Boston: Houghton Mifflin Company, 2000.

Pinker, S. (1997) *How the Mind Works*. New York: W. W. Norton & Co., 1997.

Pinker, S. (2002) *The Blank Slate: The Modern Denial of Human Nature*. New York: Viking, 2002.

Plasil, E. (1985) *Therapist*. New York: St. Martins/Marek, 1985.

Plutarch (1864) *The Lives of the Noble Grecians and Romans*. Translated by J. Dryden and revised by A. Clough. New York: Modern Library.

Polanyi, M. (1962) *Personal Knowledge: Towards a Post-Critical Philosophy*. University of Chicago Press, 1974.

Popper, K. (1963) *Conjectures and Refutations: The Growth of Scientific Knowledge.* New York: Routledge, 1991.

Popper, K. and Eccles, J. (1977) *The Self and Its Brain: An Argument for Interactionism.* New York: Routledge, 1993.

Popper, K. (1982) *The Open Universe: An Argument for Indeterminism.* New York: Routledge, 1991.

Popper, K. (1983) *Realism and the Aim of Science.* New York: Routledge, 1992.

Prechter, R. (1995) *At the Crest of the Tidal Wave.* New York: New Classics Library, 1995.

Rand, A. (1967) *Capitalism: The Unknown Ideal.* New York: New American Library, 1967.

Röpke, W. (1942) *The Social Crisis of Our Time.* Translated by P. Jacobsohn. New Brunswick, NJ: Transaction Publishers, 1992.

Röpke, W. (1958) *A Humane Economy: The Social Framework of the Free Market.* Translated by E. Henderson. Chicago, IL: Regnery Gateway, Inc., 1986.

Rothbard, M. (1962) *Man, Economy, and State.* Auburn, AL: Ludwig von Mises Institute, 2004.

Ryan, S. (2003) *Ayn Rand and the Corruption of Rationality.* New York: Writers Club Press, 2003.

Santayana, G. (1923) *Scepticism and Animal Faith.* New York: Dover Publications, 1955..

Santayana, G. (1937) *Realms of Being.* New York: Cooper Square Publishers, 1972.

Santayana, G. (1951) *Dominations and Powers: Reflections on Liberty, Society, and Government.* New York: Charles Scribner's Sons, 1951.

Schopenhauer, A. (1958) *The World as Will and Representation. Volume II.* Translated by E. Payne. New York: Dover Publications, Inc., 1966.

Schumpeter, J. (1934) *The Theory of Economic Development: An Inquiry into Profits, Capital, Credit, Interest, and the Business Cycle.* Translated by R. Opie. New Brunswick, NJ: Transaction Publishers, 1983.

Schumpeter, J. (1942) *Capitalism, Socialism, and Democracy.* Second Edition. New York: Harper & Brothers Publishers, 1947.

Schumpeter, J. (1951) *Essays on Entrepreneurs, Innovations, Business Cycles, and the Evolution of Capitalism.* Edited by R. Clemence. New Brunswick, NJ: Transaction Publishers, 1983.

Schumpeter, J. (1954) *History of Economic Analysis.* New York: Oxford University Press, 1954.

Sciabarra, C. (1995) *Ayn Rand: The Russian Radical.* University Park, PN: Pennsylvania State University Press.

Shortall, F. (1996) *Economics: An Obituary*; online at http://econserv2. bess.tcd.ie/SER/archive/1996/obituary.htm [accessed April 15, 2005].

Sorel, G. (1906) *Reflections on Violence.* Translated by T. Hulme and J. Roth. New York: Collier Books, 1961.

Sorokin, P. (1942) *Man and Society in Calamity.* New York: E. P. Hutton & Co., INC., 1942.

Soto, H. (2000) *The Mystery of Capital: Why Capitalism Triumphs in the West and Fails Everywhere Else.* New York: Basic Books, 2000.

Sowell, T. (1964) *A Conflict of Visions: Ideological Origins of Political Struggles.* New York: Quill William Morrow, 1987.

Skousen, M. (1991) *Economics on Trial: Lies, Myths, and Realities.* New York: Irwin Professional Publishing, 1991.

Skousen, M. (2001) *The Making of Modern Economics: The Lives and Ideas of the Great Thinkers.* New York: M. E. Sharpe, 2001.

Steele, D. (1992) *From Marx to Mises: Post-Capitalist Society and the Challenge of Economic Calculation.* La Salle, IL: Open Court Publishing Company, 1992.

Stove, D. (1999) *Against the Idols of the Age.* New Brunswick, NJ: Transaction Publishers, 1999.

Thorton, M. (2003) "Who Predicted the Bubble? Who Predicted the Crash?"; online PDF at http://www.mises.org/journals/scholar/Thornton6.pdf [accessed April 14, 2005].

Vivas, E. (1955) *Creation and Discovery.* Chicago: Henry Regnery Co.

Weaver, R. (1948) *Ideas Have Consequences.* Chicago: University of Chicago Press, 1948.

Weaver, R. (1987) *The Southern Essays of Richard M. Weaver.* Indianapolis, ID: Liberty Press, 1987.

Wilson, E. (1998) *Consilience: The Unity of Knowledge.* New York: Alfred Knopf, 1998.

Yi, M. (2007) "Spank a little kid, go to jail, if bill becomes law Critics blast effort as intrusive and difficult to enforce" *San Francisco Chronicle.* January 19, 2007.